T0278310

UNSETTLING ■

Gilberto Rosas

UNSETTLING

The El Paso Massacre, Resurgent White Nationalism, and the US-Mexico Border

JOHNS HOPKINS UNIVERSITY PRESS
Baltimore

Printed in the United States of America on acid-free paper
9 8 7 6 5 4 3 2 1

Johns Hopkins University Press
2715 North Charles Street
Baltimore, Maryland 21218
www.press.jhu.edu

Library of Congress Cataloging-in-Publication Data

Names: Rosas, Gilberto, 1968– author.
Title: Unsettling : the El Paso massacre, resurgent white nationalism, and the US-Mexico border / Gilberto Rosas.
Description: Baltimore : Johns Hopkins University Press, 2023. | Includes bibliographical references and index.
Identifiers: LCCN 2022024610 | ISBN 9781421446165 (hardcover) | ISBN 9781421446172 (ebook)
Subjects: LCSH: Emigration and immigration—Government policy—United States. | Mexican-American Border Region—Government policy—United States. | Social justice—United States. | BISAC: SOCIAL SCIENCE / Emigration & Immigration | SOCIAL SCIENCE / Activism & Social Justice
Classification: LCC JV6465 .R58 2023 | DDC 325.73—dc23/eng/20221117
LC record available at https://lccn.loc.gov/2022024610

A catalog record for this book is available from the British Library.

Special discounts are available for bulk purchases of this book. For more information, please contact Special Sales at specialsales@jh.edu.

To the recent past: The twenty-three people who lost their lives on August 3, 2019, in El Paso, Texas, and the some 10,000 others who have died trying to cross the US-Mexico border, and the thousands upon thousands more who have been detained, deported, refused entry, or otherwise expelled.

And to Teo, Maya, Kora, Niki, and Mom and Dad,
for a better future.

CONTENTS

unsettle, *v.*

Pronunciation: Brit. Hear pronunciation/(ˌ)ʌnˈsɛtl/ US. Hear pronunciation/ˌənˈsɛd(ə)l/
Frequency (in current use): Show frequency band information
Etymology: UN- *prefix*[2] 1a, 1

1. *transitive.* To undo from a fixed position; to unfix, unfasten, loosen.

1598 J. FLORIO *Worlde of Wordes* *Discasciare*, .. to make loose the teeth, to dismount artillerie, to vnsettle anything.

[1755 S. JOHNSON *Dict. Eng. Lang.* *To Unsettle*, v.a., to move from a place.]

1818 J. KEATS *Endymion* IV. 179 He .. strives in vain to unsettle and wield A Jovian thunderbolt.

2. To force out of a settled condition; to deprive of fixity or quiet:

a. a state of things, institutions, etc.

1651 T. HOBBES *Leviathan* II. xxvii. 154 Such as .. take upon them .. to unsettle the Lawes with their publique discourse.

1678 V. ALSOP *Melius Inquirendum* I. i. 78 To set Religion upon its proper Basis, and unsettle it from the feeble foundations upon which former Ages had erected it.

1695 J. EVELYN *Diary* (1955) V. 209 Never so many Private Bill<s> passed for unsettling Estates, shewing the wonderfull prodigality & decay of Families.

1704 F. ATTERBURY *Serm. House of Commons* 7 Those Mighty Events, that fix, or unsettle the Peace of the World.

1803 W. WORDSWORTH *England! the Time is Come* 4 Old things have been unsettled.

1849 T. B. MACAULAY *Hist. Eng.* I. i. 71 This theory, though intended to strengthen the foundations of government, altogether unsettles them.

1884 *Leeds Mercury* 15 Nov. 6/4 Such a struggle .. must unsettle all the institutions of the country.

b. beliefs, thoughts, the mind, etc.

1644 J. MILTON *Doctr. Divorce* (ed. 2) 19 They should but seek .. to unsettle our constancie with timorous and softening suggestions.

1662 E. STILLINGFLEET *Origines Sacræ* III. i. §2 When men bent their wits to unsettle the Beleef of such things as tended to Religion.

1671 in F. P. Verney & M. M. Verney *Mem. Verney Family 17th Cent.* (1907) II. 354 My thoughts are unsettled.

1759 S. FIELDING *Hist. Countess of Dellwyn* II. 261 His Father had unsettled his Resolution.

1794 A. RADCLIFFE *Myst. of Udolpho* IV. ix. 173 The long struggle, which Agnes suffered .. at length unsettled her reason.

1816 W. SCOTT *Black Dwarf* xix, in *Tales of my Landlord* 1st Ser. I. 346 The shock was even sufficient to unsettle his wits.

1839 C. DICKENS *Nicholas Nickleby* iv. 26 None of those ill-judged comings home twice a year that unsettle children's minds so.

1885 *Spectator* 25 July 971/2 That his mind had been unsettled by his peril.

c. persons (in respect of beliefs, etc.).

1833 S. T. COLERIDGE *Table-talk* (1884) 225 What is the spirit which seems to move and unsettle every other man . . at this time?

1851 A. HELPS *Compan. Solitude* xii. 236 Provided they do not, as they would say, unsettle their neighbours.

1880 R. G. WHITE *Every-day Eng.* 140 A phonetic printing of those two words would unsettle all these people.

3. *intransitive.* To become unsettled.

1608 W. SHAKESPEARE *King Lear* xi. 149 His wits begin to unsettle. View more context for this quotation

1624 R. SANDERSON *Serm.* I. 102 The house cannot but unsettle apace, and without speedy repairs fall to the ground.

1643 J. MILTON *Doctr. Divorce* 8 Their wild affections unsetling at will, have been as so many divorces to teach them experience.

*a*1859 T. DE QUINCEY *Posthumous Wks.* (1891) I. 14 He gazes, and slowly under the blazing scenery of his brain the scenery of his eye unsettles.

4. *transitive.* To clear of settlers.

1895 *Advance (*Chicago*)* 11 Apr. 991/1 Probably no [other] section of our country has ever been un-settled so rapidly.

Source: Oxford English Dictionary, online version

UNSETTLING ■

INTRODUCTION

August 3, 2019, was a Saturday morning like any other for Guillermo Glen. It became a day he was condemned to remember.

He had stopped at the local Walmart to buy dog food and other odds and ends before heading home. He recalled seeing young people out in front of the store fundraising. He couldn't remember for what. They were with their parents.

The store was bustling. It was full of people from El Paso and Ciudad Juárez, Chihuahua, the latter the major city across the Rio Grande, in Mexico. They shopped for inexpensive milk and eggs, meat, and chicken. They were buying lunchboxes and backpacks, pencils and pens, and other supplies. School would begin the next week.

Other shoppers hunted for bargains in televisions, diapers, and clothing. Mexican soccer jerseys, cans of chiles and salsa, and Mexican, American, and Texas flags filled the aisles. Spanish and English rang through the store. "Spanglish" doesn't do it justice.

Guillermo remembered being in the back of the store when he heard what he thought was a series of loud pops. Was someone shooting fireworks out front, perhaps leftovers from the Fourth? Was a car backfiring? Had something fallen?

Then he heard the horrendous screams.

People began running.

Guillermo ducked. He knew to stay low.

His voice shakes as he describes what he saw: "I saw a woman . . . she'd been shot in both her legs . . . Me and another woman we ran to the pharmacy to get gauze for her." They bandaged her. They put shopping carts around her, trying to shield her, as the shooting continued.

They then took her out of the back of the store in another cart. "She was bleeding."

He recalls seeing "a body of one of the parents of the children who had been fundraising was on the pavement."

"A woman was crying. She had lost her kids."

After a long pause, Guillermo says, "I wasn't shocked."

The longtime community activist pauses before he continues witnessing. He takes in a large breath.

"Crusius [the killer] was methodical." He had chosen his rifle—a technology with deep ties to the settling of the United States—"down to the kind of shells he was using." He had purchased special bullets, the Russian-developed 8M3 rifle rounds, known for their extraordinary lethality, known for their ability to ravage bodies on impact.[1]

Guillermo relates that the killer had driven to this store some 650 miles over ten hours from his family's home in East Texas. "The killer wore dark clothes. He wore ear protection and safety glasses."

"He stalked us, hunting us in the aisles."

■ The store is some five miles from one of the busiest international ports of entry in the world. El Paso—the pass—had regularly been regarded as one of the safest cities in the United States for a community of its size.[2]

Until that day.

The Drug Enforcement Agency, Immigration and Customs Enforcement (ICE), US Customs and Border Protection, United States Border Patrol, and local police and sheriff departments are some of the law enforcement agencies that work in this city. The First Armored Division at the Fort Bliss military base makes this city on the international divide its home. It has trained hundreds of thousands of soldiers.

Crusius penned a manifesto seething with white nationalism.[3] He posted it on the online message board 8chan before the attack. The manifesto avowed support of two other mass shootings, which occurred at mosques in Christchurch, New Zealand. Some fifty people were killed and another forty-nine wounded during Friday Prayer on March 15, 2019. That killer had ties to the alt-right and white supremacy groups. He live-streamed one shooting. That killer was the first to publish an online manifesto. I excerpt Crusius's declaration:

> This attack is a response to the Hispanic invasion of Texas. They are the instigators, not me. I am simply defending my country from cultural and ethnic replacement brought on by an invasion. Some people will think this statement is hypocritical because of the nearly complete ethnic and cultural destruction brought to the Native Americans by our European ancestors, but this just reinforces my point. The natives didn't take the invasion of Europeans seriously, and now what's left is just a shadow of what was. My motives for this attack are not at all personal. . . . Actually, the Hispanic community was not my target before I read The Great Replacement. This manifesto will cover the political and economic reasons behind the attack, my gear, my expectations of what response this will generate and my personal motivations and thoughts . . . immigration can only be detrimental to the future of America. Continued immigration will make one of the biggest issues of our time, automation, so much worse.

> Some sources say that in under two decades, half of American jobs will be lost to it. Of course some people will be retrained, but most will not. So it makes no sense to keep on letting millions of illegal or legal immigrants flood into the United States, and to keep the tens of millions that are already here. Invaders who also have close to the highest birthrate of all ethnicities in America.

The manifesto refers to the "Great Replacement." French ideologue Renaud Camus coined this term in an influential 2011 book of the same name. The book draws on a century of white supremacy thinking. Camus contends that "white genocide" is occurring in France. Immigrants, in this case largely from Africa and the Middle East, are bent on the conquest of the country's white European population. Experts fear the doctrine of replacement may be activating lone wolf terrorists and informing the mindset of some politicians.[4]

In an ominous email to the *New York Times,* Camus wrote that nonviolence was central to his convictions. In his correspondence, he held that people of white European descent were endangered, at risk of being obliterated by immigrants and people of color. Camus added, "If white supremacists held those views, Good for them. That is indeed my belief."[5]

Camus's book echoes *The Passing of the Great Race* by patrician Madison Grant. Published originally in 1916, the book espouses "scientific racism." It ranks groups as races according to their physical, mental, and personality traits. Adolf Hitler termed *Passing* his "bible." The book served as evidence in the Nuremberg war crimes trials in the defense of Nazi physicians to demonstrate that American theories of white supremacy legitimated "crimes against humanity," including compulsory sterilization and unnecessary, experimental surgery, performed without anesthesia.[6] *Passing* espouses eugenicist warnings about degenerate immigrant masses, the dangers of miscegenation, and *Great Replacement*–like contemplations of white race suicide.

Passing served as fodder for the Johnson-Reed Act, or Immigration Act of 1924. This legislation has been recognized, as Cacho writes, the "greatest triumph of the eugenics movement."[7] Johnson-Reed placed strict limits on new arrivals from less desirable Southern and Eastern European countries, though migration from the countries of the Western Hemisphere continued relatively unabated, and it prohibited Asians from naturalization. The historical record bears ample testimony, as the act was being debated, to a preoccupation in national identity policy with maintaining the "white" or "Caucasian" racial purity of the "American" population and with anti-Semitism. Indeed, the Ku Klux Klan favored the law. President Calvin Coolidge observed when signing the act into law that "America must remain American."[8]

The 1965 Hart-Cellar Act eventually superseded Johnson-Reed. Hart-Cellar abolished discriminatory quotas. It established equal quotas for all countries that migrants were from, a move hailed at the time as progressive. It introduced civil rights into immigration policy. The 1965 act included, however, a ban on "sexual deviants," including queer migrants. It took until 1990 for the ban to be rescinded. Edward Kennedy, lionized as a liberal Democrat and progressive force in the US Senate, held that the bill "would not inundate America with immigration from . . . the most populated and economically deprived nations of Africa and Asia."[9]

■ I grew up in El Paso. It was where my parents returned after my father's time in the military and his medical internship in California. My parents, in-laws, and much of my extended family still live in the city. I attended primary, middle, and high school there. The store where the shooting occurred was close to where my grandparents once lived. I'd visit their home on Sundays and most Christmases and other holidays. A white-brick two-story on the city's east side was where my aunt and uncle grew up, after their older brothers left the city on their military tours. I'd enjoy chiles rellenos, beans and tortillas, made rich with Manteca, and some roast beef or another meat at my grandparents. I'd sip a cold Texas Pride or Pearl

Light on hot summer days with my grandfather, when I grew older. I remember walking into the old home and finding my grandmother, teary-eyed, peeling the skin from jalapeños she was roasting.

My mother's side of the family also has deep roots in El Paso. My great-grandparents Eduardo Delgado and Amelia Lunduza del Delgado fled northern Mexico and sought refuge in this border city early in the twentieth century. They were refugees before the category gained legal and social purchase.

They were fleeing the country's civil war, called the Mexican Revolution. They wound up living on what was then the city's western edge, on Mesilla Street, close to where the University of Texas at El Paso is today. Delgado, my family's story goes, had been a judge in Mexico. He was charged with hunting down the notorious bandit and revolutionary figure Pancho Villa. The revolutionary put a price on my great-grandfather's head.

Pancho Villa, the story continues, also had a hand on the other side of my family's exodus from northern Mexico to this border city. They worked in the silver mines in Camargo, a small village in Chihuahua. One of my great aunts disappeared. It is believed she was a victim of the followers of the revolutionary bandit.

Crossing international boundaries was much easier back then. The Border Patrol did not begin until the 1920s. Concerns about Chinese migration across the northern and southern borders of the United States and the influx of people fleeing Mexico's revolution kindled it. No legal distinction between economically motivated migrants and people fleeing persecution existed then, as it does for those seeking refuge at the US-Mexico border today.

The border was meant to be crossed.

One of those seeking refuge was my great aunt Ignacia Delgado. I can remember seeing her long black outfits when I was a boy. I can remember the gold leaf she always wore pinned at the crest below the gold cross around her neck. She would whisper prayers in the halls of our home before returning to a room she rented at a convent in downtown El Paso.

My mother describes how, when my grandparents would go out for an evening, Ignacia, whom we called Lobitos or Lobo (little wolf or wolf), would sit with my mother and her siblings. She would walk by the windows, ordering an imaginary army to guard the home. "Oye, Juan cuidas esta ventana" (Hey, Juan, you watch this window). She would then walk by another and say, "Oye, José tú cuidas esta ventana" (Hey, José, you watch this one). Every window in the home had an imaginary guardsman at the ready.

My parents, my sister, and I moved back to my parents' homeland in the early 1970s.

We lived in El Paso.

We thrived in Ciudad Juárez. It was *the* major city in the area.

We moved back and forth, and forth and back, over the Rio Grande, across the international boundary.

We were a few of the hundreds, if not thousands, who crossed the international boundary every day at all hours. It was *the way*.

We would pile into the car on the weekends. We would drive a few minutes on the interstate. We would head across the bridge spanning the river and indulge in fantastic meals of mole, flautas, tacos, steak, and sopapillas.

My mother would shop in Ciudad Juárez. She would disappear for a few hours and return with sodas made with real cane sugar and rich and pillowy-soft flour tortillas. When family visited us from out of town, we would head south of the border for the meals and the mercado. The market exploded with brightly colored ceramic cups and saucers, plates, and clothes. My parents and relatives would sometimes buy us small, cheap toys for us kids. I remember the Mexican prints always for sale: a young woman, eyes longing for the viewer's attention, or the Spanish-inflected scenes of a matador engaging a raging animal at a bullfight, or a Mexican flag.

Ciudad Juárez became even more enticing as I grew older. It was where young people from the United States rushed to adulthood. The city was where the pleasures of the taboos north of the border could be indulged south of it.

We were models cruising down the main drag of Calle Juárez. Young men in baggy shirts and balloon pants, hair gelled up a mile high, would parade next to young women doing their best Madonna impersonations. We moved to the disco techs and nightlife. And we would dance. And dance. And dance. Then, anywhere from midnight to 5 a.m., we would head back over the bridge, brown bodies aglow with last night's excitement. If you were lucky, you would have a new phone number in your pocket. I experienced my first kiss in Juárez.

We would declare our citizenship to border guards and head home. No passport was required.

There would also be those moments when my friends and I would be hungry or thirsty, or simply bored. We would cross into Mexico.

We would park in downtown El Paso, walk a couple of blocks toward and then over the bridge, over the river, and spill into Mexico. There we would press against the day laborers and other regular crossers, moving down the streets. They commuted across the international boundary to work in construction, in homes, and in restaurants in El Paso. All of us moved along the avenues that lead to the official ports of entry, next to the long lines of vehicles waiting for entry into the United States. To return to the United States meant pushing through a cranky turnstile and having to deal with a few crankier border agents.

■ Today borders and their crossers provoke. They instigate. Borders—and what they portend—unsettle.

They have become instrumental in national and global politics, where they become portrayed as sites of racial invasion. Borders cloud predatory processes of capitalist exploitation and its handmaidens. Indeed, he that would become the forty-fifth president of the United States began his candidacy for that office with a fiery speech to his supporters. He stated early in his speech, "The US has become a dumping ground for everybody else's problems. . . . When Mexico sends its people, they're not sending their best. They're not sending you. They're not sending you. They're sending people that have lots of problems, and they are bring those problems with us [*sic*]. They're bringing drugs. They're bringing crime. They're rapists. And, some, I assume, are good people."

He continued for another forty-five minutes. The speech culminated with his pledge to "make America great again."[10]

Donald J. Trump's call to "make America great again" became inextricable from the related call to "build the wall," which promises to insulate the United States from Latin America and keep the migrants—particularly Latinx migrants—out. He coupled those calls with the specter of an "open" US-Mexico border. Indeed, "the border" rarely refers to the northern border with Canada or the country's water borders of the Pacific or the Atlantic. This coupling became pivotal in his crass mobilization of vulgar anti-immigrant ethno-nationalism. The forty-fifth US president amplified US white nationalism and a corresponding agenda in terms of hard borders and pure cis-hetero bodies. Trump's rhetoric cast Mexican migrants specifically and border crossers generally as criminals. It shifted public perceptions of what was permissible when government bureaucrats carry out his heinous policies. The then soon to be president's bellicose call to fortify the US-Mexico border was simultaneously linked to anti-Muslim racism. It raised the dramatic spectacle of "terrorism" and invoked the specter of a porous border with Mexico exploited by border-crossing Middle Easterners.

But to focus solely on the policies of the Trump administration is to fall prey to a deep mystification. The stark reality is that US-Mexico border policy under recent Democratic administrations was already smoldering. To focus solely on the Trump administration overlooks the ramping up of military-grade tactics, technology, and equipment by the US Border Patrol, a process that has been occurring for decades, a process that I have studied, witnessed, and analyzed both in my hometown of El Paso and elsewhere along the US-Mexico divide. To focus solely on the Trump administration ignores the long-standing and cruel processes of detention and deportation. Trump's speech and subsequent policies and practices threw gasoline on the tinder of US immigration and border policy. I recognize how dominant people in the media, academia, and other positions of authority fail the border. They often fail its people. They cast the region as rife with graft, crime, violence, and death.[11]

To this end, I draw on works critical of the all too familiar histories of the founding of the United States and its contemporary reverberations in this book. The "discovery" of the Americas by European explorers such as Christopher Columbus, the valiant struggles of European settlers who worked the land, their uprising against European crowns, the creation of a new nation, and the westward expansion told in pioneer narratives and sanctioned by scholarly and intellectual authority—this founding myth all too often whitewashes the elimination of Indigenous peoples actually and symbolically. The concept of settler colonialism critically highlights how the original inhabitants of the land are cast as rudimentary folks to be conquered, how dominant currents of thought cast them as people in need of resettlement, reeducation, and other kinds of elimination. It helps capture why they must be dehumanized as savages or brutes, however noble, or reduced to mascots for sports teams. Settler colonialism as a body of academic thought contributes to the analysis of the organization, expansion, and ideology of market economies and liberal societies, and the disproportionate and asymmetrical work of racial and related differences within them.[12] Settler colonialism speaks to a collective blindness to the land dispossession of Native populations in contemporary society, the abrogation of their rights, and other diminishments of their being. Borders in settler colonial societies mark the boundaries of stolen land.

Among its many contributions, settler colonialist studies illuminates how European settlers and their ancestors came to see themselves as natives.[13] This identity includes deep commitments to private property and to fundamentally orthodox family arrangements as well as restrictive gender and sexual relations.[14] European American identity as native helps clarify the valuing of fertility and reproductive power, making salient the emphasis on the nuclear family in immigration law, border policy, and in the home, as well as the molten anxieties about replacement in migrant birthrates. Ethnonationalism or white nationalism fuels contemporary border enforcement and its myriad complexities. *The Great Replacement* must be considered ethnonationalism retold, revealing an anxiety about the linkages among peoples and territory where borders become the jagged edges of ethnonationalist projections.[15]

Settler colonialism is integral to the complex dispossessions of those seeking refuge, their loss of biological and chosen family, their loss of home, friends, and particular ways of life. The processes that the concept helps consider include the enslavement of some thirteen million Africans and some five million Indigenous people in the Americas. Those who today experience the jagged edges that borders have become attest to the renewed urgency of understanding these processes.[16] Indeed, I refrain from using the term "migrant" in this book. I prefer "the dispossessed" or "border crossers" as better speaking to the complexities.[17] Migrants, it seems, never arrive, and a certain specificity can be lost as compared to those who challenge regimes of border enforcement, now taken for granted. Migrants are always already predetermined as being within a system, often cast as labor or in relation to finance. They can never get beyond that designation.

Since 1990, if not before, militarized enforcement policies and practices have intensified at the southern border of the United States. They coincide with the United States, Canada, and Mexico joining the North American Free Trade Agreement (NAFTA), and the accompanying economic crisis brought on by the structural adjustments it demanded in Mexico. Beginning on December 19, 1994, Mexico slid into a severe economic crisis, the worst since the Great Depression. The national currency lost 70 percent of its value between 1994 and 1995. Unemployment doubled. It approached 50 percent of the economically active population. Over the following year, Mexico's gross domestic product shrank 6.9 percent. Approximately one-third of Mexico's businesses went bankrupt, leaving industry operating at 40 percent of its capacity. The crisis threatened the integrity of the global financial system and triggered financial panics as far away as Argentina.[18]

Then US president Bill Clinton, a Democrat, managed to organize a $50 billion aid package, the largest since the United States' post–World War II investment in Europe. Conditions for the relief included deep structural adjustments, including further cutbacks in public expenditures, increased taxes, and further reductions in workers' wages. The number of impoverished Mexicans increased from fifty million in 1994 to nearly seventy million by 1999. Migration to the United States and the remittances it afforded became a central force in the country's economic survival.[19] That NAFTA was justified to the American public as a way to stem immigration speaks to a nativism fanned by economic pressures.[20]

The trade agreement accelerated the movement of goods and services across borders between the three countries. It desiccated agricultural life in much of Mexico. A scene from my research in Nogales, Sonora, Mexico, opposite Nogales, Arizona, in the 1990s is revealing:

Javi, in between his forays into the dense traffic, tells me that he is from a small agricultural village in Sonora . . . when I approached him this morning to ask him if I could talk with him, he asked me for "*una milpa*," by which he meant a peso, Mexico's currency. The term translates literally as "cornfield."

The vernacular use of "milpa" for currency hints at how the agricultural communities of Mexico in the 1990s experienced the crisis instigated by the government's obedience to neoliberal structural adjustment policies. Javi, like the dozens of other young people whom I worked and wrote about in my first book, left his family in the 1990s. He was looking for a new life in the United States. They were part of the mass flows of the recently dispossessed trying to move through the border.

Javi and the thousands who have since come to the international divide found a hardening border. It is fused together by a police agency drawing on the advice of outside entities such as the Department of Defense Center for Low Intensity Conflict. The border has become a site for deploying and perfecting of militarized tactics and technologies of law enforcement and population control, driving border crossers into deserts and other weaponized terrain, thus exposing them in peril.

In the El Paso area, Operation Blockade, later given the more politically palpable name Operation Hold the Line in response to popular protest, started in September 1993, on the eve of NAFTA. In a show of force, four hundred Border Patrol agents and their vehicles positioned themselves along a twenty-mile stretch of the border, and helicopters hovered overhead. The Border Patrol placed agents at roughly fifty-yard intervals along the urban boundary between El Paso and Juárez. Shortly thereafter, the Immigration and Naturalization Service (INS) Operation Gatekeeper in Southern California, Operation Lower Rio Grande in South Texas, and Operation Safeguard in southern Arizona on "Operation Hold the Line. All of these maneuvers are entangled with white nationalist or settler replacement anxiety.[21]

The *Border Patrol Strategic Action Plan 1994 and Beyond* is telling. In it, the Border Patrol advances a strategy of border and migration controls called "prevention through deterrence." The document ominously holds that "violence will increase as effects of strategy are felt." Furthermore, "the Border Patrol will achieve the goals of its strategy by bringing a decisive number of enforcement resources to bear in each major entry corridor." The document predicts "that with traditional entry and smuggling routes disrupted, illegal traffic will be deterred, or forced over more hostile terrain, less suited for crossing and more suited for enforcement."[22] Subsequent Border Patrol operations channeled those attempting to cross into the United States away from southwestern urban centers into the desert, effectively weaponizing it.

Some ten thousand would-be border crossers have died in the deserts since the 1990s.

The remote areas to which militarized border enforcement channels migrants are conducive to extralegal, rogue practices of enforcement on the part of Border Patrol agents, as well as other ruthless individuals. Agents and others commit rapes, beatings, and other depredations. They murdered some 130 of the dispossessed in the decade since 2010, though that number represents only a small fraction of all the encounters between agents and migrants. According to the Southern Border Communities Coalition, Customs and Border Protection agents' use of force includes fifty-five deaths caused by shooting, asphyxiation, firing a Taser, beating, or applying a chemical agent. Another thirty-nine deaths were due to vehicle collisions involving Border Patrol, the majority of which occurred during high-speed car chases initiated by patrol officers. Twenty-two of the deaths were related to medical emergencies or to failure to provide adequate medical attention, either while individuals were in Customs and Border Patrol custody or directly after an encounter with agents. Off-duty officers killed eleven people. Four were due to other causes, including alleged suicide (two) and drowning (two).[23] A former agent–turned–human rights advocate holds that within law enforcement circles the Border Patrol is known to operate with little oversight and the agency's reviews of such incidents are largely ineffective.[24]

These tactics have a history. Consider that John Logan, a onetime police officer in Oklahoma, was a Border Patrol officer in the 1940s and 1950s. He worked near the Mexican border. The officer was well known for violence, as were many of his fellow patrol officers. As the Cold War engulfed Latin America following the 1959 Cuban Revolution, Logan went to work for the Central Intelligence Agency (CIA), providing security assistance to anti-Communist allies. His job was to teach local police and intelligence agencies tactics that he'd used earlier to capture the dispossessed at the US-Mexico border. He arrived in Guatemala in late 1965 and organized a paramilitary unit that would eventually carry out what he called Operation Limpieza, or "Operation Cleanup." The unit undertook some eighty raids and multiple assassinations, including an action that, over the course of four days, lead to the apprehension, torture, and execution of some thirty prominent left-wing opposition leaders. The military tossed their corpses into the sea, while the Guatemalan government denied any knowledge of their whereabouts.[25]

Such actions smolder in the dominant rhetoric and creeping militarization of border enforcement and often into other international boundaries across much of the globe. They have real political implications: migrants, refugees, asylum seekers, and their loved ones can be separated; mass deportation and indefinite detention of immigrants make too much sense to citizens and those otherwise positioned legally in the United States, as do the brutal and downright lethal border enforcement practices. These practices serve as a potent reminder that the fundamental human rights of such border crossers are put in jeopardy. Always already subjected to imperial power, vulnerable populations at the US-Mexico border become subject to the legal and extralegal government occurring in the border region.

The sheer density of border policing proves difficult to convey to someone who does not live in the region. Stadium lighting, fixed and mobile cameras, radar, helicopters and other aircraft, aerostat balloons, drones, motion sensors, cell signal sensors, license plate readers, all cast a wide, fine-mesh net on the region with little accountability. There are also some 16,700 Border Patrol agents. Some are stationed at fixed sites, others patrol the desert, but most rove densely inhabited areas. With such scrutiny comes a greater likelihood that a crosser will be arrested for a federal law violation, which is especially significant when we note the inequities of exactly who and which localities are most intensively surveilled in the border region. Agents lord over a predominately Latinx region. The results include a greater likelihood of becoming subjected to the US criminal justice system.[26]

Regular movements across borders, the kind that people from the region know well, interrupt the nexus between land and people that is integral to nativist mythology and contemporary society. Such movements interrupt the interconnection between blood and soil so central to settler claims of nativity and the accompanying paranoid anxieties of racial replacement. Such movements call into question the spectacle of border enforcement: of migrant suffering and the concomitant moral panics about out-of-control borders. Large-scale movements of nonwhite bodies across international boundaries, those who tunnel under or climb over walls, or cross rivers or oceans, those who seek asylum or some other Orientalist legal status, have been cast as threatening, as signifying disorder.[27] They become disposable.

Borders, frontiers, and similar supposed margins of countries prove instrumental in such processes.[28] Governments across much of the globe render border regions anti-democratic zones where those who cross international borders, and too often those resembling them, are subject to distinct orders of legal powers and extralegal vulnerabilities.

Inspired by certain critical intellectuals and concurrent struggles of other dispossessed peoples, I write for a reading public as well as scholars. I do not simply recount my analysis of the shooting and its linkages to the complexities of US-Mexico border policy. I am not a neutral party, much less a neutral observer. Nor am I participant observer, a methodological convention in sociocultural anthropology. Rather, I walk alongside, *sigo acompañando*, the global movement that is Black Lives Matter and other movements against the global system of white supremacy, aligned with asymmetries of wealth and related kinds of power and privilege. I walk alongside *las caravanas*, those traveling in mass from Central America as they make the treacherous journey north to the United States. Such collectivities tell of their quest for dignity and of their politically organized vulnerability. It tells of the import for a collective reckoning with militarized border enforcement and its deep and perverse reverberations across much of the globe.

I cannot look away.[29] I am positioned, by my community, my family, my friends, and my ethical and political commitments, and as a Latinx anthropologist struggling with the complex legacy of this discipline.

I witness.

I recognize concerns about reproducing certain representations of marginalized communities in too much contemporary scholarship as well as other forums. Scholarship such as this book risks reproducing the pornography of violence that mischaracterizes certain overstudied and marginalized communities that have long been grist for the academic mill and related exercises of voyeurism and extractive modes of knowledge production. I will not peddle the pain of real-life flesh and blood. Indeed, the act of witnessing in anthropology largely attempts to (re)establish the authority of those ethnographers who evoke the figure of the witness in order to necessarily position themselves as an authority. The figure of the witness and the practices of witnessing serve to legitimate painful, devastating, and complex histories about the survivors of violence, persecution, and oppression. Nevertheless, despite the noblest intentions of those in the discipline, such ethnographic productions may have perverse reverberations.[30] One strategy I practice to avoid this end is not interviewing actual border crossers, asylum seekers, or those otherwise rendered victims. They are already dispossessed enough.

My concern about what the border risks becoming drives my writing and my thinking. It demands that I witness, with all that term's ablest complexities. It demands I write this book and analyze and recount what I learned, saw, and heard. It demands that I represent the eyewitness accounts of activists and legal workers who seek to make a more just world—accounts either in their own words or, when they ask, in my words absorbed from our conversations. I privilege the voices of those challenging what the border has become, drawing on compelling accounts and analysis from activists to attorneys to authors. I also offer up scholarship, news reports, and *testimonios*, a genre of popular storytelling prevalent in Latin American studies circa the Cold War.[31] These sources document the struggles of oppressed peoples with military governments that were often supported by the United States.

I do all of this to dispute an exceptionalism that holds that the recent pathologies of the powerful exhibited at the US-Mexico border are extraordinary. They are not.

The horrific mass shooting that occurred on August 3, 2019, at the

Walmart in El Paso marks the culmination of years of hardening the US-Mexico border and reflects how legal and extralegal practices forge it and other contemporary international boundaries. They are inextricably tied to larger settler processes that underpin liberal societies, which border crossers ultimately unsettle.[32]

What further unsettles is how border enforcement practices fuel white nationalism, including those purveyors of it pulling the levers so effectively behind the scene in the Trump administration. The kindling of border enforcement implicates Democratic and Republican administrations alike. Policies supported by either or both parties have led thousands of immigrants to perish in the deserts as part of our government's efforts to harden the southern border of the United States over the past thirty-odd years.[33] The fuel includes the long and complex history of immigrant detention and the thousands more now experiencing it every night. It includes the thousands upon thousands who have experienced deportation. It includes the unsettling spectacle of children in cages. And it includes the practice of separating children from their parents, grandparents, aunts, uncles, brothers, sisters, and other caregivers.

Legal and extralegal terror would solder shut international borders. They prompt those who lack the appropriate documentation to cross international boundaries and expose themselves to the searing powers of border law enforcement. Or they face criminal forces, including vigilantes who hunt migrants in the deserts of Texas and Arizona.

Trump's presidency accelerated these conditions. It gave emotional license to speak, purvey, and exercise the disturbing and rapacious resentments representative of white ethnonationalism. It fueled a nihilistic mythology of blood, soil, and orthodox patriarchal family arrangements, embroiling an aggressive and aggrieved settler masculinity bent on protecting the homeland. This mythology smolders in the foundations of US history. It is baked into immigration and border policy. The Trump administration amplified the expansive powers, laws, and policies at the US-Mexico border. It hailed a white nationalist fixation on borders as sites of official exclusion and chaotic crossings. And it incited the mass execution of August 3, 2019, and related practices of a rapacious, anti–border crosser sadism.

The horrific shooting and the politically organized material and carceral conditions that have transpired at the US southern border and other international boundaries across the globe demand that we reimagine the globe. Borders once were the edges of governments and states and meant to be crossed. They are no longer.

Hardened borders have become integral to a national order of things.[34] They have become integral to the view of the world as a series of countries each with discrete and seemingly always salient international boundaries.

We must reimagine our communities.[35] We must disrupt the deep and disturbing linkages between a resurgent ethnonationalism and the legal and extralegal production and exploitation of the kinds of life that cross borders.

We must break the cages of an oppressive and, for too many people, death-dealing present, a global apartheid that severs polity from polity and life from life. The percentage of migrants as a share of the total population across the globe continues to grow. In the next twenty-five years, the rate of migration is predicted to speed up. Environmental catastrophe may cause international migration to double over the next forty years.

Borders and their deep reach must be reconsidered. They can be sites of crossings. They can be spaces of encounters. They can be where people live and learn from one another, as they once were not so long ago.

And as they can be again.

Migrants and others of the dispossessed do not need to suffer. Their humanity must be recognized, their human rights affirmed.

We must reimagine international boundaries as sites of the regular and normal movement of people of all kinds. We must reimagine the movement of people across the edges of countries as banal, as it once was for much of the globe, and as I and many other people like me live and know, where refugees, migrants, and other kinds of crossers are welcome. We must imagine borders so they are not horrendous sites of violence, despair, and exclusion for the "wrong kind" of crossers or for those who resemble them.

Borders so reimagined douse white nationalist embers that smolder beneath the surface of contemporary territorial arrangements. They could also help douse related ethno-nationalisms.

■ KINDLING

Some twenty thousand agents on foot and on bikes, some driving SUVS, ATVS, and other machinery, others flying in helicopters and planes, still others monitoring drones, remote sensors, and X-ray cameras, accentuate the crimes of the US-Mexico border. Too many of the men, women, children, families, queer, and disabled and others who are seeking haven become criminalized. They become subject to detention, to deportation, or to electronic monitoring, such as wearing a bracelet that tracks their movements.

Deemed "arriving aliens," they are technically "refused entry." They are detained, unless they are pregnant or for some other humanitarian reason. They are held in immigration prison.

I witness.

Five brown-presenting men enter the courtroom in this their "appearance" in immigration court. They are shackled.

"Raise your right hand," states the judge. He swears them in.

An interpreter sits in the corner, a headset linking his utterances to those of the defendant and judge. He interprets for all of them. Headsets grip their chins, pressing on their ears and lips.

Law and the dispossessed antagonize each other.

I witness.

One of the five men holds his right hand in the air, long after convention would require. He seems unaccustomed to the rituals of the court.

Those bound in shackles watch the proceedings. They witness, too.

They listen to the proceedings on headphones.

"You're here to plead guilty to unlawful reentry," states the judge.

This court does not permit phones or other devices that could document the proceedings.

My pen slips from my fingers.

Three of the shackled are from Cuba. One is from Mexico.

The last respondent is from Guatemala. His Indigeneity draws the ire of the state's attorney. The latter presents as Latinx. "I don't know how to pronounce his name," he says of this respondent. "She-take . . . She-took. I don't know." He spits it out, rolls his eyes, then scoffs.

The "Deportation Diner," in the Mexican border community of Nogales, Sonora, Mexico, in 2008, captures the normalcy of deportation. Photo by author

The judge states to those bound in shackles: "To plead guilty, you must waive your rights. Are you pleading voluntarily?"

His question, spoken in English, is interpreted into Spanish.

It also ricochets electronically to somewhere else in the globe before returning to the detainee's headset. He then interprets it in what may be Q'anjob'al, a Mayan language that is spoken in parts of Guatemala and Mexico and is increasingly evident in parts of the United States.

The first respondent says in English, "Yes."

The second shackled individual states, "*Culpable*," or "guilty" in Spanish. The courtroom interpreter says "Guilty."

The third and fourth respondents also reply, "Culpable." And the interpreter does his work.

The chained Guatemalteco with the spat-out name states, "Bey."

To hear an Indigenous tongue in such a proceeding invokes five hundred years of resistance. It severs the room. It evokes a collective resistance to accommodating the impositions of the colonial languages English and Spanish. It evokes an accompanying resistance practiced through the wrong kinds of movement that immigration law and border policing struggle to cage.

A split second later, his response is interpreted. "Guilty," states the interpreter.

The immigration judge banishes those who are shackled to detention, where they await deportation. They leave through a dark hallway.

Another handful of young men appears before the court. One of them has his face covered with black and green tattoos. His carved body bulges in a white T-shirt and jeans. His torso presses against the chains.

He is lucky. He has an attorney. Most people in these situations do not. She wears a black ponytail and a striped pantsuit. She greets her peers, then makes her way to her client. Taking the seat next to the young man, she acknowledges him.

I think she says to him, "¿Cómo estás? [How are you?]"

A smile breaks through the ink tattooed on his face.

Officialdom interrupts. The court calls the young man to the stand. All the chains are telling. Officialdom cuffed his wrists to his belly, his ankles together, a chain around his waist. The chains scrape the floor when he stands and makes his way to make his case.

Immigration courts are not courts in the sense that most Americans imagine them. They do not honor due process. They do not administer impartial justice. They are not neutral arbiters of law. Immigration judges are not even real judges. They are attorneys. They are employees of the Executive Office for Immigration Review. It is in the Department of Justice. The nation's top law enforcement agency runs a court system in which it regularly serves as a party.

After some preliminaries, the judge intones: "Illegal entry into the United States is a misdemeanor. Reentry is a felony. . . . How do you plead?"

Senator Coleman Livingston Blease of South Carolina—unrepentant white supremacist, defender of lynching and segregation, and neo-Confederate, notorious for appealing to the prejudices of impoverished whites—authored the part of Title 8 of the United States Code making it a misdemeanor to enter the country without authorization, as an attorney explained to me. According to this law, people who arrive in the United States without proper documentation are subject to criminal prosecution.[1] So much more appears to be occurring than the exercise of law and its enforcement.

Another round of whispered consultation occurs between the chained young man and the attorney.

"No culpable."

"Not guilty."

After a few minutes in the proceedings, the judge remands the chained and tattooed individual to detention.

Such scenes were regularly occurring in El Paso and all along the border. Five, ten, twenty, fifty, ninety, of the dispossessed faced immigration court in mass trials.

They come to the edges of Mexico and the United States. They risk crossing through volatile Mexico or swimming across the roaring oceans.

Many do not speak English. They do not speak Spanish. They do not speak French.

They speak Quiche, Lengala, or another subordinated language.

They come to the border, where seeking asylum or otherwise crossing for refuge, or work, or pleasure was once not so heavily policed, criminalized, or pathologized.

Now they present themselves to Customs and Border Patrol officials. They are stymied.

Many end up "detained." The term exemplifies how the United States government and its unreal immigration courts rely on opaque rationales and terminology. The capaciousness of "detention," its innocence, masks its tyrannies.

Regular people fleeing persecution or torture, or those seeking work or a better life or escaping the violence of poverty, are not being held up on their way to the store or the library. They are not being delayed from getting a cup of coffee or from getting to work or an appointment. They are not held up by traffic.

"Detention" in practice reflects a far more consequential intention. Border crossers are caged.

Often indefinitely.

Cities and towns compete to hold women, men, and children. They compete to "detain" individuals and families, all too many of whom face material conditions that force them to abandon their way of life back home. The dispossessed, having lost so much, having left so much behind, now have what little they have left taken from them. Their time is stolen.[2] They are deprived of hours, days, weeks, months, and some lose years. They are caged in public, private, and semiprivate facilities.

Many of them are then "returned." They are "removed."

"Detention" exemplifies the bureaucratized language of state-produced unfreedom, of routinized violence that is "law-affirming."[3] It is the terminology of bureaucratic malaise, of indifference, of cruelty that is institutionalized and, taken as routine procedure, agentless.[4] "Detention," "detainee," "voluntary departure," "removal," "deportation," and similar terms cloud the gray-sky procedures. Their grammar demands no subject. The agent is the state. The state is the agent. The state detains. The state returns. It removes. It deports.

Even shelters can become implicated. They and other temporary-but-not-temporary sites where migrants end up hold them. The dispossessed, having lost their way of life, their homes, their families and friends, now lose their freedom.

Their human rights are put in jeopardy. Those held in detention are less likely to get legal counsel. They are less likely to succeed in their asylum bids or related efforts to stay in the United States. No statutory limits exist for the time different agents can hold a noncitizen. Detention as a practice puts in doubt the rights, human relationships, and connections to humanity of those who have been captured and confined. Organized political subjection forces detainees into some lesser condition, some lesser place, unfree and under guard.[5]

"Detention" signifies nothingness. It is a scorching abyss beyond the safeguards of criminal law. The term represents an exercise of state power against citizens from other countries, or power exercised against those for whom the US government should bear some accountability.

"Detainees" have no real trial.[6]

Detainees are not officially imprisoned. Prisons are meant for accused persons convicted of crimes after a trial. Prisons require a certain recognition of rights, including those to legal counsel. Detention holds the surplus humanity that falls through the molten cracks of the contemporary globe, before they are expelled.

The Department of Homeland Security banishes them to places where they may face serious persecution, death, or hardship. Some returnees have been in the United States for days, for weeks, for months, for years, some for almost all of their lives. Many have deep roots in the

United States. Nevertheless, they are banished from their homes and loved ones.

The government exiles them to countries that they may not know or may not have visited since childhood, where they often have no biological or chosen loved ones. They are returned to places where they may not speak the dominant language.

Immigrants lack protection against retroactive changes in the law. Guilty pleas to minor offenses based on the correct advice of counsel can lead to deportation should Congress change the rules the next day, week, or year. People who have lived nearly all of their lives in the United States have been deported for possession of small amounts of marijuana or shoplifting, without regard to the constitutional limits on disproportionate punishment. People who made the difficult calculation to leave their homes, if convicted of certain crimes classified as aggravated felonies, face mandatory deportation without a discretionary hearing where family and community ties would be considered.[7]

The Department of Homeland Security detains those seeking asylum or otherwise trying to cross the border more often than the Justice Department incarcerates people suspected of white-collar crimes, most of whom have the resources necessary to flee. The government more regularly detains or, better, incarcerates those seeking haven or those having crossed the southern border of the United States without authorization, one advocate told me, than it does people accused of violence. Asylum seekers include some of the most vulnerable members of society. They include children, single mothers, victims of domestic violence or torture, and other individuals who have suffered persecution and trauma. Some of these individuals live in the United States while their application is processed, while others—including children and families—are detained for some or all of this time, as I learned in my conversations with immigration attorney Virginia Raymond.

Detention often begins early for the dispossessed. The Border Patrol holds people it catches in *hieleras*, or freezers. These sites are so named for their air conditioners, which are cranked up so unbearably cold that migrants freeze, despite the desert heat of the US Southwest. The pens are often so packed that migrants often are forced to stand. They typically have one toilet.

States of emergencies—typically cast along racial, national, ethnic, and related axes taken as immutable—infiltrate these practices. The racial, ethnic, religious, or national emergencies rarely speak to the specificities of what brought the dispossessed to such borders.

Spaces of civilian detention and the emergencies they are linked to rarely end. Guantanamo Bay detention camp, one such space of detention resulting from the War on Terror of so long ago, persists. Detainees and nationals from other countries, as well as United States citizens, remain "detained" there.

To concentrate women, men, and children, of different colors, creeds, and nations, who often speak different languages, in such spaces, in such temporary-but-not institutions, brings to life a righteous indignation that such practices are not who we—the collective "we" of the United States—are.

Yet persist they do.

Witness.

In June 2014, well before the forty-fifth presidential administration came to power, attorney Raymond told me, hundreds of thousands of dispossessed children and families risked the journey to the United States. They arrived at the southern border of the United States. The Department of Homeland Security (DHS) implemented an extraordinarily punitive response. Although the Obama administration had promised to prioritize criminal aliens in its enforcement practices, it grievously disappointed and angered advocates.

The Obama administration incarcerated families.

Dilley, Berk, and other detention centers in the southwestern United States filled with Central American families. Central Americans did not have a constituency to struggle on their behalf like other groups such as the “Dreamers,” a group of undocumented young people mostly from Mexico who made sophisticated use of the media to cultivate advocacy groups on their behalf.

The Obama administration ignored the lessons from before. The Bush administration had then detained some five hundred mothers, fathers, and children, many of whom were asylum seekers at the T. Don Hutto Family Detention Center in Taylor, Texas in 2006. It was once a medium-security prison operated by the Corrections Corporation of America (CCA).

The CCA held families in deplorable conditions under essentially a penal regime. Children and their parents were compelled to wear prison uniforms. They had no freedom of movement within the facility. They were subjected to multiple daily prison counts and prohibited the children from having toys or writing implements in their cells. Until ensuing media attention and litigation, CCA provided only one hour of education per day, as reported in testimony on July 29, 2015, of Barbara Hines, then a senior fellow at the Emerson Collective, a coordinating member of the RAICES/Karnes pro bono project, and a clinical professor of law at the University of Texas School of Law, where she codirected the immigration clinic. This harrowing testimony on the detention of children and their mothers—before Trump's ascendance—and the complaints that were reported at Hutto, including “inadequate medical care, weight loss, inedible food, threats of separation as a disciplinary tool, and more[,] are remarkably similar to conditions and complaints at today's detention centers.”[8]

A sustained legal effort involving the American Civil Liberty Union, the University of Texas Immigration Clinic, and the law firm of LeBouef, Lamb, Green & McRae challenged these practices. They sued to enforce the *Flores v. Reno* settlement agreement. *Flores* favors the release of immigrant children and requires that if immigrant children are detained, they must be housed in the least restrictive alternative setting in a facility that is licensed under state law. The parties in the Hutto litigation reached a settlement that lasted for two years. In August 2009, as the expiration of the settlement approached, DHS, under President Obama's newly elected administration, made the humane decision to end family detention, except for a small, ninety-bed facility in a former nursing home in Berks County, Pennsylvania. Families were released into the community to pursue their immigration cases.

Family detention ended.

Or at least it did temporarily. But the holding of civilian migrants in temporary-but-not institutions ultimately continued. For example, Virginia Raymond tells of "a detention center–slash-prison [that] was an old jail. It was a disgusting facility. It was in Robstown [Texas], outside of the current moment; the current moment keeps . . . as moments do, they keep moving forward." Raymond continues, describing one of the detainees: "She was a young woman from Guatemala who had never come into the United States before. There was not any indication that she was trafficking, carrying weapons, carrying drugs, engaged in human trafficking or other forms of smuggling. She was a person who crossed the border and was looking for asylum."[9]

When she approached the border authorities, "she asked for asylum, completely peaceable, young woman, barely not a child; she was locked up in this dark and dingy hellhole in Robstown. . . . It was like being in prison, where you're looking at somebody who's separated from you. There's a plexiglass wall and then there's an opening: you're sitting on one side, and the person is sitting on the other side."

The young woman had surrendered herself and sought to exercise the internationally recognized right of asylum.

Again, these instances occurred well before the forty-fifth president of the United States threw gasoline on the border. The border region was already experiencing the acceleration of its police forces, kindling for the white nationalist flames flickering below.

The histories of ten mothers in the declaration of Luis H. Zayas, a highly regarded scholar and dean of the School of Social Work at the University of Texas at Austin, is telling. The mothers ranged in age from twenty-four years to forty-seven years, and their children from two years to seventeen. "Eight of the families were from El Salvador," Zayas reported. "One was from Guatemala and one was from Honduras." All the families he interviewed had

> fled severe violence in their home countries in order to seek refuge in the United States. The pre-migration histories of most [of] the families included domestic violence and sexual abuse of the mothers by their partners. Several of the mothers also reported being raped, robbed, and/or threatened by gang members. The teenage children appeared to suffer the greatest difficulties because of the gangs. Adolescent girls reported being accosted by gang members who insisted on forcibly taking them as their "girlfriends," while adolescent boys reported being told that they must become members of the gangs. In both cases, the teenagers reported that the consequence of refusal would be their own death or the death of a parent or sibling. (Teenage females were naturally more reluctant to discuss the situations of their sexual assaults with a male interviewer.)[10]

The Department of Homeland Security characterized such mothers and children as lacking merits necessary for refugee claims and thus as illegal border crossers. It insisted that all families should be detained without any individualized consideration of the need to detain. The DHS neglected its domestic and international obligations to protect families seeking refuge in the United States, though the vast majority of the families had credible asylum claims. Many ultimately won their asylum cases on the merits. Obama's Department of Homeland Security, per Hines's testimony, argued that mothers and children, the most vulnerable of all migrants, should be detained without the possibility of release.

Karnes and Dilley and many other detention sites are in remote rural areas, as Raymond explained. Their distance from urban centers produces a significant impediment for appropriate legal representation. Per Raymond, the Karnes detention center, operated by the GEO Group, Inc., is in the small town of Karnes City, Texas, approximately one hour from San Antonio and two hours from Austin. Karnes currently has capacity to house 532 mothers and children, with plans to expand to almost 1,200 beds. The Dilley detention center, operated by CCA, in an even smaller community, Dilley, Texas, is located over one hour from San Antonio and over two hours from Austin. Dilley has the capacity for 2,400 mothers and children. Most disturbing, DHS awarded another contract for the care of families to CCA, the very entity that designed the penal-like regime at Hutto.

Neither the Karnes nor the Dilley facility is licensed to house children under child welfare standards in the state of Texas. The absence of licensing means that there is no independent oversight, binding child welfare standards or child care expertise, to ensure children's safety and well-being. Guards do not have training in addressing the needs either of mothers and children seeking asylum or of trauma survivors. Women have no control over their children's lives. Both facilities are secure-lockdown detention centers run on a rigid schedule, including mealtimes, wake-up and lights-out times, and multiple body counts and room checks during the day and night.

Raymond explains that this new instance of family detention "started in Texas."

> New—not the beginning of, because there had been an earlier period at Hutto, the former prison in Taylor during the more recent Bush administration when families had been detained there. Of course, if we're going to talk about families being separated and families being detained, there's a much longer history beginning with both the genocide of Native peoples in what is now the United States and beginning with slavery. And believe me, the irony was not lost on me that this was happening in Karnes, because you know whose family was incarcerated in Karnes County. . . .
>
> The family of Gregorio Cortez. When Gregorio Cortez went

on his ride on that little mare. Was it a mare? It was a mare that he was riding on while the Texas Rangers were looking at him. For a time, his family, including his wife and children and I don't know who else, was incarcerated in the Karnes County Jail, which is right across the main road, or one of the [word inaudible] from both the heavy-duty barbed-wire Karnes Detention Center, which has both people who are accused of federal crimes such as smuggling and bringing in drugs and whatever, and the security-light, low-security, minimum-security facility that was, up until the summer of 2014, the Karnes County Civil Detention Center. Then magically, after August, [it became] the Karnes Family Residential Center.[11]

Raymond refers to an account of an early detention imposed on a family with a prominent history in Chicana/o-Latina/o studies. Cortez was mistaken for an outlaw by law enforcement in the Lower Rio Grande Valley because of a "cultural misunderstanding" in the nineteenth century.[12] He shot the sheriff and then fled the Texas Rangers, a law enforcement agency with a long history of anti-Mexican, anti-Black, and anti-Native violence. Mexican communities along both sides of the Rio Grande aided Cortez, as sung in a *corrido,* typically an oral history of working-class Mexicans in Texas, Mexico, and elsewhere.

US Immigration and Customs Enforcement (ICE) readied the detention centers for incarcerating families by adding new coats of paint in 2014. Raymond describes the process for Karnes Family *Residential* Center:

It took them a while to paint that sign, but that's what they did. They put out some blue benches that they hadn't had before that were like right at the entrance to the lobby. They put up a covering that provided a minimal amount of shade and that's blue. So they made cosmetic changes. I have been told that they painted big vegetables on the cafeteria to make it more child friendly.

Unlike in 2006, in 2014, ICE did not require the families to wear prison garb. Nonetheless, they were incarcerated in devastating and deteriorating conditions.

Hines, in her testimony, tells how some 250 children received adult dosages of a hepatitis vaccine:

> On the day of the vaccination incident, I met with a mother at Dilley, whose abusive, gang-member domestic partner had kidnapped her and broken her fingers. She removed the cast from her fingers during her flight from her home country because the cast impeded her ability to carry her son on the journey to the U.S. When she sought medical care at Dilley for the pain in her hand, she was forced to wait for hours to see medical personnel, received no treatment, and was repeatedly told to drink water for the pain. This mother, visibly upset, reported to me that her son had been vaccinated that morning and that he was feverish, had no appetite, and was in pain when he walked. As she instructed her young son to show me the injection marks on his legs, his eyes welled up with tears.[13]

Indeed, ICE was refusing to set bond except in extraordinary circumstances. An exception was a young girl. She had contracted brain cancer. ICE eventually capitulated, allowing her to seek medical care, following enormous public pressure and given her severe medical needs.

ICE insisted on incarcerating these families even though they passed credible-fear interviews and were eligible for release on recognizance or bond. Many of them had close family or other sponsors willing to house them or provide support at hearings. Attorney Raymond recalls that when she challenged an officer about these practices, he confirmed that ICE was refusing to release families that were being detained at Karnes: "He told me 'Our directive is no bonds on anyone. We are keeping them here through the entire process, unless an immigration judge orders otherwise.'"

Raymond also recounts an instance when an "ICE lawyer present[ed] pages and pages and pages of—let's call it nonsense"—to an immigration court, "arguing that all of these women and children, all of these Central American women and children, are a threat to the national security of the United States. The judges are like, 'Why are they are a threat?' I remember very well Grace Garza [assistant chief counsel for the Department of Homeland Security] saying, 'They are drinking our water.'"

Zayas's declaration exemplifies witnessing in its account of the drudgery of daily life in the spaces where the families were concentrated. It documents the bullying and cruelty of practiced by certain staff members and exercised against detainees.

Beyond that is the remarkable banality of the caging of Central American families. There were census counts three times a day, Zayas reported. "[I]f a child, typically an adolescent, was found in her or his mother's cell and not in the one assigned to the teenager, they were given some sort of demerit. This was the case with one teenage female who was separated from her mother and two younger female siblings and was often weepy and fearful of being separated from her family. When I met her, the girl had received two warnings and was told that a third time would bring upon her a serious penalty."[14]

All the families Zayas spoke with manifested

> feelings of despair and uncertainty. Among the younger children, [he] detected high levels of anxiety, especially separation anxiety (fear of being away from their mother; fearful that they would be moved and children not told; fear of losing their mother). The mothers showed mostly signs of depression with such vegetative signs as lack of sleep, loss of appetite and weight loss, and hopelessness. Some of the same symptoms were evident in the adolescents, especially girls. . . . At least three mothers with young children were distraught in thinking that they brought their children from one nightmarish situation to another.

Zayas saw signs that the experience of family detention had produced regression or arrests in the development and major psychiatric disorders among the children. These included "suicidal ideation." He witnessed developmental regression in one infant: "Although he had previously been weaned, he had reverted to breastfeeding and needed to be held by his mother constantly." Other, older incarcerated children manifested separation anxiety and other "regressions in their behaviors. . . . Several children reported nightmares."[15] At least three of the teenagers whom Zayas spoke with exhibited major depressive disorders: "[O]ne teenage male I interviewed expressed suicidal ideation, telling me that he would rather take his life than to return to his hometown and face the gangs that had tried to recruit him."[16]

■ Other Orders of Detention

Beginning in early 2019, tens of thousands of the dispossessed, primarily from Latin America, who arrived at the border and requested asylum have been returned to Mexico following the Orwellian "Migration Protection Protocols," also referred to as "Remain in Mexico." The program's dynamics varied from border city to border city, but people swept up in the Migrant Protection Protocols in Ciudad Juárez were made to cross the border early in the morning. There they were taken into Customs and Border Protection custody, where they were held for processing to appear at trial, then returned to Mexico at night.

Metering was common in Juárez, according to this observer. An 1-800 number was given for court dates, the more informal but nonetheless related regimes of metering. Officialdom assigns them a numbered place in line, where they must wait—a detention of a different order. Crystal Massey, a human rights activist, reported that in one border city where people came to request the internationally recognized right of asylum, some were being processed on the same day at the ports of entry. Other people were having their place in line recorded on their bodies with a

Sharpie.[17] I repeat: US officialdom was writing numbers on the dispossessed in black permanent markers.

Massey also reported that in another border community individuals who arrived at the port of entry and requested asylum entered a different kind of limbo. "There wasn't the infrastructure to call US officials to check on the progress of cases." The dispossessed relied on "some random dude's cell phone number that nobody at the shelters even trust. And so it's just a crap shoot . . . you've made it that far, what are you doing to do?"

She notes that in Nuevo Laredo, Tamaulipas, Mexico, the city offered them tents in a flood zone.

The would-be border crossers waited in camps. They waited in shelters. They filled the churches, the hostels, and other encampments, in Ciudad Juárez and other ports of entry, places where human rights are suspended, the places that contemporary borders have become.

They waited, subject to extortion, kidnapping, and being ransomed.

■ Blackness "Detained"

I must note an important distinction regarding detention: the Department of Homeland Security largely did not situate African asylum seekers in the Migrant Protection Protocols program. Instead, for asylum seekers from Cameroon, the Democratic Republic of the Congo, Guinea, Ghana, and Sierra Leone, it used privately run detention centers, jails, and prisons.[18] Although all of the dispossessed, including Latin Americans, are vulnerable to losing their identity documents, the long, arduous voyages that Africans undertake make it likely that they will arrive at US borders without current, valid passports or other government-issued identity documents, thus accelerating their detention.

The Department of Homeland Security and immigration courts also likely factor in questions of interpretation in legal representation. It is easier to find Spanish-speaking legal counsel than it is to find speakers of Hausa or Arabic, or even—in South Texas and Central Illinois—French, as well as speakers of all Indigenous, noncolonial languages, rendering African asylum seekers and related kinds of border crossers subject to detention.[19]

Those people who seek parole from DHS must show, to that agency's satisfaction, that a bond seeker is not a danger to the community, not a national security threat, and not a "flight risk." A DHS officer's perception of the "dangerousness" of especially Black-presenting men and of the probability of their presenting a "flight risk" appears susceptible to anti-Black racism.[20]

On Detention in Perpetuity

I am still witnessing. I am at the scene with the judge in the El Paso immigration courtroom where I begin this chapter. Another group of migrants, again all men, appears before the judge. He swears them in. After some brief proceedings, he remands them into "detention." Chained, they exit the courtroom through a doorway, part of the fifty thousand–plus banished into the burning abyss of nonbelonging, of unfreedom, of detention today.

Another group of men appears before the imaginary court. They are sworn in. I think I detect Caribbean-inflected Spanish. The court remands them to the temporary-but-not spaces of detention, where they must wait.

As someone concerned with the asymmetries in anthropological knowledge production, particularly its extractive relations, here I briefly turn the narrative over to Diana Martinez. She is a longtime activist, born and raised in El Paso, with family on both sides of the border. She is principally affiliated with the Coalition to End Childhood Detention but regularly works with other allied organizations. Her critical insights and deep knowledges about the region proved invaluable as I researched and wrote this book.

■ INTERLUDE

White Supremacy in El Paso before August 3, 2019

Diana Martinez

White supremacists kept coming to the border before August 3 all year long. It felt as if it was one tragedy after another. The people of the border were overwhelmed with the trauma of blatant racism and cruelty toward Latinx peoples. El Paso was under target all year. Before we could recover from one thing, some new trauma would come up. At times I felt helpless to do anything.

On December 23 we were at Tornillo, calling for the children to be reunited with their families. After the protest the Witness Tornillo Team had stayed to be sure that the facility did close as promised by Kevin Denin, the president and CEO of BCFS, the organization contracted by the US government to run the Tornillo Influx Facility.[1] However on December 24 and 25, ICE began dropping off migrants without coordinating it with nongovernmental organizations like Annunciation House. They were dropped off at odd hours, making it difficult for volunteers to care for migrants arriving at the Greyhound station downtown on Overland Street. White supremacist and conservative politician Anthony Aguero came to harass and record migrants at the station. He chased migrants and volunteers who were transporting them with his video camera.

He tried following them to the shelters. El Paso came out and set up transportation to the shelters and emergency food and supplies for the migrants. People coordinated donations of food and clothing in many locations around this time. I know I volunteered at the Borderland Rainbow Center, transporting food to shelters and making a massive amount of cinnamon toast at once. The Borderland Rainbow Center also had coffee donated from Starbucks too. Throughout the early part of the year, the center was coordinating donations for migrants and volunteers having to respond to ICE chaotically releasing migrants. People coordinated an Amazon wish list and online fundraising for immigrant advocacy groups in El Paso. This kept going until Migrant Protection Protocols kept all migrants in Mexico.

Trump came to El Paso mid-February to attract attention to a border town he called dangerous and criminal. He told the lie that the wall had made us safer. He stiffed us with an unpaid bill of more than $500,000. This visit was his campaign kickoff. He held it at the County Colosseum. The Women's March, Border Network for Human Rights, Las Americas Immigrant Advocacy Center, the El Paso Democratic party, team Beto, and forty or so other organizations coordinated a counterprotest called the March for Truth in a nearby baseball field. I got off work late and had to go through the back way to join the protest. My friend and I encountered a lot of people from out of town who were clearly here to see Trump. It was a bit nerve-racking as older white people with southern accents told us that the colosseum was full and we would not get to see him. People were waving all sorts of flags, such as the American flag in black and white with a blue line. They had Nazi swastika flags, Confederate flags, and Trump flags. In the middle of one side street to the colosseum a Latina woman was waving a flag and yelling "Latinos for Trump!" She was dressed in all red, white, and blue.

Out of the thousands of people who came from out of town, some stuck around for a bit longer. A couple stuck around and waved Nazi, Confederate, and Trump flags from their RV on Sunland Drive and Mesa

Hills. It stayed there for weeks. They made themselves very much visible from a busy intersection on Sunland Park Drive. Nearby was access to the highway. Down the road was the town of Sunland Park, New Mexico, and access to the border on Paisano. The area is a busy commercial center with a mall, restaurants, and shopping centers with lots of traffic. They wanted to rub in Trump's visit a bit longer, along with the hate their flags represented. They wanted to make sure everyone could see them. We wanted them to go home.

US Customs and Border Patrol (CBP) commissioner Kevin K. McAleenan came to the Paso del Norte Bridge in late March to say, "We cannot let in more migrants." Behind him the Border Patrol constructed a tragic scene of migrants under the Paso del Norte bridge surrounded by a barbed-wire fence. The nights were still cold. We were horrified as we watched people of all ages, exposed to the cold, rounded up under the bridge. They had no showers, no toilets, no mats. They had only hard rock to sleep on. One man held onto his four-month-old child behind a barbed-wire fence in the chilly air. I think they were held there for two or three weeks—maybe more. We could not figure out why they were not processing and releasing them to Annunciation House. That is, until McAleenan used the scene as the backdrop to a press conference where he announced that the border was saturated with migrants. They manufactured a border crisis. Shortly thereafter, the militia groups came to town in the name of helping the Border Patrol protect the nation from invasion.

The United Constitutional Patriots came to El Paso heavily armed in March, April, and May. Some of the members were felons. They dressed in paramilitary uniforms with big guns slung across them. They terrorized hundreds of migrants seeking asylum on our borders. They wanted to act as the Border Patrol. I guess being white with a gun gave them that self-sense of authority that they can do that. At night they pointed their guns at hundreds of migrants to "detain" them in the area around Executive Drive and Sunland Park. I watched the saved video of a Facebook live-stream as they pointed guns at migrants sitting and coughing on the street curb. The militia guys talked about the migrants as if they were diseased pests that they were arresting. Not until June was their leader arrested for impersonating the Border Patrol. It gave us a sense of relief when they all started to disperse. This was five minutes from where I lived at the time. I felt that if I had confronted them, I would not have been safe. I had wished that our mayor or some authority would have said something to discourage them from hanging around our town. But we also had no faith that our mayor would speak up against the Trump followers, since he was part of the same party that encouraged these white nationalists to come to town. The fact that no authorities acted early to get them out of there upset me. These guys were holding very big guns in the open in our community, acting as if they had authority.

The We Build the Wall group came and kept bringing white supremacists to El Paso from the spring through the summer. Conservative Anthony Aguero was the local guy in El Paso bringing in all sorts of conservative white nationalist groups in here. The project was to build a section of the border on private property on Mount Cristo Rey in the Anapara section of Sunland Park, the town in New Mexico. This is an area that zigs in and out between Texas and New Mexico directly on the border with Mexico. The project violated several permits. The mayor of Sunland Park was going to halt the project by saying that it violated a permit and zoning concerning the height of the wall. However, the white nationalists called in full force with death threats to him and his family. The permit was passed through and allowed shortly afterward. How is it that they got away with that? I do not know. Why were the authorities not investigating this? I do not know. How could they keep getting away with not being accountable to the law? This terrified me. They broadcast the project on Facebook live and YouTube so all white supremacists can have their eyes on El Paso. They scarred our sacred Mount Cristo Rey with a monument to hate. Everyone felt that our little mountain between two countries and three states was a shared place. It had always been an amazing, beautiful place with the beloved statue of a compassionate Jesus on top. People from all the communities made pilgrimages up the mountain to the top on Easter. It was seen as a peaceful place of convergence. Now it was ruined by their hate for us as immigrants and their descendants.

Rather than releasing migrants in a coordinated and gradual manner, Customs and Border Patrol would build up a bunch of migrants at once and then release them at odd hours. It was an erratic release of migrants, rather than a steady flow. It was hard to estimate how many migrants to prepare food for and when. There would be no one, and then suddenly 500 migrants at once to feed in the middle of the day on a Wednesday. And for a while there were migrants coming to the port, but where were they being released to or transported to? Were they holding on to them? In May the Department of Homeland Security's Office of Inspector General reported that an El Paso processing center had been filled beyond capacity. The facility was built to hold 125 people but was packed to the brim with 900 people. Some people had been in there for several weeks rather than the required seventy-five hours. There was standing room only. They were squeezed together in inhumane conditions. Shortly afterward, in the middle of June, it was uncovered that the Clint Border Patrol station was holding 255 kids in horrible unhygienic conditions. One report talked about how a child remained in the same diapers for two days. The older kids were expected to take care of the younger kids. They all slept on concrete floors with only mylar blankets. They were let outside for only fifteen minutes a day. Most of them had been there long past the seventy-five hours.

The continual protest and horror against these inhumane actions created anxiety for me and other organizers. What more can we do? How much more fuel did we have to keep reacting to each of the dreadful human rights violations? Pressure, anxiety, frustration, and anger over all this was building up. How can we stop the cruelty from happening to people looking for safety and the will to survive? How can our society allow this to happen? Why aren't more people outraged by this? How do they keep getting away with this inhumanity toward people? If they were not Latinx Brown people, would they still be able to get away with this? Thus far, the year had been filled with shock, anger, and heartbreak.

Two weeks before August 3, an online conservative disinformation site released a story that Antifa was coming to El Paso to attack the Border Patrol. Mayor Dee Margo released a warning to stay safe and be vigilant that Antifa was coming and that he would keep them out of town. It was not Antifa. They were protesters coming to protest the abuse that Border Patrol, ICE, and CBP subjected migrants to all year. In just a few weeks El Paso was not attacked by any Antifa group, but by an outsider coming again to our border to bring Trump's hate to our city. This time he did use his gun on our people in a Walmart filled with beautifully binational people from both Juárez and El Paso. This man came alone physically and pulled the trigger that killed and ruined so many lives. But it was also the hate rhetoric targeted toward our city. It was also the Border Patrol and CBP, which staged a crisis on the border to create a narrative about the border being overrun by migrants as if they were a "horde of Brown people ready to invade." The next day the city got on its feet to donate blood, protest, and mourn those who were killed. The year 2019 was trauma after trauma in El Paso brought on by DHS's rhetoric and actions that spurred white nationalists to come here.

■ THE LLORONX

Ay mis hijos! Baytal ayik' eb' unin?

She screams: *Ay mis hijos!* (Oh, my children!)

The cries reach me here, hundreds upon hundreds of miles from the US-Mexico border, spurred by the recent reports of children crossing borders alone, unaccompanied: *¿Dónde están mis hijos?* (Where are my children?)

La Llorona is a mystical, crying woman, a wailing specter, whose ghostly presence haunts Mesoamerican folklore and children alike in much of the Americas. Garbed in white, she wanders the darkness, seeking her lost children. She terrifies. Her howls crack through the nights. She scares children who are out late, unsupervised, alone, or in a small group, causing them to run back home.

She was once a beautiful young woman. Her name was María, and she lived long ago in a rural village. She came from a poor family. One day, a wealthy nobleman traveled to her village. Her beauty stopped him in his tracks.

She charmed him, and he charmed her. They fell in love, then married, and the couple had two sons.

The romantic bliss eventually subsided. Her husband traveled frequently. He stopped spending time with María and the children. When he was home, he paid attention only to the children.

One day, he returned to the village with a younger woman. He bid his children goodbye, and he left María.

Spurned, hurt, and angry, she took her children to a nearby river, so the legend goes. Blind and enraged, she lost them.

Ay mis hijos!

Or did the river take them? Did she drown them? Did she kill her children?

The story is ambiguous. The guilt, the rage, the anguish are not.

She soon realized what she had done and returned to the river. She couldn't find them.

Ay mis hijos!

Days later, her lifeless body was found on the bank of the river.

God damned her. She was guilty of committing two cardinal sins: murder and suicide. He condemned her to wander through the purgatory that the Americas have become, seeking her lost children, crying for them, wailing for them, screaming from them.

She hunts for them at night. *Ay mis hijos!*

Latinx parents tell this ghost story to their children. But her invocation haunts some adults. She appears by rivers or lakes. La Llorona will get you.

When her wails sound close, she is far. When she sounds near, she is near. Run the other way when you hear her. To hear her cries means misfortune or death, so go some versions of the story.

She'll take your children. She'll kidnap you. She'll drown you. She begs the heavens for forgiveness.

The legend of Llorona tells of colonial mothering. It represents the seduction—or the horrendous rape?—of Indigenous women by the Spanish and other tormentors. It is another rendition of the infamous Malinche, a woman infamously cast as the betraying mother who births the mestizo race.[1] Her cries signify the birth of the mixed-race mestizos. Loss, longing, betrayal, and violence mark them.

Her cries reverberate across the Americas, from homes in the southwestern United States, to Mexico City, to south-side Chicago, to New York, to California, to Guatemala and elsewhere. She represents the colonial past. But the story sears the unsettling present.

"Officers would come into the cells and literally just take the kids away from their arms and say goodbye. 'We don't know when you're going to see them again,' they would say."[2]

Sergio Garcia is a force of nature. This assistant federal public defender for the Western District of Texas in El Paso earned his law degree from Indiana University. He clerked for ten years, for six different federal judges, including two circuit judges in the United States. He is from Mexico City. Garcia told me he believes in the law and its strict interpretation. Juan Gabriel croons over the stereo as we talk during his lunch hour.

Garcia becomes a witness. He tells of a woman he thought was in her forties or fifties. But her worries, or the demands of working in the fields in Guatemala, or escaping what was her homeland, or resisting her and her family's caging in the United States, had taken a toll. They spoke to each other in Spanish. He realized during our conversation that it was much more of an imposition for her.

"The officers told my client that they were taking the child to get a shower . . .

"They never brought the child back [she said]. They took him."

And she cried.

This incarcerated caregiver from an impoverished region of Guatemala recalled signing a document with an "X."

> The elderly woman couldn't write or read in Spanish, much less get on a website. The government said, we'll give her the website of the . . . How the hell is she going to get on the website there in jail when she's cannot read English or Spanish?
>
> "Where is the child?" she pleaded.

> I didn't know. They took him. That was the end. It was the last time she saw the child, to the best of my knowledge.
>
> I was heartbroken.

The document she had signed likely gave the US government custody of her child, according to the attorney.

> I had to give her the bad news because she asked me, all confused, What happened, Mr. Garcia? Where is the child? I said, We lost. How come they couldn't help me? I said, We tried. I couldn't help her. I couldn't help her. I saw this woman cry like a baby, screaming at me, Why have I let her down? Why did I let her down? I promised I would help her, because I did.
>
> It broke my heart.
>
> It broke my heart.
>
> It was just horrible. She grabbed me. She grabbed me with her handcuffs. She put her hands on my shirt and my tie, and she said, You promised that you would help me.
>
> I said, I tried.

Another assistant federal public defender, Alex Almanzan, bears witness:

> [*C*]*hildren were screaming and crying*. . . . We saw families being taken apart. We would have individuals that were charged with the 1326 [the code governing reentry of removed aliens], and they were telling us, "Where's my son. Where's my daughter? Either the agents, the Border Patrol agents, didn't know what happened to the children, or just were indifferent.
>
> I would ask, "Well, was this person with a child?" And the agent would say, "I don't know who the child is."

"Where was the child taken?" Almazan would ask.

The Border Patrol agent would reply: "I have no idea. We turned them over to someone else. They got picked up and we don't know where they are."

El Paso was where such practices were incubated. It was where I grew up and my family has had roots for generations, where my black-wearing aunt, the one who fled Mexico along with my grandparents, lived; where one of her contemporaries in my extended family was kidnapped by a group of men; where she pretended that armed men patrolled her home.

Children were "disappeared" as Garcia's supervisor, Federal Public Defender Maureen Scott Franco, put it, a term with a terrible legacy speaking to the practices of state terror in Latin America.[3]

Ay mis hijos!

This image is from the art exhibit *Uncaged Art: Tornillo Children's Detention Camp*, mounted at the University of Texas at El Paso in the second half of 2019. The exhibit featured paintings, drawings, and handicrafts composed of found materials, made by the young men and women who trekked two thousand miles from their homes in Central America and were detained in the Tornillo. Photo by author

Garcia appealed to the people he had worked with for years. "I went to the federal judges," he told me. "I thought they would help me. I presented clear, concise, legal arguments. They didn't give a shit. Nobody cared about that woman. Nobody cared about the migrants."

Ay mis hijos!

The United Nations has condemned orchestrated tactics of taking children as genocide. Certainly, the taking of children staves off the future of a people. Many fathers and other caregivers lost their children, whom they had brought with them, in their pursuit of their right of asylum, enshrined in US and international law. Officials disappeared them.

Many of their cries are in Q'anjob'al or other unsettling native languages: *Baytal ayik' eb' unin? (Where are my children?)*

Crystal Massey, a human rights activist based in Las Cruces, New Mexico, trained in anthropology and worked in Latin America. She does not want to tell me what she knows. She does not want to talk about detention, the humiliation, if not torture, of migrants, the horrendous conditions, or the rapes of the already dispossessed in detention.[4]

The practice of family separation consumed her.

She witnesses:

> I thought that I had become immune. I thought I had grown a callus on my soul sufficient to deal with migrant detention and I hadn't even grown a callus sufficient enough to deal with children being locked up under four civil guards. . . .
>
> I was working with the organization I work with now. We got a call from some folk down in El Paso, saying a ton of the separated parents are stuck here in El Paso. They're out in, they're out at Sierra de Blanca, they're in El Paso. I was going as the interpreter.
>
> I had never dealt with anyone whose soul had been crushed in the same way that these parents' souls had been crushed.
>
> The fathers. . . . it was straight from hell. Talking to those fathers . . .

And the numbers of them who had not even been in touch with their kids. . . . And a lot of the dads we were talking to spoke Spanish as a second language and had only gone to second or third grade of formal education.

Baytal ayik' eb' unin? ¿Dónde están mis hijos? Where are my children?

Nothing, nothing that I had worked with, not torture survivors, not people who had survived the murder of a family member, not seeing children mistreated by guards, not rape survivors [in Latin America]. None of that prepared me for talking to a father who had their child taken out of their arms.

None of it.

None of it.

Government officials gave the detainees a paper with an 800 number on it. It was where they were to receive information on their taken children. You couldn't call 1-800 numbers from those hell holes. And so you have these dads stuck detained hundreds of miles away who had been handed a paper saying, "If you want to talk to your kid or find out where they are, you need to call this number."

And they had no way to call.

There was nothing they could do.

Now the 1-800 numbers, they were for security purposes, which makes total sense. They don't tell you. So you can call them and say, Hey, I'm looking for Juan. This is his date of birth and this the country he's from. They're not going to tell you, Oh yeah, he's at such and such facility. This is the number. Call them. For security, if they don't know who you are and you're just calling a random number, they have to verify. So what they do is they take down the information and they send the facility where the child is detained a message.

Sometimes the organization that Massey works for would have the resources to advocate for the incarcerated parents and other caregivers and allow them to make such phone calls.

> They would come back beaten and distraught.
>
> It would be the first time they had spoken to their child in six or eight weeks. The child believed their parent, their aunt, their uncle, their brother, their sister, or other family member had abandoned them.
>
> The children believed they were forgotten.

Fathers, according to Massey, who "were doing everything in their power to keep their children safe faced impossible choices." They were told to "sign documents and [they] could pursue the right for asylum for themselves and their children." The documents were in English, a language many of them could not read.

> They hadn't spoken to their child. They didn't know where their child was. They didn't know if the child was safe. They were given the option to seek asylum for both them and their children, and if they lost, they would both be deported.
>
> Or the parents were given the option of signing a deportation order, and the state would then keep the child safe with whomever the parent chose and the parent would be sent back. Some were told "sign here and we can send you all back together now and then you can be reunited right away. You miss your child? We'll reunite you and deport you within 48 hours.

Attorney Virginia Raymond bears witness. She describes a scene when it dawned on her that an asylum officer was unaware that the Department of Homeland Security was separating children from their parents in 2018 during "a credible-fear interview," when government agents first assess a noncitizen's stories in their quest for asylum.

Her client had been asked a series of routine questions: her name, her age, her country of origin, her domestic arrangements.

Then, the officer asked, "Do you have any children?"

"Yes."

Asylum officer: "How many?"

"One."

Asylum officer: "What is your child's name?"

The woman replies.

Asylum officer: "What is your child's birth date?"

The mother replies.

Asylum officer: "So your child is living in Guatemala?

She says, "No."

Asylum officer: "Then, where is your child?"

"They took him."

Asylum officer: "Who took him?"

"They took him. They took him when we got here."

"Who is 'they'?"

Silence.

Asylum officer: "Who took your child away, and why would they do that?"

Silence.

And then, "It's been a month since I've seen him."

Contemporary appearances of La Llorona resonate with family separation for those who arrive at the US-Mexico border seeking refuge, but the moment demands a redrafting. The contemporary manifestation of this apparition coincides with the demands by nonbinary Latinxs for recognition and an accompanying acknowledgment that helps us consider the shortcomings of nationality as an identifier.[5] These currents trans-figure this icon of betrayed and betraying motherhood. She has become nonbinary, a term for those either refusing or unable to fit into the dominant male-female gender opposition so normalized, so natural, so given to us.

The situation demands a reckoning with other wretched episodes of this practice. They include the ruthless divisions of enslaved black families, such as the taking of children at slave auctions; the deportation of Native youth from their homes to boarding schools; and the removal of children from largely Black "welfare mothers" deemed unfit to parent in the twentieth century.

The cruel histories of security forces of certain authoritarian regimes that the United States supported in the "dirty wars" in Central and South America further fuel such practices. Such regimes often colluded with the US government and US-based corporations in taking children from civilians: practices of state terror as rule. Attorney General Jeff Sessions, as documented in a Department of Homeland Security review of the practice, told US attorneys of the border region: "We need to take away children; if care [*sic*] about kids, don't bring them in; won't give amnesty ~~to kids~~; to people with kids (strikethrough in original)"[6]

The Trump administration characterized Central American children as threats to national security. They were sometimes denied basic dignities such as soap, toothbrushes, and potable water, treatment capturing how contemporary international boundaries are instrumental in the disavowal of humanity. Authorities at the border separated young people, toddlers, even babies, from their parents, putting them in different detention camps or expelling the parents.

Baytal ayik' eb' unin? (Where are my children?)

The lloronx marks tragedy. Heartache. Pain.

This transformed figure puts flesh on the story of a Honduran father separated from his wife and child. He suffered a nervous breakdown at a Texas jail. Locked in a padded cell, as detailed in an incident report filed by sheriff's deputies, the father killed himself.

He had fled Honduras with his wife and their three-year-old son after his brother-in-law's murder left the family terrified. His suicide caused deep apprehension about the vicissitudes for irregular border crossers who face family separation in government custody. The couple had resided in the United States. Their child is an American citizen. The family went back to Honduras voluntarily several years ago to raise coffee beans.[7]

They and others like them represent the damned, searching for their and their community's lost children. Parents and other caregivers of those who have lost their children, whose children were taken, have tended to be from Guatemala, where they have their own stories of La Llorona.

Massey witnesses that parents had to make excruciating choices under such pressures. Government agents and prison guards would tell parents of disappeared children,

> You don't qualify for asylum. You don't have an asylum case. You're not going to win anything. Why are you fighting? . . . the single worst day was actually being there working with the parents who were being reunited after a month, after two months, and they were bringing kids in dirty. They were bringing kids in with lice. There were dads who had just been reunited with their kids two hours before and then they . . .
>
> It was incredibly rare to see a joyous reunion . . . it's mostly children who thought they'd been abandoned and children who had not even been allowed physical touch or comfort for two months while they were traumatized going through this.
>
> What we did is sick and irreparable. My first experience in Dilley was with a woman who had her little kid, her two-year-old with her, but she was trying to figure out what had happened to her other kids, because they had all gone as a family group with other families to the port of entry, asking for asylum. They got to the midpoint and officials are pushing people backwards, and her ten-year-old and twelve-year-old were in front of her going forwards and they were just getting pulled apart. And her kids were screaming back to her and she's screaming up to them. She ended up back, thank God, instead of getting deported.
>
> And so she ended up back there, and she didn't know what

had happened to her kids. They'd just gone on. And so, when she got to Dilley a few days after this . . . Because the priest walked back with her the next time . . . Good old Italian dude. He was walking along with her and he gets her in and then the US officials process her and send her to Dilley with her two-year-old, and all she can think about is, where are my kids? What happened to my kids?

Massey recalls that a Japanese American author visited Dilley in 2016. She grew up in a Japanese internment camp during World War II. She came out horrified. "This is levels and levels worse than what we suffered in the internment camps" Massey remembers the author saying.

> That was her words, and she has written about it. She said in the internment camps they were kept together, not always initially but they were eventually brought together as groups, family groups. And they have family groups even up to extended family; both parents, et cetera, together with the children. And our government sent Dad off one place, 18-year-old kids another place, Mom and minor kids to Dilley, and they've completely upended the family unit. They put people in space where they cannot easily communicate with one another and given them a lot of misinformation. And so, we were regularly hearing from people there.

Massey describes one scene:

> So they flew the kids back out with their caseworkers from ORR [the Office of Refugee Resettlement] to wherever the hell they had been after hours of sitting in the desert sun in this fucking parking lot in July last year. And then they brought them back the next day. There was also a case where they reunited parents and kids in the parking lot of the ICE Detention Center there, and then they put them on a bus and they told all these parents,

> "You've got to sign this paperwork or we're going to re-separate you." And it was deportation stuff they were asking. So [there] was a whole group of parents who refused to sign, and they literally dragged the parents off the bus in front of their kids. It was straight from hell, nightmarish. But the parents are like, "I'm not going to let you kill my kid. I will not sign shit that's going to mean . . . that I can't read. And that I know . . . Because I don't trust any of you motherfuckers. It would mean that you're going to deport my kids, too. I did too much to keep them safe.

Some advocates refuse to talk about the family separation. Their faces would quiver. Their voices would crack. Others seemed to have repressed the memories, refusing even to try to remember what happened. To hear the testimonios about family separation is to listen through the silences and to read the pained expressions of attorneys and other advocates.

Advocates for the people who experienced family separation or for those who witnessed it as it occurred disagree on some details. They differ, for example, as to whether it was prosecutorial overreach or some other legal calculus at play that allowed US officials to "separate" children from their parents. But they agree that it was the Trump administration's aggressive and punitive enforcement of what had previously been routine administrative return of people in the United States without permission was what set the stage for the screams of children being taken from their families and the conjuring of the lloronx.

Maureen Scott Franco, the federal public defender for the Western District of Texas, recalls the first time she learned of the state-implemented practices of family separation and the specter of the lloronx. Some attorneys in her office approached her with the news that a husband and wife had crossed the border into New Mexico with a young child. The Department of Homeland Security prosecuted the father. But the couple was distraught about their missing daughter. "They didn't know where the child was," Scott Franco witnesses.

> Typically, what would happen is that the case would be handled administratively. They would have been detained in ICE custody, where families are held, and they find a sponsor. The father, a Mexican national, did have minor run-ins with the law. They were typical of someone who crosses the border to work. The little girl, the office learned after a month ended, up with family in New York. Eventually that child was okay. That was the first recollection that I have of it.
>
> Before then a lot of times the lawyers would be able to work out a deal with the government where the case would get dismissed or they would be able to—they would get a reduction. But the children were not disappeared, so to speak. I mean they knew where they were.[8]
>
> Many advocates tellingly adopted the language of state terror, when describing these events.

The US government had been separating children from their parents in 2017—again, before the Zero Tolerance directive had been implemented. A government report documents a conference call on May 1, 2018, with Attorney General Sessions and Southwest border US attorneys in which the possibility arose of prosecuting adults in family unit. According to notes from a US attorney who was present on the call, Sessions expressed concern that illegal entry numbers "are [rising] again" and mentioned the need to "look to changing the situation." The notes further reflect that the concept of family unit prosecutions was discussed; specifically, the notes state, "prosecute parent and not kids of family units."

Scott Franco recalls:

> The agents would show up and they were like, "I don't know where the child's at," just this nonchalant attitude. Eventually a meeting was called involving community stakeholders that Congressman [Beto] O'Rourke's office organized in September or October 2017. It included immigration practitioners, nonprofits,

faith-based groups, and the like. They asked the immigration authorities if these practices constituted a new policy.

The officer said, "We're doing it. It's not a new policy. We take the president's directive, that he had issued in, what, January of that year, "to mean that we should be enforcing the law to the full extent of the law."

He said it's anything—zero tolerance.

I hadn't really seen that ardent of a response by the government when the president made an edict before. I mean I certainly hadn't seen that in the past eight years under Obama. I hadn't really seen any immediate—they opened up the jails and let out everybody who had been under a mandatory minimum or something. Where the majority of people come in is the Southern District [of Texas]. They weren't seeing family separation. They weren't seeing them really in New Mexico. I hadn't heard about it in Arizona or California, so I asked the border patrolmen that were there. I said, "Well, is this something that's just peculiar to the Western District?" And they said yes. They were enforcing that.

So, I said okay. "It is a priority for us that we're doing this... normally we don't take children. We don't prosecute if the child is 10 or under."

I said, "I had a four-year-old." They looked at me. Everybody else in the room couldn't believe—they were just kind of like, And? They then totally hijacked that meeting because then it wasn't just me talking about it, now the nonprofits, everybody was up in arms that this was going on. There were a lot of direct questions. "Well, what kind of information are you giving to the parent when their child is taken away from them?" "Well, they're not in our custody anymore." Because remember, this was back in the day where Border Patrol would only keep them for seventy-two hours, and then they were like, "They're out of our

> hands." Now they can't do that because they're too full. Well, who does the child go to?" "Well, HSI [Homeland Security Investigations, part of ICE], or it goes to HHS, or it goes to ORR"—all these different other abbreviations were coming up.
>
> I said, "You don't provide the defendant or the alien any information about how to get in touch with their child?" "Well, if they give us information as to where family is, then they already have that information. Why do we have to give it to them, because that's what we'll try to do?"
>
> One of the counterparts on our side asked, "Well, there are a lot of sponsors who now are very afraid to sponsor a child if they're here illegally because they've heard, we've heard that you're also prosecuting sponsors."
>
> He's like, "Yeah. If we check out [the matter] and a child goes to a sponsor and we find out that the sponsor is here illegally, yeah, we're going to file orders on them, a notice to appear.

Scott Franco also recalls a magistrate pointing out that in a proceeding, "if you took a respondent's property, a baseball cap or a belt, they [the attorney] would know how to get it returned." But how to reclaim the children swallowed up in border law enforcement was unclear.

Assistant Public Defender Sergio Garcia recalled when Scott Franco called him to her office in 2017 because of some irregularities. Agents of the state were taking children of parents who had no prior criminal history whatsoever and were being charged with a misdemeanor. As Garcia remembers:

> It sounded like a horror movie, so I dove in, and I started looking at it. There were five cases. I immediately filed a motion to dismiss, because I found out that in these cases, the parents had made a credible-fear claim. They actually crossed the border not at a port of entry but when they encountered the immigration officers. As soon as they did, they said, Hey, we are fleeing [our]

countries; we are being persecuted. The respondents made what in my mind were credible-fear claims. They should have been referred to an asylum officer.

Garcia witnesses. He describes going before the judge to argue that the cases should be heard in immigration court. The court denied his motion. The government attorneys denied that family separation was novel. A supervisor appeared at the proceedings and put three lawyers against him on these cases. The supervisor told the judge that there was nothing new, that this is something the government had a right to do and, per Garcia, they were going to do it.

Garcia continues:

> I begged the magistrate to see the fact that they were children. The oldest was being—I think he was 14, if I recall. I knew the youngest was seven. My clients were mortified. The supervisor looked at me, and she said, well, we offer you plea deals. Have them plead.
>
> I replied to her something to the effect that we're worried about the children. We're not worried about the plea.
>
> Furthermore, we can't plead because you're putting my guys in an impossible spot. They will be pleading not voluntarily; they're pleading because they're afraid of where their children are. They need to go, they need to see their kids.
>
> I reminded the court that they were minor incidents; they were misdemeanors, the equivalent of, I don't know, a traffic violation. I don't know, something small, a misdemeanor.
>
> These people had never been in the country. Those are my first memories of this tragic, tragic way to enforce, or disregard, immigration laws.

Attorney Garcia elaborates:

> Even parents who commit the most horrible felonies have rights to ensure that their children aren't taken from them indefinitely.

> What was occurring among immigrants was indefinite. Neither the parents nor their attorney knew where the children were. We didn't know where the children were. We had no idea, and neither did my clients. We had no idea.

The government suggested that the parents were traffickers in these proceedings. Garcia recalls saying, "If you have any evidence as to that, the most remote evidence, charge my clients with a felony, and charge them with trafficking children." "My clients were petrified," he recalls. They became the new lloronx.

Garcia continues with the following analysis:

> The punishment is not a conviction. The punishment is that they're going to be sent away to their countries without their children, and we don't know whether they're going to see them again: that is excessive for the commission of a misdemeanor. That is legally excessive, to literally terminate parental rights. That's what they were doing.
>
> I know in four of the five cases, those parental rights, to my knowledge today, the government has never informed me if they got reunited. I don't know if the parents will ever see these children again, because how are they going to travel all the way again from El Salvador with the fear that if they get caught again? They're going to be deported. They won't even be allowed to get to the bridge. Why? We know from reports from the news—journalists who report that there are actually officers at the port of entry saying, Hey, don't come in, don't even come and ask. They're being deterred from coming.

El Paso was where the Trump administration first piloted family separation. Maureen Scott Franco remembers that in the late summer or early fall of 2017 she began hearing rumors. A lawyer had told her about their clients, a wife and husband who had both crossed, the latter with a small child. The wife crossed in New Mexico. The husband was caught in El Paso. Scott Franco couldn't recall if the wife was apprehended or not, but the husband was caught with the child. Federal Public Defender Scott Franco witnessed: she recalled that they were prosecuting the father, and he was very distressed because he didn't know where the child, a little girl, was. The family was Mexican.

Scott Franco noted that typically, cases involving children would have been handled administratively. The dispossessed would go through the civil process. They would have been detained in ICE custody, where they would have some sort of family arbitration or find a sponsor, or be sent out somewhere else. Sometimes one family member would be deported while another remained in detention, or another family member would be deported through a different port of entry than the one through which they had entered the country, making it more difficult for them to find their family members. Their belongings, such as cell phones, would be confiscated, making it impossible for them to reach their family, and only legal guardians would be allowed to "retrieve" their children from detention centers, thus barring other kinds of family members from helping.

Kindling for the making of the lloronx qua family separation lurks in reports, studies, and scholarship. For example, Tanya Maria Golash-Boza, a sociologist, has documented a major immigration raid in March 2007, well before the rise of Trump's white nationalist administration. On March 6, just after the workday had begun, some three hundred heavily armed ICE agents stormed into the leather factory of Michael Bianco Inc. in New Bedford, Massachusetts.[9] Panicking, people began to run and hide. ICE agents ran after them, eventually capturing them. Reports indicate that some employees became ill and vomited. Others testified that they were mistreated and abused both at the factory and later during detention.

After screening each of the employees, the agents placed hundreds in ICE custody. Of these, 361 workers were taken to Fort Devens, in Ayer, Massachusetts, for processing around 3 p.m. The following day, 60 of these workers were released for humanitarian reasons, and 90 were sent to a detention center in Harlingen, Texas, thousands of miles away. On March 8, another 116 workers were flown into a detention center in El Paso, Texas. Over the following few days, 31 more employees were released from Texas for humanitarian reasons, primarily because they are the sole caregivers of children.

Nevertheless, many children experienced separation. They spent at least one night without their parents. Many of the children were in the same child care facility. Family and community members took charge of those children whose parents did not come to pick them up. At least one mother was not able to convince ICE that she had a toddler; that child was not released until late at night. About twenty other parents were flown to Texas and waited several days before they could be reunited with their children. Among these was Marta Escoto, the mother of two young children. Both Daniel, age two, and Jessie, four, were born in the United States and were in day care when their mother was arrested. Jessie suffers from a debilitating illness and cannot walk. Marta's sister, fortunately, was able to care for Marta's children in her absence. On Wednesday, March 14, more than a week after the raid, Marta was released pending her trial and was flown back to Massachusetts.

Golash-Boza also documented that another woman was being sent to Texas with other detainees, where on the following day she was able to explain that her six-year-old daughter was ill and was to be taken to the doctor the following week. On the second day of her detention in Texas, she was permitted to contact her babysitter, who did not know what had become of her. A few days later she was released.

The same woman also reported that some of the women who were the sole or primary caregivers of their children and who claimed they were breastfeeding were compelled to prove it by showing milk secretions. She said that the guards made fun of the women when the milk was excreted, laughing and asking other guards to bring them Oreo cookies. At least one of the children of these mothers ended up being hospitalized for dehydration. The child would not take up the bottle.[10]

White nationalist lloronx creation smolders in the disturbing reports about the treatment of Haitian children asylum seekers in the 1980s and 1990s. Haiti, is a land of green mountains, is the country founded by former enslaved Africans. France forced the country to pay reparations for its audacity.[11] In the late 1980s Haiti underwent a political struggle that resulted in the ouster of Jean-Claude Duvalier and, in 1990, the election of Left president Jean-Bertrand Aristide. A subsequent military coup in 1991 generated a large number of Haitians seeking asylum in the United States. President George H. W. Bush ended up creating temporary safe havens for them outside US sovereign territory. They were onboard Coast Guard cutters and at the Guantanamo Bay Naval Base. Under the policies of Bush and his predecessor, Bill Clinton, much of them couched in homophobic terms about preventing the spread of HIV, Haitian children became subject to excessive force and verbal abuse, as the US Atlantic commander admitted. A New York–based advocacy group, Guantanamo Watch, which included several high-profile Black freedom and cultural legends such as Harry Belafonte and Danny Glover, alleged that the children suffered abuse and terror at the hands of US military authorities. The United States eventually repatriated many of the children, sending them to relatives, who reported feeling coerced to sign documents indicating they would care for them.[12]

A report authored by No More Deaths / No Más Muertos documents how migrants are put at risk by the Border Patrol's practice of "lateral repatriation," or deportation through ports of entry that are distant from the location of apprehension. The report shows that 1,051 women, 190 teens, and 94 children were repatriated after dark. It adds: "Children were more likely than adults to be denied water or given insufficient water. Many of those denied water by Border Patrol were already suffering from moderate to severe dehydration at the time they were apprehended."[13]

A 2011 report estimates that at least 5,100 children whose parents had been detained or deported were living in foster care. This figure was a projection based on data collected from six key states and an analysis of trends in fourteen additional states with similarly high numbers of foster care and foreign-born populations. The linkages between border protection enforcement and such areas are remarkable: per the report, where local police aggressively take part in immigration law enforcement, children of noncitizens were more likely to be separated from their parents. Indeed, in counties where local police have enforcement agreements with ICE, children in foster care were, on average, about 29 percent more likely to have a detained or deported parent than in other counties. This report also finds that the impact of aggressive enforcement remains statistically significant when research controls for the size of a county's foreign-born population and its proximity to the border.[14]

Immigrant victims of domestic violence and other forms of gender-based violence face a high risk of losing their children. Approximately one in nine of the stories recounted to the Applied Research Center (ARC) in interviews and focus groups involved domestic violence. As a result of ICE's increased use of local police and jails to enforce immigration laws, when victims of violence are arrested, ICE too often detains them and sends their children to foster care. Many immigrant victims face an impossible choice: remain with an abuser or risk detention and the loss of their children. Indeed, the study elaborates how, across the four hundred counties included in ARC's projections, more than one in four (28.8 percent) of the foster care children with detained or deported parents are from nonborder states. Whether children enter foster care as a direct result of their parents' detention or deportation or were already in the child welfare system, immigration enforcement systems erect often insurmountable barriers to family unity.

Of course, there are cases that warrant separating children from their parents. I acknowledge instances when parents were abusive, detrimental to their children's well-being, or incapable of caregiving.

■ Zero Tolerance

On April 6, 2018, months after the practices described above were carried out, Attorney General Jeff Sessions issued a memorandum. Titled "Zero-Tolerance for Offenses under 8 U.S.C. § 1325(a)," it ordered "each United States Attorney's Office along the Southwest Border—to the extent practicable, and in consultation with DHS—to adopt immediately a zero-tolerance policy for all offenses referred for prosecution under section 1325 (a)." It accelerated the lloronx-making practices of family separation across much of the US-Mexico border region.

"Zero tolerance" has a history. It's encountered in schooling, for example, when children face expulsion for carrying a knife in their lunchbox, to spread jam, sandwich spread, or the like. Zero tolerance refers to the maximization of punishment for the slightest infringement of rules or breaking of laws. A particularly relevant example is the inflexible repression against minor offenses, as implemented in New York City under onetime mayor Rudolph Giuliani, later Trump's personal lawyer. The city's police force targeted the impoverished, the dispossessed, those of the wrong color, creed, sexuality, or nationality, though poverty is endemic to our current way of life. Zero Tolerance focused on "street crimes." After his time in public office Giuliani consulted on such policies in Mexico. Other countries in Latin America adopted similarly rigid law-and-order responses, often as a state response to social demands for increased security and a firm hand against crime. Global North "experts," including criminologists, police officers, and politicians, often design these policies, also known as *mano dura* (akin to "iron fist"). They are financed and promoted by multilateral organizations that are heavily invested in implementing and naturalizing predominantly capitalist ways of organizing social and economic life.[15]

Zero Tolerance had been used in the US-Mexico border region before. A Bush II–era program, for example, called Operation Streamline, removed prosecutorial discretion and continued well into the Obama administration. It required the criminal prosecution of all undocumented border crossers, regardless of their history. Border Patrol agents voluntarily returned first-time border crossers to their home countries or detained and removed them from the United States through the civil immigration system.

I underscore that what happened after the Sessions memorandum was *not* zero tolerance. The state did not punish the dispossessed at the US-Mexico border to the fullest extent of the law. The dispossessed were not forced to pay a fine and then subjected to six months of detention, as would be the case under a true zero-tolerance scenario.

Instead, they became subject to state terror.

As attorney Virginia Raymond explained to me, the memorandum allowed those caught to be sentenced to time served. They were then put into removal proceedings.

The state took their children.

"They're unaccompanied because you made them unaccompanied. That's the big difference between what happened with Obama and what's happened now."[16] The state disavowed parental or custodial rights. It negated the familial bonds between children and parents or other caregivers, creating "unaccompanied alien children." *This constituted a strategy of undocumenting kinship relations.*[17]

Several interlocutors emphasized this point. Family separation occurred through the draconian weaponizing of long-standing administrative practices. In deporting or putting parents in removal or related proceedings, the Trump administration rendered unaccompanied the children of asylum seekers or those involved in another immigration proceeding. This effectively created lloronx, those now seeking their children, seeking redress, many having been banished to their homelands.[18]

Diana Martinez explains that even when the Trump administration relented in pursuing family separation, following expressions of deep outrage and a sophisticated legal challenge of the practices, normative expectations of what made up the family continued to allow the family separation in a different form to occur.

Dónde están mis hijos? Baytal ayik' eb' unin?

■ WITNESSING TORTURE

Father Bob Mosher wears a brown long-sleeve shirt when we meet on a hot summer day in 2018 at a home not far from the international boundary. Goateed and speaking with reassurance, the priest offers a disquieting analysis of migrant detention in the United States. We are in a small home in downtown El Paso, where the Detained Migrant Solidarity Committee (DMSC) often meets. The house is a few miles from a bridge that goes over the Rio Grande into Ciudad Juárez, Mexico. He has me sit to his right as we talk.

He bears witness. He states unequivocally, "*We're torturing migrants.*"

Mosher joined physicians writing in the journal *Pediatrics: Official Journal of the American Academy of Pediatrics*, psychologists, and experts in the United Nations in finding that the Trump administration's treatment of the dispossessed amounts to torture.[1] Observers who visited immigration detention facilities in the US Southwest had the same conclusion. They reported that children were being held in cruel conditions, according to the *New York Times*. They witnessed children as young as seven sleeping on concrete floors. They were denied soap and toothpaste, and older children were being forced to care for younger children. One doctor specifically termed the detention centers "torture facilities."[2] The United Nations defines torture in its Convention against Torture and Other Cruel, Inhuman or Degrading Treatment or Punishment as

> any act by which severe pain or suffering, whether physical or mental, is intentionally inflicted on a person for such purposes as obtaining from him or a third person information or a confession, punishing him for an act he or a third person has committed or is suspected of having committed, or intimidating or coercing him or a third person, or for any reason based on discrimination of any kind, when such pain or suffering is inflicted by or at the instigation of or with the consent or acquiescence of a public official or other person acting in an official capacity.

The definition contains three additional elements of note:

> No exceptional circumstances whatsoever, whether a state of war or a threat of war, internal political instability or any other public emergency, may be invoked as a justification of torture.
>
> An order from a superior officer or a public authority may not be invoked as a justification of torture.
>
> No State Party shall expel, return ("refouler") or extradite a person to another State where there are substantial grounds for believing that he would be in danger of being subjected to torture.[3]

Mosher is careful to explain how the DMSC works to end migrant torture. The organization, he explains to me, leads fundraising efforts to pay the bonds of detained migrants. Its members visit the detainees qua prisoners. They commune with the mothers, fathers, and other relations in detention, who were experiencing a deeper sense of dispossession. Some had lost a child. They were experiencing family separation; they were becoming le lloronx.

It was around the time of this conversation that 900 migrants in a processing center in El Paso, Texas, were, as reported by the *New York Times*, "being held at a facility designed for 125. In some cases, cells designed for 35 people, were holding 155 people."[4] One observer described the facility to *Texas Monthly* as a "human dog pound."[5] The DHS's Office of Inspector General found that ICE was feeding expired food to detainees. The office further uncovered "nooses in detainee cells," "inadequate detainee medical care," and "unsafe and unhealthy conditions."[6]

Mosher continues bearing witness. He tells me of migrants being beaten while handcuffed, of migrants being locked up in solitary confinement for extended periods, of migrants being stripped of their clothes and left nude and shivering in cells.[7] There are also repeated allegations both in my interviews and in certain human rights reports of the sexual abuse of the dispossessed.[8]

Father Bob described detention centers as being constructed of painted-over cinder block:

> The centers have cement floors, razor wire on top of all the walls, double fencing around the enclosure. They look like a prison.
>
> Inmates have to wear color-coded overalls according to their degree of conformity. Although some of them are coded in red and orange to indicate past criminal activity, they are a minority. Blue indicates those who have committed no crimes.

According to Mosher, many of the detained and dispossessed have no criminal background. They have been detained anyway because, he says,

> private companies have arrangements to fill 43,000 beds every night.
>
> They have a contract with the US government. It's a figure established quite randomly by Congress. There's really no reason why that number is so important, except that it's the number of beds that Congress has required to be filled. So that's why even people with no criminal history go into these detention camps. They're not that well organized in the sense that they could get a

situation of overcrowding in these camps. . . . So they sent the overflow to a federal prison or a county jail where they're mixed in with the public.

Mosher's description of the incarceration of the dispossessed echoes that witnessed by attorney Virginia Raymond.

Mosher and others with the DMSC struggle to help detainees feel human. "We're sitting in front of a glass partition," he recalls, "we're talking on these phone pieces . . . to each other. We're sitting down on these metal fixed stools. There's a table underneath the glass partition. Just like what you see in the movies. As if this was a dangerous person. Can't have any contact of any kind with people outside."

Most of the migrants held in detention are from the so-called Northern Triangle of Honduras, El Salvador, and Guatemala, but many are also from Mexico. There are also Chinese, Africans, and Russians.[9]

The priest wearing brown turns his head leftward and continues: "What concerns us is the abuse by the guards. There have been many abuses that the people have described. It's pretty savage in these detention camps."

He bears witness to migrants being yelled at with racial epitaphs, their labor being exploited, their being spat on; to the difficulty they have with visitations; to the homophobia exercised on queer inmates; and to the use of solitary confinement while they are in detention.

Detainees, he underscores, "live hungry."

> Visitors reported [that] individuals appear to have lost weight during their incarceration. . . . A few individuals with dietary restrictions, for either religious or health reasons, complained that their dietary needs were not met. For some, the spicy seasoning was difficult on their digestive systems. . . . Textured vegetable protein, or "soy meat," is served, and sometimes it is not completely rehydrated. Potatoes, another common food item, were also reported as being frequently undercooked. According to two individuals, food often has an "off" taste or smell.

It was reminiscent of pesticide.

Father Mosher explains that movements to resist the torture and detention of the dispossessed grow out of previous struggles for migrant rights. They flourished before the Trump administration. They flourished during the Obama administration. The latter was deporting large numbers of people and faced opposition from those supporting migrant communities like the Dreamers.

Opposing torture is in the priest's blood. His liberation theology took him to Chile in the wake of General Augusto Pinochet's coup in 1973 and during his subsequent oppressive regime, which the US government and its business class supported. Following the democratic election of Salvador Allende in 1970, his Popular Unity government had rejected both Soviet-style suppression of civil liberties and American economic dominance. The Unity government sought to begin a peaceful transition to socialism for Chile while preserving political freedoms. Allende became the first elected socialist president in the Americas, sparking an array of political passions and fueling what Josefina Saldana might call the "revolutionary imagination of the Americas"—and, arguably, of the world.[10]

Allende's election offered up the promises and possibilities of mass-scale struggle on a "democratic path to socialism."[11] The 1959 Cuban Revolution, along with anti-colonial, Indigenous, Black, Third World, and feminist mobilizations, including ones vested in beating the U.S. empire from within, such as Black Power and the American Indian Movement, fertilized energies and passions across historical and geographical divides in much of the Americas and elsewhere in the world. The late twentieth century saw large-scale movements for decolonization, US-based civil rights struggles, national liberation movements, and feminist critiques within many of these movements. Revolution within Chile's own borders was the result of a much more heterogeneous set of struggles, including the armed revolutionary left (MIR), struggles for gay liberation, feminist currents within and outside a popular coalition, and a much broader Mapuche struggle against colonization.[12]

Chile's challenge to the United States was not that it would be turned into another left wing, Soviet-allied, Castro-style dictatorship. The challenge was that it would *not* turn into such a regime, as the historian Greg Grandin notes. And so President Richard Nixon instructed the CIA to "make the economy scream."[13]

Following the coup, the newly imposed bureaucratic authoritarian regime relied on torture to maintain its rule. State terror demobilized political opposition. People were rounded up. Soldiers brought them en masse to sports stadiums, army hospitals, and police barracks. Enemies of the state, of "progress," and members of the Communist and Socialist parties were systematically hunted down. Soldiers regularly pointed machine guns at the "detained." Cattle prods seared the bodies of those condemned to be standing in the country's way. Rape became common. Detention too.[14]

Padre Bob Mosher went to Chile to oppose torture. He felt compelled to do the same in the United States. He explains:

> I have to oppose torture. I protested in Chile. How am I not going to protest it here? I found myself living in a country where torture was practiced, which is huge.
>
> We used to be the country that would protest torture, but now we have no basis for that. . . . [T]he one thing that people found themselves able to overcome their fear and mobilize against, is now a problem here. I came back to the states in 2009 and found that the use of torture was debated in this country. It's something I never imagined.[15]
>
> I remember the Chilean police, and they would repress us and see that there were foreigners in this movement. And they were saying, "Why don't you go back to your own country and protest torture?" and of course, it would just roll off us because we were from the United States. We didn't torture.

Indeed, public opposition to torture has gradually eroded in the United States, particularly since the War on Terror. President George W.

Bush concluded that the Geneva Conventions did not apply to certain enemy combatants in that war. He approved the use of "enhanced interrogation techniques" and, bypassing Congress, issued an executive order that established a new parallel system of justice to deal with "terrorists" through military commissions, most notably at Guantanamo Bay in Cuba. The president, vice president, and secretary of defense made several official statements calling for interrogators to obtain results.

The hardening of borders across the West and prominent calls for increasing the use of enforcement in the Americas and in Europe are inextricably linked to an imperial racism, a pernicious collapsing of domestic concerns about immigrants and "aliens" with international concerns about terrorists and criminal elements. As a result, inequalities, specifically the rights of some populations to thrive while situated closer and closer to death, become naturalized as part of the global order of things. They converge in a profound sensibility that borders are out of control and that citizenship and sovereignty are threatened. And they legitimate tactics such as channeling noncitizens who cross the southern border of the United States without documentation into the scorching desert by day or, with recourse to contemporary detention centers, incarcerating families and children. Militarized border enforcement sears the life of the dispossessed. Migrants experience harsh crossings, depredations by criminals, and abuse by ruthless officials. The vast majority of the wretched who cross the US-Mexico border irregularly survive, coming to labor as imperial subjects in the United States. They unravel the boundaries between life and death.

Anti-migrant torture smolders within militarized border enforcement. Thousands of would-be border crossers have been killed by a weaponization of border environs organized through the US government's deliberate policies, which began during the Clinton administration.[16] Indeed, the "Border Patrol Strategic Action Plan: 1994 and Beyond" advances a strategy of border and migration controls it calls "prevention through deterrence": "The prediction is that with traditional entry and smuggling routes disrupted, illegal traffic will be deterred, or forced over more hostile terrain, less suited for crossing and more suited for enforcement."[17] Border Patrol campaigns such as Hold the Line and Gatekeepers—with their armed officers, helicopters, ATVs, and other equipment—have channeled many of the dispossessed away from southwestern urban centers such as El Paso and San Diego. The effects of this policy cannot be exaggerated: it is the kindling, violence that US policy makers of varying political persuasions organized well before the Trump administration. It implicates presidential administrations from at least the Clinton administration to the present.

Consider that on June 12, 1992, five agents of the US Border Patrol were surveying an area near Nogales, Arizona. In a remote canyon, they encountered three Mexican men. The agents took them to be lookouts for Mexican narcotics smugglers. In violation of Immigration and Naturalization Service (INS) firearms policy, agent Michael Elmer fired three shots over the head of one of the men. The three men fled toward Mexico. Agent Elmer then shot a dozen times at one man, Dario Miranda Valenzuela. He was unarmed. Miranda was hit by two bullets.

Doctors estimate that Miranda may have been alive for thirty minutes after the shooting. Elmer became the first Border Patrol agent to be charged and tried for murder. Other troubling allegations against Elmer came forth during the trial, including the sexual harassment and brutalization of another Mexican man and the alleged wounding of another Mexican man when Elmer shot into a group of thirty undocumented immigrants.

Elmer's lawyer successfully depicted the shooting of the unarmed Valenzuela in the back as an act of self-defense. The jury found that Valenzuela's murder was reasonable at the border. Elmer was acquitted. Eventually, the agent pleaded no contest to a charge of reckless endangerment. Having already spent six months in jail after the shooting, Elmer served little additional time.[18] This is certainly not a lot of time for causing the death of another human being.

Or consider that on the evening of May 20, 1997, a unit of the US Marines was engaged in training in an area of the border known as Polvo Crossing, outside Redford, Texas. At about 6:05 p.m., Corporal Clemente Banuelos, a US citizen of Mexican descent, reported by radio that he had spotted an individual, Ezequiel Hernandez, shepherding goats. He was carrying a rifle. At 6:07, Banuelos reported that his unit was taking fire. Investigators presume that Hernandez, a shepherd, had mistaken the camouflaged marine for a predator and opened fire. After the marine unit then stalked Hernandez for another twenty minutes, Banuelos aimed his high-powered, military-issue rifle at Hernandez and fired a round that entered the shepherd's body below his chest on his right side. It caused severe damage to internal organs and major blood vessels. Hernandez died shortly thereafter. He was a US citizen.

Or consider the following scene from my earlier research in Nogales, Sonora, Mexico.

■ I look up as "Román" points toward the rolling hills that brush up against the fence of the international boundary on this Día de los Muertos, or Day of the Dead, a popular Mexican holiday that honors the deceased. A Border Patrol vehicle parks, close to a tower that shoots video of Nogales, Sonora. We can make out two Border Patrol officers exiting the vehicle. Román, sixteen years old, with a goatee and squared shoulders, flips them off. He laughs.

He lived in Chicago and Seattle before his father's deportation landed him in Nogales.

Since then, Román has struggled on the edges of the Nogales economy. As the border hardens, he and other youth seek work on the edges of Mexico and the United States, selling tacos or small packages of gum, washing the windshields of cars heading north at the port of entry. Indeed, one of Román's many jobs involved working with a man who tied a rope around his waist as the young man was lowered into dark, hot factory chimneys to clean them. Eventually he and other young men and women became involved in the underground economy, where they terrorized the dispossessed trying to cross surreptitiously into the United States, mugging them.

Helicopters buzz the sky above us during our conversation.

Surveillance cameras mounted on border towers aim at the terrain below. Border Patrol in SUVs and all-terrain vehicles move up and down the dusty streets. Infrared sensors report intrusions onto US territory.

Although undocumented migrants were delayed in human way stations such as Nogales, Sonora, on the Mexican side of the international boundary, the undocumented population in the United States grew robustly throughout the 1990s and continues to grow.[19] In these way stations, they steel themselves for the crossing, and the vast majority of them succeed. They seep over, around, and, in this and other cases, under the militarized regimes of boundary enforcement, facing the brutal management of bodies lacking authorization and the multiple exposures that the edges of US racial nationalism demand.[20]

The beauty of the rolling hills, mesquite trees, and saguaro cactus and the brilliant sunshine that beats down on the sand, where temperatures even in the 1990s routinely exceeded one hundred degrees, belied how deliberate border policy rendered the environment deadly. The human body needs at least a gallon of water a day in these ovens of a neoliberal order—the killing deserts.

I tell Román about a University of Houston study soon to be published. It estimates that at least 1,600 immigrants trying to cross the border irregularly between 1993 and 1997 died from dehydration, hypothermia, or other maladies as they tried to avoid the deepening regimes of border enforcement. Hundreds of others, the study reports, simply vanished; whether they were dead or simply unaccounted for is not known.[21]

The number of deaths has grown and grown. Today, an estimated 10,000 border crossers have perished due to US border policy since 1993.

Román replies, "And that does not account for the violence. I bet you Beto's death doesn't count."

He then tells his story of Beto's death. The young man left his home in central Mexico in 1996 when he was fourteen. The country was still suffering from the repercussions of its worst economic crisis since the Great Depression, and people then commonly referred to the country's dire financial situation as *la crisis* (the crisis). As Mexico's onetime corporate state was torn asunder, community farmland was being sold; corn, a staple, grew increasingly expensive. What remained of starved welfare programs did not help Beto's family. He and his parents decided he would join hundreds of thousands of other migrants by going to the United States and helping the family by sending money back home. He would find work in Los Angeles, probably bussing tables at the same restaurant where his aunt worked.

Yet he could not make history as he pleased.

Beto knew that *los chiles verdes* (the green chiles—the Border Patrol in local vernacular) were making crossing difficult in El Paso and San Diego. He headed to the then newly formed clandestine route through Sonora, where he hoped to slip through the border at Nogales. He arrived during one of the high points of Operation Safeguard, a Border Patrol campaign built on the political success of similar ones in the El Paso and San Diego regions. He tried to cross and was quickly apprehended.

Eventually, Beto and the other young people were sent to the juvenile authority of Nogales, Sonora. The defunded public welfare programs such as the Sistema Nacional para el Desarrollo Integral de la Familia (or DIF, as it is commonly referred to) were then exploding with young people who, like Beto, had migrated from points throughout Mexico and Central America looking for work.[22] Eventually, he was back on the streets of Nogales with a few pesos in his pocket and fewer options.

Some two weeks after his original attempt to cross the border, and while the Nogales region remained "hot," Beto tried to cross again. Román explains that this time Beto chose another route. He literally undermined the border through the moist underground world of a transnational sewer system. As luck would have it, when Beto exited the sewer system via a large drainage ditch in Nogales, Arizona, the authorities caught him again.

Beto soon tried again. On his third attempt—his second navigating the below-border, subterranean sewer tunnel—he succeeded. He exited the tunnel into the drainage ditch and climbed up into the light of the United States. He then hopped a freight train. As he jumped from one boxcar to another, probably trying to hide from the Union Pacific Railroad police, who were on high alert for immigrants, he slipped and fell onto the track.

"Lo cortó así." It cut him like this, Román reports. He makes a chopping motion across my waistline. The train severed the young man in half.[23]

■ No More Deaths, a human rights organization based in southern Arizona, reported in 2011 certain "inhumane" practices used by the Border Patrol and in detention against the dispossessed. It resonates with Padre Bob's analysis.

The report substantiates a litany of abuses. It draws on 4,130 interviews with 12,895 individuals who were in Border Patrol custody, including 9,562 men, 2,147 women, 533 teenagers (ages thirteen to eighteen), and 268 children (up to age twelve) from the fall of 2008 to the spring of 2011, primarily in Arizona border communities. Per the report, the documented abuses have "remained consistent from year to year, interviewer to interviewer and site to site."[24]

They include officials slashing humanitarian-provided water bottles of those crossing the weaponized deserts of the border, thus depriving those captured in the scorching desert of water. The report contains testimonies of people who witnessed officers denying border crossers medical care, even if they were afflicted with life-threatening illnesses. The report has testimonios of children and adults who experienced beatings during apprehensions and in custody. The report includes testimonies people who observed agents denying children water after apprehending them in the desert.[25] Children were more likely than adults to be denied water or given insufficient water. Keeping vehicles transporting captured migrants extremely hot or cold, playing traumatizing music (*migracorridos*) about people dying in the desert and other kinds of sensory overstimulation, and exercising other verbal, physical, and psychological abuse, including death threats, are documented in the report. So is cramming the undocumented into cells and subjecting them to extreme temperatures. Patrol officers deprived the captured of sleep, an abuse sometimes characterized as torture; threatened them with violence; and failed or refused to provide medical treatment or access to medical professionals.

Interviewees consistently reported inhumane and unsanitary conditions in detention centers. Many were held in cells so packed that the detainees could not move or lift their arms or lie down. Toilets were in a common area.[26] Migrants were refused blankets. Those who received them described them as filthy or riddled with cactus spines. Officers told women they were going to be left alone with a group of men whom they did not know, threatening them with the possibility of sexual violence.

I excerpt several testimonios from the report to bring further flesh to theory:

> June 14, 2010, with Gerardo, 47, from Nayarit, Mexico. His feet were severely blistered and were being treated by a volunteer EMT during the interview. He stated that he was detained for two days at a Border Patrol detention center near Why, Ariz., after walking through the desert for three days. At the detention center, agents went through Gerardo's belongings and those of others and threw away identification, cell phones and lists of phone numbers. He was able to rescue his cell phone from the trash can and had it in his possession during the interview. Gerardo requested medical treatment for his feet but was only told "Later" and never received any care. Migracorri-

dos, songs telling morbid tales of death in the desert, were played over the loudspeakers 24 hours a day at high volume, he said. Every two hours, guards would come in shouting at the detainees and require them to line up for inspection. These measures prevented the detainees from sleeping.

April 24, 2010, with Diego, 21, from Oaxaca, Mexico. He stated that he tried to cross into the United States for the first time to join his parents and siblings. When he was apprehended in the desert, an agent asked Diego how many were in his group. When he said, "It's just us," the guard struck him in the face with a flashlight. In the Border Patrol vehicle, agents mocked him. He never received medical treatment for injuries sustained in the assault or for wounds on his feet. At no point while he was in custody was he told where he was being taken or held. Diego described the site where he was detained as a small center in the desert. Women and minors were held inside, but the men were held in a pen outside in extremely cold temperatures with no blankets. After a day and a half, he was deported to Nogales.[27]

Feb. 19, 2010. Three women were held in custody Feb. 17–18 in Tucson. One woman, 24, was from Chiapas, where she has three children ages 8, 10, and 12. She was attempting to cross for the first time to find work to support her children. She was brought in chains to Operation Streamline at the federal courthouse in Tucson, where guards pushed detainees who were chained together. One guard held her nose in front of the detainees and said they smelled. Another woman stated that when she was apprehended with a group in the desert, a Border Patrol agent accused them of carrying drugs and threatened to shoot them. The third woman reported that guards shouted at them and used racist language. Agents took their clothes and then held them in extremely cold temperatures while in custody.

Sept. 21, 2009, an anonymous woman stated that she had lived in the U.S. for 17 years with three children. When her parents died in Mexico, she returned for the funeral, and was apprehended on July 23 near Nogales, Ariz., while trying to re-enter the U.S. In the processing center, guards laughed at her for being Mexican. They had her strip naked; then they took her clothes and touched her breasts in the presence of both male and female guards. Her belongings were taken and not returned, including $20, jewelry, and make-up. She was detained for two months in Florence. She was given papers in English to sign, without a translator, and was deported Sept. 18 to Nogales, Sonora.[28]

The report also documents lloronx making, the separation of family members. The Border Patrol deported 869 family members separately, including 17 children and 41 teens.

A 2011 report by the Applied Research Center documents the following:

> Josefina's baby was just 9 months old, and Clara's children were 1 and 6, when they were placed in foster homes with strangers. Clara and Josefina, sisters in their early 30s who lived together in a small New Mexico town, had done nothing to harm their children or to elicit the attention of the child welfare department in the late summer of 2010, when a team of federal immigration agents arrived at the front door of Clara and Josefina's trailer home in New Mexico. Immigration and Customs Enforcement (ICE) had received a false tip that the sisters, who were undocumented immigrants, had drugs in their home. Though they found nothing incriminating in the trailer and the sisters had no criminal record, ICE called Child Protective Services (CPS) to

take custody of the children, and ICE detained the sisters because of their immigration status.

For the four months that ICE detained them, Josefina and Clara did not know where their children were. In December, the sisters were deported, and their children remained in foster care. Josefina was very quiet as she talked by phone from Mexico a year after she was de ported: "I don't know where my child is; I have no contact with my baby. I didn't do anything wrong to have my children taken away from me.[29]

There is also the harrowing complaint against the Border Patrol for the beating and tasing to death of Anastasio Hernández-Rojas. The complaint went before the Inter-American Commission on Human Rights on behalf of his family. The petition draws on US federal law and the United Nations Convention against Torture.[30]

Born on May 2, 1968, to Porfirio Hernández-Rojas and Maria de la Luz Rojas Olivo in the city of San Luis Potosí, Mexico, Anastasio was the third of nine children. At age fifteen, he moved to San Diego, California, to seek work and help support his family. He met Maria de Jesus Puga Moran when he was twenty-one. The couple conceived five children, over the course of twenty years. All of them were born in San Diego.

On May 10, 2010, Hernández-Rojas was arrested for shoplifting and detained in the United States. He was removed from the United States to Mexico two weeks later. He attempted to rejoin his family in San Diego by reentering the United States with his brother, Pedro Hernández-Rojas on May 28, 2010. Customs and Border Patrol, after apprehending Anastasio and Pedro, took them to the Chula Vista Border Patrol Facility and Detention Center. The agents searched them and found that they were carrying a gallon of water and ham sandwiches. Upon arrival at the Chula Vista facility, Border Patrol agent Gabriel Ducoing directed Anastasio Hernández-Rojas to put the water he was carrying into a trashcan. The officer grew angry when Hernández-Rojas did so. The officer slapped the water jug out of Hernández-Rojas's hands, pushed him against a wall, and repeatedly kicked his ankles apart.

Hernández cried out in pain and asked, "Why are you doing this to us? Why are you hitting us? We haven't done anything wrong" (14). Ducoing retorted, "You don't want to be beaten?" Ducoing then handcuffed and took him to an interview room. There, Hernández-Rojas complained that Ducoing had injured his ankle, which was held together by a metal screw, having been broken years before. Hernandez complained about the pain, rubbed his ankle, and requested the opportunity to appear before an immigration judge during the interview (19).

At no time during the interview did Ducoing inform his supervisor that Hernández-Rojas had complained about mistreatment or requested medical attention, as required by US Customs and Border Protection policy. He was then taken to a processing area and handcuffed to a bench. While in processing, he repeatedly requested medical treatment, asked for the opportunity to make a phone call, asserted his right to appear before an immigration judge, and complained about mistreatment. After several hours, the facility supervisor, Agent Ismael Finn, spoke with Hernández-Rojas, who repeated his request for medical care and complaints of mistreatment. Rather than taking action to address those complaints, Supervisor Finn ordered his agents to remove Hernández-Rojas from the United States to Mexico. The agents later stated that Hernández-Rojas did not behave like a "typical alien" during processing. Unlike "typical aliens," who quietly face the wall, agents reported that the man talked loudly, looked directly at the agents, and complained about the agents' mistreatment (24).

Another agent, Philip Krasielwicz, reported feeling much "disdain" for Hernández-Rojas because he had complained in a loud voice and failed to show the agent the respect that the officer expected. Another agent, Jose Galvan, testified that Hernández-Rojas's behavior during processing was "out of the norm." He did not comply with instructions to remain quiet but gesticulated and talked loudly. Finn testified that Hernández was "vocal and argumentative." Agent Sandra Cardenas explained that Finn arranged for Hernández-Rojas to be transported to Mexico right away because he was disrespectful and problematic. Finn instructed Ducoing and Krasielwicz to transport Hernández-Rojas in handcuffs to the Whiskey 2 area at the San Ysidro Port of Entry for removal to Mexico. Hernández-Rojas's brother Pedro, with whom he had been detained, remained at the Chula Vista facility. As Hernandez-Rojas limped toward the vehicle, he complained that he had difficulty walking (31).

Once at Whiskey 2, Ducoing and Krasielwicz exited the vehicle and removed the handcuffs from Hernández-Rojas. The agents testified that as they removed the handcuffs, the young man lowered his hands to his waist instead of putting them on top of his head as instructed and "moved around too much" (34). A struggle ensued. Two ICE agents, Andre Piligrino and Harinzo Narainesingh intervened. They used retractable steel batons to strike Hernández-Rojas's chest and diaphragm.

Agent Piligrino had been trained in baton use at the Federal Law Enforcement Training Center. He testified that he knew that the proper areas for baton use were the thigh, calves, and arms and that secondary strike areas were the body's midsection and joints. He was trained to not strike the cranium, sternum, spine, or chest.

According to agent testimony, Hernández-Rojas and four agents fell to the ground, with Hernández-Rojas on his stomach. A fifth officer, Agent Derrick Llewellyn, arrived on the scene. Hernández-Rojas's hands were handcuffed behind his back as Ducoing, Krasielwicz, and Piligrino pressed him facedown onto the pavement. They held him by the legs, the waist, and the side of his body.

Hernández-Rojas could not move. He cried out for help in Spanish.

His cries drew the attention of passersby, and a group of witnesses gathered on a pedestrian bridge that overlooked the scene. They began using cameras and cell phones to record what was happening.

Two additional CBP agents arrived and joined the five other officers. Together, the officers tried to force Hernández-Rojas into the back seat of an SUV, but the man braced his feet against the door of the vehicle. Officers then dragged the man, who was still handcuffed, behind the SUV and again placed him facedown on the pavement (47).

According to the eyewitnesses, agents kneeled on the back of the man's neck and on his lower back, while others repeatedly punched, kicked, and stepped on his head and body.

Two more vehicles arrived on the scene, and according to witnesses, an agent exited one of these and "went straight to Hernández, who was still on the ground (in handcuffs), and kicked him . . . hard, like a soccer kick" (5).

Witnesses then observed CBP agent Jerry Vales arrive at the scene and yell at Hernández-Rojas to "stop resisting," though he was handcuffed on the ground and not moving.

More agents arrived on the scene, and by this point, between fifteen and twenty-five agents were present. Vales then warned the other officers that he intended to use his Taser X26 weapon. The agents surrounded and partially obscuring the scene.

A recording by a witnesses captured Vales administering multiple shocks with the taser while Hernández-Rojas lay on the ground in a fetal position with his hands handcuffed behind his back and multiple agents forming a circle around him.

The taser sent electric currents surging through his body (5–6).

Vales activated the taser at least four times, according to the Taser's log, a program on the device that records the occurrence and duration of each shock. This log recorded that the first and second administrations lasted five seconds, the third thirteen seconds, and the fourth for twelve seconds. Of these four Taser X-26 activations, at least two successfully shocked the immobilized, handcuffed father. In the last application, the agent set the taser to "drive stun" mode and put the twelve-second shock directly to Hernández-Rojas's chest. Piligrino testified that this final shock "caused Hernandez to convulse."

A witness video-recorded Hernández's cries for help:

Hernández: "Que les hago?" (What did I do?)

Hernández: "Ayudenme." (Help me.)

Hernández: "Ah. No! No! Ayuda! Ayudenme! Ya! Por favor! Se ores ayudenme! Ay, ay, ay." (Ah. No! No! Help! Help me! Please! People help me! Ay, ay, ay.)

A command: "Stop resisting."

Hernández: "Ayudenme por favor!" (Help me please!)

[Hernández:] "Me tratan como un animal. Ah, ah, ah. No. Ayuda. No! Ay ay." (You're treating me like an animal. Ah, ah, ah. No. Help. No! Ay ay.)

Female voice: "Ya dejenlo!" (Leave him alone!)

[Hernández:] "No!"

Female voice: "Hay, esta mierda!" (Damn, this shit!) (6).

After the last shock from the taser, officers swarmed the subdued detainee and again pressed him facedown with their knees on his head and back, preventing him from breathing (6). A witness testified that he observed officers punch Hernández-Rojas repeatedly in the ribs. Unlike other settings on the taser, which primarily aim to immobilize the victim, the "drive stun" mode does not incapacitate. Its purpose is to cause localized pain, or ensure "compliance," as law enforcement refers to it.[31]

Video footage shows a flashlight illuminating the scene, with Hernández-Rojas on the ground face down and the legs of an officer kneeling on his head and neck. Video also captures officers taking off Hernandez-Rojas's pants. Officers then zip-tied his ankles to his handcuffed hands.

Face down, handcuffed, and effectively hogtied, the man went motionless. Officers nudged him with their feet. He did not move. Officers stood by for approximately two minutes before trying CPR. An ambulance arrived on the scene anywhere from five to fifteen minutes after Hernández-Rojas became unresponsive.

Hernández-Rojas was taken to a local hospital. The beating and tasing had deprived his brain of oxygen for eight minutes. He was diagnosed with an anoxic brain injury (the death of brain cells due to oxygen deprivation), secondary to his resuscitated cardiac arrest, and was pronounced "brain dead" by physicians on May 29, 2010. He remained briefly on life support until he flatlined and was pronounced dead on May 31, 2010, at 4:30 p.m. He was forty-two years of age. The forty-two-year-old father's death certificate reports cause of death as anoxic encephalopathy, or brain damage produced by a lack of oxygen to the brain. The secondary causes of Hernandez's were deemed "resuscitated cardiac arrest, acute myocardial infarct, and physical altercation with law enforcement officers" (7)

White nationalism intensified by border enforcement is the comorbidity.

On June 1, 2010, Glenn N. Wagner, the chief medical examiner for San Diego County, performed an autopsy of Hernndez-Rojas's body. Dr. Marvin Pietruszka, a board-certified anatomic and clinical pathologist and the civil plaintiffs' medical expert, did a second autopsy, a few days later. The first autopsy confirmed:

> blunt force injuries of the forehead, right side of face, lips, flank, abdomen, hands and lower legs. . . . The abdominal injury which shows underlying soft tissue hemorrhage is consistent with a collapsible baton strike. . . . The puncture marks over the right flank and left buttock are believed to be Taser marks.
>
> Dr. Pietruszka noted there were contusions, abrasions, and bruises on the following areas of Hernandez's body: the right jaw, the upper jaw, the cheek area, both hands, right wrist, right thigh, extensive hematoma extending into the posterior paravertebral musculature near the left scapula (running along the upper left side of his back), abrasions of both knees and buttocks, contusions and abrasions of the upper and lower lips, the upper gum line, the left anterior chest, the left upper abdomen, the right pelvis, the left inner thigh, the right forearm, and the right anterior tibial region of the leg. Dr. Pietruszka additionally noted that Hernandez-Rojas sustained five broken ribs.

Both autopsies ruled Hernandez-Rojas's death a homicide.

When asked if the use of Tasers contributed to Hernandez-Rojas's death, Dr. Wagner was unequivocal: "There's no question in my mind." He concluded: "I have no choice but to determine the manner of death as homicide. . . . [His] heart attack . . . is clearly the result of oxygen deprivation to the heart. . . . And the only way I know that you can get that is with an arrhythmia that oftentimes is triggered by a surge of norepinephrine or a blow to the chest."

Although the FBI decided to investigate the incident following the release of video by an eyewitness, the Department of Justice declined to prosecute, allowing a pattern of obstruction of justice on the part of Customs and Border Protection to persist. Officials dispersed witnesses without recording their contact information at the incident, and they failed to collect the government's own video surveillance footage, and impeded the investigation.

The family of Hernández-Rojas, represented by Alliance San Diego, a member of the Southern Border Communities Coalition, and international law experts from the International Human Rights Law Clinic at the University of California, Berkeley, would eventually file a petition with the Inter-American Commission on Human Rights (IACHR) in Washington, DC. This action followed six years of failure to hold CBP agents accountable for Hernandez-Rojas's murder. The IACHR eventually announced that it would move forward with the case. It gave the US government the opportunity to respond to allegations of extrajudicial killing, torture, and obstruction of justice. This was the first case alleging an unlawful killing by law enforcement opened by the IACHR against the United States.

The Trump administration maintained that the IACHR lacked jurisdiction to hear the case. On July 23, 2020, the Inter-American Commission on Human Rights (IACHR), the investigative arm of the Organization of American States, found that it has such authority. In January 2021,

Hernandez-Rojas's family, represented by Alliance San Diego and the UC Berkeley International Human Rights Law Clinic, filed a brief with the IACHR that included new testimony from three former Department of Homeland Security officials who pointed to a cover-up (7).

The case is moving forward.

None of the officers involved have been disciplined or fired.

■ Enter the figure of the refugee into the crosshairs. Enter those seeking to exercise the internationally recognized right of asylum, who want and deserve their day to be heard and who often present themselves to the border authorities, at which point they become subject to detention, or worse. I return to Padre Bob Mosher:

> Trump is our Pinochet. Obviously he's not a military professional, and there's no violent military coup that brought Trump to power. But the oppressive actions of this administration... some of them are merely intensifications of things we have seen before.
>
> The separation of families has taken place before. Obama used to be called the "Deporter in Chief" for good reason. That administration deported more people than any other president before him. The Obama administration caged children and families and it continued the militarization of the US-Mexico border enforcement, the weaponization of ICE, in tandem, culminated in Zero Tolerance and the insidious conditions for migrant suffering.
>
> But it's at a new level now, and there are parallels with the racism of Pinochet's regime, with the repressive measures, with the instances of torture, if you can consider the separation of parents and children as a form of torture, which I do.
>
> So General Pinochet was a difference in degree rather than kind. In many ways, not absolute on that. 'Cause, again, Trump

> was elected, maybe not by the majority of voters but by the majority of electors, anyway. And Pinochet never even received a single vote for anything. It was often pointed out during his regime. And then he established—we would say that Pinochet ran as the only candidate, and he still lost. So I guess it's the whole anti-democratic kind of regime here in the states that makes me think that my time in Chile was like a preparation for what's going on in my own country.

Mosher continues: "People come to the border and ask for asylum and are being told, 'We can only take three of you, so your [last] child can't come in with you, you're going to have to leave a child behind.'"

Migrant torture demands accountability. It demands to be documented. It demands to be recognized as sadistic. Family separation approaches the UN's definition of torture.

Family separation "may have severe consequences in a child's developmental processes and psychosocial functioning," Cristina Muñiz de la Peña declared in remarks delivered to the Subcommittee on Oversight and Investigations of the US House Committee on Energy and Commerce. The intense fear, sense of helplessness, and vulnerability that a child experiences who is forcibly separated from their parent can lead to a state of hyperarousal, attention deficits, depressive symptoms, and interference in their ability to communicate and relate to others.

"Overall, it has been my observation that children who endured separation at the border are more likely to develop symptoms of post-traumatic stress and depression, which are reflected in their negative perceptions of the world as unsafe and uncontrollable and their self-perceptions as helpless and endangered," she said. "These perceptions affect how children navigate the world, how they communicate with others, how they learn and how they develop relationships with peers and other adults in their life."[32]

Muñiz's testimony provided several real-world examples, including that of a two-year-old boy who was separated from his mother while he was sleeping and kept from her for two months. Even after mother and son were reunited, the boy demonstrated signs of separation anxiety and hypervigilance. In another case, the government separated a sixteen-year-old girl from Honduras from her mother after she displayed symptoms of depression.[33] "The experience of total lack of control and terror during the separation," Muñiz testified, had left her with a severe sense of helplessness, which she described as feeling like others would always have control over what happens to her, and hopelessness, which she described as feeling like her life would never get better."

Research shows that the longer the separation, the greater the reported symptoms of anxiety and depression are for children, reported Muñiz. Long-term separation also can result in ongoing difficulty in trusting adults and institutions, as well as lower levels of educational achievement, according to a report by the APA Presidential Task Force on Immigration. Muñiz continued:

> Over the past five years directing the mental health services at Terra Firma [Immigrant Youth Clinic, in New York City], I have observed the impact of recent immigration policies on children and families, both positive and negative. I have seen an increase in anxiety in children and families due to the potential separation, detention and deportation. . . .
>
> I would urge this committee to consider the serious mental health impact of parent-children separation on both children and parents and put an end to the practice of family separation and help to ensure that immigrant children and their parents receive needed mental health care.

■ I return to Padre Bob Mosher and his description of the case of one young woman:

> She did not present herself voluntarily at the bridge, which many asylum seekers do. She asked for its consideration after she was

caught in the country. Her case doesn't look good. But you have to respect that petition and investigate and let her have her day in court before a judge. So that much at least is working, although very slowly. She could be years in the detention camp before she gets to see a judge. But the criminal or the unjust thing happening to her, is this separation from her boy. And her boy, I think because she had said she had a family who would put them up in New Jersey, they shipped the boy, flew him up to New York and he's there at a shelter there, run by the government, two thousand miles away from here. She hasn't seen him for two months. And she just says there's no greater pain, and she hardly ever sleeps; she can't stop wondering about him. She was able to speak to him on the phone once a week, and he recently turned ten, so she really felt it then. She said to me very plaintively, "I wish I could make him little again." Of course any mother knows what that's like, doing something for your child on the child's birthday. The pain these people feel over something so arbitrary, and barbaric. The pain is so great that it creates a trauma for both the mother and the child. And you could see this. All I do is keep her company and listen to her as much as I can.

And she just, she appreciates that it gives her a chance to talk about what she's going through, and that's helpful for her, but she doesn't experience any resolution.

The priest in the long-sleeve brown shirt continues to witness:

Family separation used to be the kind of thing that would shock us so profoundly as a society. When the movie based on the book *Sophie's Choice* came out with Meryl Streep . . . this was the central dramatic element of the book, that you wouldn't even get to until you're very deep into the end of the movie . . . this Polish woman who had been imprisoned in a concentration camp under Nazi-occupied Poland . . . was forced to leave one of her three children by the Nazis. She experienced family separation.

. . . What was Sophie's secret was the whole thing, and Meryl Streep played the part of Sophie in the movie, and the movie too kept you going with, What was it that this character, this Polish woman who had been imprisoned in a concentration camp under Nazi-occupied Poland, what was her big secret? How was she so deeply marked by that experience that she kept getting into this destructive relationship with her boyfriend, and eventually by the end of the book, spoiler alert, she takes her own life at the same time as her boyfriend.

Well, Sophie's choice refers to the fact that she had to choose, at one point, between her son and her daughter.

Who was she going to take with her to the concentration camp? And the Nazi guard that was forcing her to make that choice was staring at her and forcing her to do it, and she chose her son, and her daughter was dragged away, screaming. The movie shows it in such an impactful way, as the girl is screaming, being dragged away, Meryl Streep's character, holding onto her son.

That won the Academy Award, it was a huge thing . . . very celebrated.

The priest wearing brown continues:

Now that's taking place all the time with thousands of kids, people coming to the border, asking for asylum and being told, "We can only take three of you, so your child can't come in with you; you're going to have to leave that child behind. . . . They come up to the bridge or the gate, they ask for asylum, and they're often turned away by the officers or they're told, we can take three people, and in your family you are five members, so two of you are going to have to stay.

> There's Sophie's choice right there, the trauma [of], Which children do I choose to bring with me? They won't accept it, as far I can see; nobody's coming into the states to separate their families. It used to be so moving. The whole US society was shocked by this novel that came out. The movie was based on something that actually happened.

His analysis captures the sadism behind the practice: *"It was the Nazis . . . but now it's us. We're the Nazis.*[34]

Here I respectfully disagree with the brown shirt–wearing, leftward-looking Padre Bob. I don't liken the Trump administration to Nazis or a similar exceptional force pulling the levers of United States government. The militarization of the border enforcement—and particularly "prevention through deterrence," which channeled border crossers into remote areas, weaponizing the beautiful desert, where thousands upon thousands have died and disappeared—have created the conditions for abuse, beatings, and other tactics that approach torture. Militarized enforcement creates the conditions for deepening dispossessions of the wrong kind of border crossers. These include family separation. They birth le lloronx.

As our conversation was ending, I think Padre Bob detected my despair. He stopped me as I was readying to leave. He told me he had witnessed Chile change. The priest had witnessed the democratic transition from an authoritarian government to a better Chile. "People have come together," Mosher pointed out,

> from a great diversity of perspectives in order to oppose the ideology and the inhumanity of the president and administration. People are waking up, not just to the policies of the president's administration, but also to some of the structural injustices. We see progressive political movements actually gaining new strength now in the country, offering a greater variety of political options to the American electorate in the future. It's very prom-

ising. People thirst for change, especially when there are attempts to take it away from them. There's an air of—what should I say—urgency about removing all restrictions and just meeting and talking and getting your voice out, because in Chile's case, it was being repressed in other places.

Change can happen.

■ WITNESSING THE JOAQUIN DEAD

Witnessing in brown captures the dilemmas of working with those who risk sacrificing their lives in fleeing home, crossing borders, and seeking refuge. The concept captures how these migrants must be made dead in order to live, or, even more complexly, how they make themselves dead by experiencing brutal conditions—what I am calling necrosubjection. Necrosubjection sheds light on a neglected history of subjection, its linkages to the politics of death. In contrast to the often-flattening notions of power that interested certain followers of Foucault, necrosubjection as a concept brings flesh to the analysis of how certain kinds of power capture and kill; how they generate psychic and somatic effects; and how these effects may birth resistance or, more likely, usher in unrecognized refusals at the level of life itself. Necrosubjection underscores not the politics of life and death but those of death and life. I have witnessed its birth in the ever-increasing violence of undocumented border crossings, the exposure of the individuated self to deadly environs, the complex demands to depict oneself as a victim in immigration proceedings, and, as recent tragic events in my hometown of El Paso show, resilience in the wake of killer white nationalism.

I elsewhere practiced what I now see as witnessing:

> The grainy shots of the gray cement drainage ditch capture the sinewy subterranean scatological connection between Nogales, Arizona, and Nogales, Sonora. The scene is being filmed by an officer of the Nogales, Arizona, police department. . . . The footage shows police officers and Border Patrol agents (most of whom are Hispanic), hands on their holsters, asking the youths what they are doing, telling them to go back to Mexico. . . . The grainy footage then shifts to the flash of a light cutting through the darkness of the sewer tunnel behind the youths. A group of the undocumented materializes on the screen as they make their way toward the bright sunlight of Nogales, Arizona. El Enano (the dwarf, a nickname of one of the youths) wields a metal pipe. He repeatedly strikes one of the migrants in the leg. A child in the group screams. Another of the young men of Barrio Libre seizes a migrant by his lapel. With his other hand, he rips a chain from the neck of the unlucky man, who is wearing a cowboy hat—a telltale sign of a chúntaro. The officers above, once again on the screen, order the youths to stop.[1]

These *chúntaros*, the uninitiated border-crossing hicks in Chicanx drag, make themselves subject to death.[2] Beaten and brutalized but alive, they escape into the United States. The videotape sits on my bookshelf—further documentation of the complex reverberations of border enforcement practices that speak to profound disruptions and orders of cruelty that reach back at least to the 1990s.

What of other irregular border crossers? What of the men, women, children, and families who attempt to cross the weaponized environs that the deserts of the southwestern United States have become? "The border is where thousands of those have died; social violence will increase," predicts the "Border Patrol Strategic Action Plan: 1994 and Beyond" in outlining a strategy of "prevention through deterrence." People risking life and limb in such conditions lack the cultural acumen of long-standing "border people."[3] As I wrote about in *Barrio Libre*, they end up in treacherous geographies such as the "killing deserts."[4] Or they may suffer other kinds of violence, taken or normalized as natural, such as that which Jason De León describes in *Land of Open Graves*.[5] Neither random accidents nor natural disasters produce the deaths of noncitizen border crossers: the United States and its agents situate certain groups as deserving of attrition, exhaustion, the burning up of their insides, as they make their way ever northward.

I chart these and related modalities not of life and death but death and life. I assume a politically depressive pessimism of the intellect to this end. Witnessing necrosubjection insists so.[6]

People disappear forever in the killing deserts. Animals, heat, cold, smugglers, "delinquents," Border Patrol agents, all conspire in the death and the degradation of border crossers. Rain and sun cause their corpses to wear away, slowly, deteriorating into the most elemental of human remains.

The US-Mexico border kills. Experiences of crossing it without documentation pervade the contemporary social science of the border region.[7] These experiences deepen relations of illegality and deportability, what some aptly term "deportation terror."[8]

But, many noncitizens succeed in crossing it. They live.

What does it mean to almost die? What does it mean to expose oneself and possibly one's loved ones to death and other cruel fates? What does it mean to be disappeared, erased, to be made dead, socially if not politically? What does it mean to be detained or, more accurately, incarcerated and separated from parents and other kin? What does it mean to be the subject of death and its politics?

Necrosubjection involves representing those who are made—and who make themselves—dead in order to live, those who cannot represent themselves, those who must be represented. Making dead in order to live is part of a project of documenting and expressing contemporary brutalities without exacerbating the obscene suffering of border crossers and demands to revictimize them, both in legal proceedings and in certain traditions of scholarship. In this way, we analyze, recognize, and ultimately struggle against violence and oppression, both spectacular and mundane. This project—a historically and politically derived critical analysis of expert testimony provided in immigration proceedings on behalf of people seeking asylum and related legal status and their methodological and theoretical implications and dilemmas—thus recognizes the complexity of working with groups struggling against systemic oppression and of the ways oppression often infiltrates them and activist-scholars alike.[9]

I made a conscious political choice in my witnessing work to break with protocol. As an expert witness, I am not supposed to discuss the specifics of cases. I have made a point of negotiating with the clients and attorneys and explaining that I want to document what is occurring in my capacity as an expert witness.

To write about these experiences and to draw on the respondents' stories is to commit a kind of betrayal. But ethnography, if one follows certain feminist directions in the discipline, must betray. For Kamala Visweswaran, the assumption of a universal sisterhood among women demands betrayal, and in this she echoes other feminist ethnographers, such as Patricia Zavella, who work on "the inside," being of the same race, ethnicity, gender, and class background as their interlocutors.[10]

In my case, as a "brown" scholar, an anthropologist, steeped in the discipline's complex currents of anti-racism and vexed by the demands of having to make people dead in order to live, I must appeal to imperial and downright racist presumptions about Mexico and other parts of Latin America as I testify on behalf of a respondent. I must speak for, rather than work with, those seeking asylum, relief from removal, or some related legal status and tell the court what I see and learn from the stories that I hear.

To be a brown witness in an immigration proceeding is to see necrosubjection in practice. Winning asylum or other relief from deportation increasingly demands accounts of deep victimization on behalf of individuals and collectivities, playing to a deeply ingrained paternalism found in Western liberalism today. It coincides with the surveillance, policing, and detention of immigrants, echoing the birth of the prison industrial complex and the hyperincarceration of African Americans.[11] This order of subjection occurs among those attempting to irregularly cross the US-Mexico border region, in politically related legal immigration proceedings, and in many other hotspots across the globe where surplus humanity threatens or appears to threaten the established polarity between us and other, between friends and enemies, where the whiteness of the social contract must be reaffirmed.[12]

Witnessing in brown involves far more than the conundrum of testifying from some middling and always compromised racial ground, the way brownness or Latinidad is too often misrecognized. The concept describes a kind of committed testimony, a political positioning born out of the dilemma of anti-racist positioning in the immigration court, a court that is not really a court, as I explain earlier in this book.[13] It contributes abolitionist anthropology, part of a larger transdisciplinary work that challenges "the state-sanctioned legal or extralegal production of politically organized premature death."[14]

The demands for necrosubjection, which I participate in as an expert witness, speak to the emergence of the living dead, those who never rest.[15] These restless undead—zombies—in popular culture flit across our screens big and small. Neither wholly living nor wholly dead, they abandon the everyday and confront the snuffing out of residual ways of life and the spectacular terror of privatized and public sovereigns, normalized as drug wars. Although many who flee Mexico, Central America, and other parts of the globe are not Indigenous, many others are. Indigenous or not, they seek to escape the genocidal logic of dispossession. They are misrecognized as traditional laborers who cross the border to work, given the longstanding imperial relationship between the United States and Mexico.[16] Their presence constitutes a refusal of contemporary tyrannies; their forms of dress, ways of speaking, kinds of clothing, and other manners of simply being unnerve contemporary normalcy.

Their persistence unsettles.

Many in this emergent current of forced migration to the United States refuse the merciless crossings through the killing deserts. They come to ports of entry and present themselves to the authorities at the US-Mexico border. They request political asylum. And the authorities increasingly deny them haven.[17]

Necrosubjective Witnessing in Immigration Court

Asylum is a protection granted to foreign nationals already in the United States or at its borders who meet the international standards of the "refugee." The United Nations Refugee Convention (1951) and Protocol Relating to the Status of Refugees (1967) define a refugee as a person who is unable or unwilling to return to his or her home country and cannot obtain protection in that country. Said person must have suffered persecution or hold a well-founded fear of persecution "on account of race, religion, nationality, membership in a particular social group, or political opinion." Congress incorporated this definition into US immigration law in the Refugee Act of 1980. As a signatory to the 1967 protocol and through US immigration law, the United States has legal obligations to provide protection and certain rights to those who qualify as refugees. To be awarded asylum involves accounting for membership in one of the protected categories, often taken as innate, such as "sex," what the law designates as "color," or kinship ties. Asylum may also be awarded through what is referred to as a "particular social group," based on shared past experiences. It can range in meaning to include land ownership or even small-business ownership. Asylum cases often hinge on a government's inability or unwillingness to protect those at risk.

Those who are seeking legal redress from deportation and detention may pursue other legal remedies, such as appealing to the UN Convention against Torture and Other Cruel, Inhuman or Degrading Treatment or Punishment (1984). It includes a provision that prevents expulsion to another state when there are substantial grounds for believing that the expellee would be in danger of torture or the infliction of pain or suffering, whether physical or mental, including punishment or coercion.

New forms of sociality crack open such legal categories. The law chases new subjectivities, as does social theory. Typically and all too problematically cast as liberal entrepreneurial subjects extraordinaire, bent on realizing the American Dream of wealth and consumption, a certain order of border crossers flees the spectacular terror of the drug war in some regions of Mexico or related kinds of dynamics elsewhere in Central America.

I sit in the witness stand and adjust the mic.[18] The judge; two attorneys representing the Department of Homeland Security; the "respondents," who are a couple and their three children facing imminent deportation; their attorney; and a small audience, including some of their family members, sit in this courtroom in San Antonio, Texas. A middle-aged husband and wife are trying to avoid deportation to their onetime home, now dominated by a ruthless cartel, which they have fled.

Many thousands of others like this couple are being held in detention centers in small towns in the United States. They refused to circumvent border enforcement and instead presented themselves to the authorities at ports of entry in Texas and requested political asylum. An administratively appointed judge wields sovereign power. He will decide their fate. He will decide who can move and who can settle—a central political struggle of our time—and whether to detain the couple, "remove" or deport them, or award them asylum.[19]

The couple from Mexico fled a massacre. They described it as the horrendous culmination of the kind of private and indirect governance occurring around the globe.

Short, quiet, and humble, the male head of household picked melons in a small agricultural village for a transnational agrarian company based in the United States. A couple of years ago, he and his coworkers began receiving threats to get off the fields where they worked. The ultimatums were written on little pieces of paper and left on stones in the field, where he and his coworkers would discover them. This man reported that if they "continued to work there they were going to be disappeared."

One day, on which he happened not to make it to work, a group of men armed with assault rifles killed some nine of his coworkers in the fields. He explained in court that "delinquents" committed the crime, a gloss for those working in organized crime. One of his close friends was killed in this event. He feared that what had happened to his coworkers would happen to him. He also worried that his children would be kidnapped and harmed. Later, a relative of this man was murdered; only his head was found. Strange men began menacing his partner, looking for the man at his home.

The couple fled to the United State. They seek asylum.

I must testify as to whether the "removal" of a middle-aged couple, specifically their deportation to Mexico, places them in imminent danger. Immigration attorneys increasingly ask social science experts like me to corroborate immigrant testimony in asylum and related proceedings.

This scenario underlines their dispossession. Their existence demands validation; not even their utterances have weight.[20] They have been rendered officially voiceless, effectively rightless in these proceedings.[21]

I consciously summon the demons—"the rapists . . . the murderers . . . the drug lords." I testify: "Mexico is experiencing the devastating effects of its drug war. Most experts agree it began near the end of 2006. The cartels rape and deploy sexual violence. They sever limbs and heads to intimidate law enforcement and civilians alike." I tell of the *fosos clandestinos*, mass graves that appear occasionally in Mexican media, and of bodies consumed in acid. Of how human rights organizations describe Mexico as rife with abuses. I explain that I am convinced the level of violence in the country is underreported.

I tell how the North American Free Trade Agreement and its asymmetric terms of trade ravaged Mexico's rural economies, transforming them into zones of undocumented immigration. Some of those who stayed behind soon cultivated marijuana and other drugs—primarily for consumption in the United States. I then rehearse the facts: the 160,000 deaths in Mexico tied to the drug war over the past decade; the 40,000 more who have "disappeared." I explain that Central American women, who are crossing the thickening border that Mexico has become, know to take birth control pills. I spew blood, telling stories of corpses, of human bodies thrown into vats of acid, of dismemberment and beheading. I seek that ripe, imperially charged sensibility.

I want to elaborate. I want to tell how the US addiction to cheap labor and cheaper drugs animates the carnage. It feeds the dead. I want to tell of racisms in this age of human sacrifice, premature death, and other orders of dispossession of both sides of the US-Mexico divide.

I feed the hunger—sated neither by the *carne* nor the carnality of power that cannot be lost—of the social hegemonies concerning Mexico generally and Mexicans specifically, as well as those from other parts of the globe.[22] I want to suggest that this hunger is tied to US neocolonial relations. I want to chart for the court the genealogies of military training and local machinations of empire.

But there is little space for complexity. I hear myself explain, "There is blurring in daily life in large swaths of Mexico among elements of the local, national, and regional government and the cartels." I explain that Ciudad Juárez, a city on the US-Mexico border opposite my hometown of El Paso, Texas, was more lethal than Afghanistan in 2010.

I paint a picture of this ordinary couple struggling in daily life. I describe how they toil; how the stained jeans that the man wears as he testifies in court on this day are likely his only clothes; how he works, plays, and, yes, provides testimony in them. I speculate about the paltry government services—such as the underperforming public education system (he finished sixth grade; she did not attend)—that have been eviscerated by the promises of a new liberalism that never came.

I paint a picture of their home, with a solitary lightbulb that glows at night, cinderblock walls, and dirt floors, homes similar to those I have seen in Nogales, Sonora, and across Mexico. The land itself and their will become subject to further dispossessions by privatized sovereigns.

I make dead to let live.

I affirm imperial and racial, late liberal common sense. Liberalism demands that my serving as a brown witness is rife with the monstrous racist and gendered imperialist projections about Mexicans. Racial liberalism demands I dance with the devil.

Violent masculinities and victimized femininities form the heart of the case, the latter invoking Lynn Stephen's notion of "gendered embodied structures of violence."[23] They must be. I must render Mexicans and their situation back in their home country as so hopeless, so bleak, so full of imminent danger, and so full of despair that the judge finds in favor of their application.

I throw gasoline on smoldering flames. I return to the mass disappearances, the decapitations and dismemberments, the clandestine graves, the tearing asunder of bodies, the spectacular violence commonly associated with narco-Mexico.

I mobilize the specter of sexual violence and rape, again and again. Liberalism demands that the cartels, officialdom, the courts, and I mobilize toxic, weaponized machismo. They also demand its corollary: victimized femininity. The lloronx haunts even here.

■ Necropolitical States

Appreciating "states" as both rich psychic interiorities and objects of deep attachment that lord over life, death, racisms, and various other power relations, always in relation to capital and empire, allows me to further unpack necrosubjection. These experiences, whether individuated or collective, capture processes of making dead to let live. They articulate complex histories of anti-Black racism generally and anti-Haitian xenophobia specifically, animating US immigrant detention and deportation practices and their deep linkages to US-Mexico border enforcement.[24] The latest fulfillment of totalitarian fantasies of racial, gendered, and sexual purification concretizes in calls for walls: modalities of prisons, the preeminent institution of contemporary carceral landscapes, as well as of borders and other spaces of detention.

A growing body of scholars and policy makers declares that the crisis in Mexico represents the failure of the Mexican state. Other scholars hold that the drug war cloaks more sinister forces, be it a clamp down on social mobilization, the latest moment of dispossession, or related, long-standing collaborations between Mexico and the United States in the unruly governance of illicit commodities and their Baudrillardian confabulations.[25] Are these simply monstrous fables?

■ What goes unremarked is the inert violence of racial capitalism.[26] What goes unremarked are histories of settler colonialism, enslavement, and other dispossessions. They are obscured in this case by social myths surrounding Mexican migration, their casting as disposable, cheap, and increasingly "detainable."

My witnessing does not document the "criminal capture of the Mexican state," a certain technocratic discourse circulating among governing elites about Mexico, other parts of the globe, and increasingly the contemporary United States. It is not that narco-traffickers or gangsters in other parts of the globe, secure in their wealth and ill-gotten gains, have undertaken or are in the process of completing a coup d'état, albeit from the side or above.[27] Imperial states, long based on slavery and Indigenous dispossession, and increasingly eviscerated of their better logics, frequently exercise terror and torture as legitimation, not as the rule but as *their* rule.

Spectacular terror is instrumental in a kind of capitalist accumulation that has reconstituted itself since the 1970s, akin to what Karl Marx termed "primitive accumulation" in chapter 26 of *Capital*. It is based on dispossession, fraud, and violence. It involves privatizing or cordoning off the commons, including Indigenous lands and related strategic resources. Rosa

Luxembourg, David Harvey, and others hold that such forms of accumulation must constantly be revitalized.[28] These modes of dispossession require accompanying modes of dehumanization that normative accountings of "the subject" or subjection may misrecognize and misapprehend.[29]

Foucault's influential *Society Must Be Defended* underlines the inextricable ties among racism, state formation, life, and death. In this never-finished genealogy, modern racism was first articulated as a discourse of social war in the eighteenth century. It developed during the second half of the nineteenth century, absorbing important impulses from psychiatry as a means to protect society against the abnormal. Racism, in this formulation, "constitutes the necessary precondition that makes killing permissible." It essentially introduces "a break between what must live and what must die."[30] The social construction of race articulates a caesura between worthy and unworthy life and resonates with the above-mentioned formulations of contemporary racism as inextricably lethal—placing bodies closer and closer to death—rather than the constructivist emphasis of racism strangling the contemporary liberal academy.[31] Although Foucault's lectures lack any substantial discussion of European colonialism or the history of the idea of race, they deserve appreciation and invite analysis of making life and death as modes of biopolitical government, which impinges on individuals in their most basic relationship to themselves and others, as it does on collectivities. The integration of sovereign power (the "right of the sword," the right to take life or give death) was complemented by a new right that did not erase the old right but did penetrate it, permeate it. This is the *power to "make" live and "let" die.*

Certain kinds of life of the dispossessed exert pressure on those competing analytics of the subject and subjection. They demand an epistemic rupture, a reversal of the modes of subjection articulated by Foucault and his army of followers in his profound and influential "The Subject and Power," modes that seem better suited to harmonious political moments than to moments rife with crisis in which hierarchies and inequalities break through normativities and challenge instrumentalist reckonings with violence. Achille Mbembe's fierce engagement with Foucault's concept of biopower from the contemporary postcolony and his demand for an analytics of necropolitics provoke a scandal.

Mbembe is concerned with certain elemental figures in the production of sovereignty. Central for him is "not the struggle for autonomy but *the generalized instrumentalization of human existence and the material destruction of human bodies and populations.*"[32] Necropolitics captures how certain lives in dark realms of jeopardy have increasingly become normalized in parts of Mexico, Latin America, Europe and its one-time colonies the United States, and other parts of the globe. The ultimate expression of sovereignty is to have the power and capacity to dictate who may live and who may die, and biopower is the domain of life over which power has taken control. Mbembe's essay draws on the concept of biopower and explores its relation to notions of sovereignty and the state of exception in order to answer many questions about the power of death in the contemporary world. He writes to this end that "war machines and states of exception are deployed in the interest of maximum destruction of persons and the creation of death-worlds, new and unique forms of social existence in which vast populations are subjected to conditions of life conferring upon them the status of living dead."[33]

Mbembe argues that biopolitics, or the politics of life, fails to explain how the threat of violence, human destruction, and death prevails as a technique of governance in many contemporary settings, challenging Foucault's reliance on Western European examples. The Cameroonian philosopher instead draws on examples from the more politically volatile states of postcolonial Africa and the Near East. These provide insights through which we can understand politics as a form of war in which the sovereign emerges through the determination of who dies and who does not die and therefore lives. The meaning of death in necropolitics appears in interpretations of corpses, killers, and those subject to killers.

My concept of necrosubjection extends this project. It speaks to the demands of both suffering and violence evident among certain orders of contemporary US-Mexico border crossings and related kinds of oppression. Nevertheless, necrosubjection refuses analytical closures of this and related schools of thought.

While Foucault's insight into biopolitical power's production and management of life remains crucial, the right to decide life and death is never completely excised from certain kinds of sovereign power, whether authoritarian or liberal democratic, the latter with its deep ties to empire. A politics of life must commit "the subjugation of life to the power of death," or it lends itself to a politics and an analysis of the privileged.[34] Necrosubjection moves to the center of analysis the subject forged in discourses and related micropolitical processes of a once-robust liberalism that is increasingly dystopic. It emerges when "the right to punish" shifts "from the vengeance of the sovereign to the defense of society."[35] It captures those subjects who regularly face the horror of death, of being made—or even making themselves—dead in order to live. From a hail of bullets raining down from the sky in imperial executions in the Middle East to the too-regular shootings of young people in public schools in the United States, what were once promises of liberal statehood now seem increasingly to secure against but also generate terror, amplifying contemporary government's deep linkages to slavery, racism, misogyny, capital, and the refusal to treat such oppressions as ancillary or superstructural.[36]

Necropolitics brings the politics of life and death to an analysis of never-ending warfare, the uneven distribution of disease, and other forms of social and discursive exclusions in modernity. Private armies, so-called war machines, states of exception, and related phenomena perversely birth death-worlds. The suicide bomber becomes recognized as a subject through her death, notes the African philosopher Mbembe.[37] It thus resonates with "revolutionary suicide" in African American thought and suggests the influence of the Black Panthers on Foucault's and perhaps subsequently Mbembe's oeuvre.[38] The corpses, both discovered and not, may be emblematic of revolutionary suicide.

Imperial sovereignty-making violence and its reverberations devastate.

They multiply. They proliferate. Nevertheless, necropolitics understates concurrent everyday dispossessions and the structural violence prefiguring these killer relations. Necrosubjection emphasizes the level of the subject, those who are birthed in and experience killer politics, as well as their kin, in drug war–governed frontier zones of Mexico and Central America, the aforementioned "killing deserts," Palestine, the Dakota pipeline, and elsewhere in the occupied Americas and related settler societies. Necrosubjection accounts for those subjectivities from which societies must be defended.

The concept also wrestles with people and their extraordinary affects that push beyond such ends of life: those who are dying to live, contending with brutal dispossession, and challenging officials and the heavily armed privatized hetero-masculine sovereigns who dictate and subjugate and all too often protect in the name of settler arrangements. Making dead to let live registers how the contemporary moment demands a theory of the subject engulfed in an extraordinarily other politics of death and life, not exceptions that become the rule, or in the naturalization of camplike spaces of liberal democracies, but in the daily workings of state and the law.

The concept chases subjectivities along axes of otherness, more precisely racism and its intersecting exclusions, and also, more pertinently, the material subjections—the subject effects—of threats over life, including the horrendous regime of violence against women termed *femicidio* (femicide), mass graves, and mass disappearances. The concept demands a reckoning with life at the margins, life subjected as illegal, criminal, queer or life cast as too Black, too brown, too Muslim. Necrosubjection is not a liberal analytic of resilience or survival. It is the contemporary subjection of the other, often individuated through violence, entangled in the death struggle of modern capital and the terrifying, often perverse, private, and indirect government of difference.

Making dead to let live, moreover, grapples with the rich interiorities of necropolitics. The concept deepens questions of the subject and power, the birth of subjectivities wracked in actual and structural relations of violence and its psychic effects, and the extraordinary affects that these processes produce.[39]

The concept invites certain politically useful caveats regarding these operations. Race and its intersections still signify; they may remain positive social identities, a position that subaltern genealogies have long recognized and pointed to as limitations of certain traditions that see race and racism only as negative trajectories. In this respect, necrosubjection in the case of immigration courts or undocumented border crossings demands recognition of long-standing or contemporary practices of escape as disruptive or potentially constitutive of new potentialities.[40] Necrosubjection thus pushes at possibilities beyond traditional binaries of resistance and accommodation, which may or may not infiltrate larger assemblages of culture and politics, those oppositional forces, affects, and practices found outside traditional notions of politics.[41]

Necrosubjectivities haunt. They inhabit the anomic zones of death and life struggles. They materialize in popular culture if one looks critically. In the television series *Breaking Bad*, mindless, ruthless young men, almost always phenotypically brown, wander through Albuquerque, bent on revenge against Walter White. There are the zombies on dystopic TV shows, always mindless, inevitably brown. These "walkers" in the parlance of television—a term that also appears increasingly in Latina/o/x studies—flit across our screens to coemerge with the anti-citizens of nowhere yet everywhere, immigrant others, the homeless denizens, damned to near-dead existence.[42]

They are Joaquin Dead: grotesque, dismembered flesh, perhaps the most fundamental of "our" resources. These ravenous subhumans devour white majoritarian flesh, ripping it from bodies with their teeth. As with most zombie nightmares, they quickly become fodder for the larger-than-life struggles, grist for the all-too-"real" human struggles among nonzombies. Protagonists practice killing for a semblance of the way things once were. Zombie fantasies mark a return of sorts, echoing Leo Chavez's assertion that representations themselves are forms of power, rather than reflections of power residing in the real.[43]

A reckoning with the Joaquin Dead demands a return to those wretched borders of death and life evident in asylum and related immigration proceedings or at the international boundary that others must cross irregularly. In either case, they all too often bring only the soiled clothes on their back. They have cultivated the land, then lost everything to the narco-governors, only to face detention, deportation, and other punishment on entering the United States. They speak nonstandard or Indigenously marked Spanish, if they speak the dominant language at all, as I sometimes must explain to the courts. They speak in short sentences. They evoke impoverishment, their need for work, unaware that everything they say can be used against them. They live a carceral regime of sovereignty beyond the walls of detention centers and prisons that bleed into daily life, as well as borders.[44] Such differences become instrumental both in their caging and in their lines of flight.

What necrosubjection and its derivatives crystallize are the continuities between liberalism and totalitarianism. They are felt first among the marginals, the Black and brown, the queer, the gender nonconforming, and always the other. The promises of liberal citizenship and of modernities, always already illusory for those on the margins, shatter into piercing hierarchies. Resurgent totalitarian logics in the Western democracies, evident in Brexit and among Donald Trump and other rulers, manifest first in cruel dealings with different life.

■ To be a pessimist of the intellect but perhaps not of the will is to recognize that those who make themselves dead in asylum proceedings or risk their lives in irregular border crossings or in other deadly ways experience their violent instantiation as the other subject so that they can live. Necrosubjection is not the imposition of false consciousness or mystification of social relations. It is the material subjugation of particular lives that are situated socially, materially, discursively, and ideologically closer and closer to death.

To become a subject in difference today all too often demands a reckoning with orders of violence that are intractable, normative, normalized.

These regimes are inextricably tied to race, or more precisely racism(s), and intersecting exclusions, recognitions, and related dynamics. Necrosubjection traces these dynamics, as in the near death experiences of those attempting to cross the killing deserts of the US Southwest; and as in immigration proceedings in which practices of expert testimony, affidavit writing, and other kinds of analysis regarding current questions of asylum from Mexico and elsewhere around the globe must underscore the horrendous. That other life must be characterized as full of pain, despair, brutality, and violence—making people dead—so that they might be freed from detention and deportation to crime-ridden homelands—letting them live—reaffirms paternal liberal social hegemonies.

This discordance reverberates in the way Black lives can be made to matter only in the wake of police violence and related banalities of evil so that Indigenous peoples, Black people, Muslims, immigrants, and those frequently racialized as immigrants, among other exclusions that others experience, are birthed into relations of normative liberal politics. It crystallizes the way specific lives must be represented as exposed, vulnerable, precarious—a characterization evident in much contemporary ethnography, which some have characterized as "dark."[45]

Necrosubjection shows how discourses about Mexican rapists and other bad hombres infiltrate immigration court, setting the stage for critical, strategic redeployments, subversions, and betrayals, following a long line of *vendidas*, *vendidx*-capturing instantiations that feed my insurgent optimism of the will.

Those who experience making dead to let live move through sewers, under borders, beyond the law, from war-torn homelands to hyperghettoes. Necrosubjects may utter and enact refusals that infiltrate larger assemblages of culture and politics or live in the shadows and refuse the contemporary. Or those who are dying to live may march in the streets of Chicago, Los Angeles, and New York or demand a new order of asylum in US immigration courts.

The killer pulse of "imperial sovereignty," to return to the words of

Mbembe, races through the concept of necrosubjection. Predatory capitalism and its intersecting prohibitions haunt practices of expert testimony, affidavit writing, and other kinds of expert analysis of current questions of removal to Mexico and the Northern Triangle and accompanying questions of asylum. To characterize other life as full of pain, despair, brutality, and violence—making people dead so that they might be freed from detention or banishment, so that they might live—reaffirms social hegemonies. It also captures a new current of immigration to the United States from Mexico—refugees—those typically thought of as coming from other countries who confront a deeply held sense in the law and civil society that Mexicans constitute a labor force.

Again, they cannot represent themselves; they must be represented. Their lives and homelands must be represented as full of despair, pain, and hopelessness; mired in relations of precarity and dispossession; replete with graft and corruption. Their representations affirm imperial racisms and liberal presumptions of the racial, cultural, and civilizational exceptionalism of the United States. They must make themselves—or they must be made—dead, like many others who cross the US-Mexico border without documentation, as well as many other kinds of border crossers across the globe.

I end this chapter by returning to the repressed. In zombie movies, shows, books, and video games, protagonists often must kill their own friends, neighbors, and families so that they do not become zombies.

But aren't they already?

Making dead to let live and its rationales demand the recognition that those who crave the flesh of the other, who make *them* sacrifice themselves so that they or their loved ones can live, those who desire them carnally——those who are contemporary zombies or the Joaquin Dead—are actually us.

Joaquin Dead is our refraction.

GRIEF AND BORDER CROSSING RAGE

I was making an early lunch when the reports appeared on my phone of the mass shooting that occurred at a Walmart in my hometown of El Paso on August 3, 2019.

"My parents!"

I frantically tried to call them.

Both of them were born, raised, and went to school in El Paso. They were now in their late seventies, increasingly fragile, and oh so set in their ways.

El Paso, a predominantly Mexican American city on the international boundary opposite Ciudad Juárez, Chihuahua, Mexico, was where they met, fell in love, and later returned to raise a family. They refused to leave their hometown that they loved so, though my sister and I had left it long ago. El Paso, literally "the Pass," was where we grew up.

No answer.

I tried again.

No answer.

I tried a third time. I heard a recording telling me that my call "could not be completed as dialed." My heart raced.

I turned on the television and a warning came on that the images I was about to see were "disturbing."

Before me the scene brought home the terror and confusion. Ambulances, paramedics, the police, a SWAT team, other agencies, and, of course, blood and lifeless bodies filled the screen. The store, which I knew was a center of border life, was right next to Cielo Vista Mall.

I knew it well. I had spent many weekends cruising through its stores, shops, and stands. I would sometimes hop on the local bus and head there with friends as a teen on the weekends. We'd grab lunch at one of the fast-food joints and go shopping. We were really there to see and be seen.

A young white man, a white nationalist, had opened fire with a high-powered rifle at the store.[1] The store was full of mothers, fathers, other caregivers, and children, buying school supplies on this weekend before school began. The store wasn't far from where my grandparents used to live.

There were rumors of other shooters lurking in the area.

I called my parents again.

No answer.

My partner, our two young children, and I had returned from El Paso only a few days before. The city was a tinderbox.

We had been there much of the summer. I had started as far back as 2014 undertaking preliminary ethnographic research on what I was then calling "the new refugees," those among the dispossessed coming to my home of long ago, not for work or for pleasure but for their security. Mexico was then enduring its latest eruption of the seemingly never-ending drug wars. Indeed, Ciudad Juárez, just on the other side of the international boundary, had experienced ten thousand homicides over the previous four years.[2] To cross the international boundary for this order of crosser meant safety for them and their loved ones. The project then was to bolster asylum claims.

The project began transforming when I returned for my research trip in the summer of 2019. Ethnographic research, particularly when practiced with an intimate, firsthand, committed approach, often demands recognizing people's rich expertise, desires, and freedom dreams—what they want to talk about and want the ethnographer to address. It can mean capturing pain and horror.

Horrendous stories were being recounted to me. Attorneys, activists, and other key witnesses described the dispossessed suffering perhaps the ultimate deprivation: losing their loved ones. Their children or the ones they were charged with caring for were "disappeared." They had been taken away from their parents and other caregivers in court, during their apprehensions by the Border Patrol and other authorities, and in other scenarios.

I would rush back to see my partner, our children, my parents, and others in my extended family after hearing such heart-wrenching testimonies.[3] I would hold my children. I wanted to be close to them. I would listen to them describe their summer days with the family, and particularly my elderly parents, over long meals. I would watch my parents smile, knowing that the children exhausted them.

My parents would reminisce about their lives in El Paso, telling our children the stories of our family, friends, and other loved ones, stories that I knew well. There was the one about how my paternal grandfather worked at Union Furniture downtown. Once he arranged for my parents to rent a refrigerator when ours was in need of repair. I remember it in the garage. And I remember when my mother drove into it, causing the appliance to bend in half. Everyone laughed.

I wouldn't say much. I didn't want to interrupt these rare and fleeting moments. I wouldn't tell them what I knew, such as of one of the stories that still haunt me today:

An officer of the court told one asylum seeker that the child they were taking care of was being taken to a shower.

They never brought the child back.

I would often awaken very early in the morning. I would try to calm myself in the darkness, listening for the reassuring rhythmic breathing of our slumbering children. I would sometimes go to their rooms to check on them and watch them rest.

I would then get up and seek to learn more the following day.

My partner, my children, and I spent the last weekend of our monthlong stay seeing family and running errands. It included several stops, right by the store turned terror scene.

■ Family separation, and the general practice of separating love ones, has a grievous history in the United States. It injured Africans and their descendants during slavery. Family members were auctioned off; children taken. Indigenous children were sent to schools sometimes hundreds of miles from their communities, as they were resettled. More recently, impoverished welfare recipients both white and not, as well as, indirectly, those experiencing mass deportation and detention also experience it.[4]

I knew as an anthropologist of borders and migrations, and as someone who grew up and regularly returned to El Paso and other communities on the US-Mexico divide, that the border region has grown increasingly violent in the wake of policy decisions both in the United States and in Mexico. I knew as a scholar that people who lacked the privileges to cross the border through normal channels risked life and limb crossing it clandestinely. They refused its enforcement. I knew as a scholar that thousands upon thousands had died, and thousands more had disappeared in the deserts of Arizona and increasingly elsewhere. Desiccated human remains could be discovered, bones picked clean of their flesh by scavenging animals dotted the landscape, as did discarded clothes and other debris, signaling humans struggling to survive in the same deserts that I used to hike and play in, now weaponized by US policy makers. I knew as a scholar that others confronted ruthless vigilantes donning military garb and that other criminal types preyed on would-be border crossers. And I was learning from my interlocutors about the cruel practices of dehumanization that communities, largely from Central America, were experiencing as they sought to cross this same border.

Just a few days before the shooting, I had attended a protest in El Paso demanding an end to the sadistic treatment of migrants and asylum seekers arriving at the southern border. I had documented the insults, the threats, the poor diet in the camps qua detention centers. I knew that the Trump administration had formally rescinded the horrible practice of family separation, its latest instantiation beginning in El Paso, but I also knew that hundreds of children were still missing. I knew of rumors circulating among the attorneys and activists with whom I collaborated that family separation continued in a different guise, under restrictive normative claims of what made up a family, so integral to immigration law and border enforcement alike.

But the terror of August 3, 2019, was even more immediate. My parents were not answering their phone. I feared the worst for my family, friends, collaborators, and associates.

■ On Grief

When I later asked my father how the mass shooting affected our hometown, this normally boisterous individual paused. His speech, typically full of playful banter that Mexicans and other minoritized individuals deploy to tell stories, grew halting.

He grew up in the city, in the underserved El Segundo barrio, what some sectors in this city on the international boundary opposite Ciudad Juárez, Chihuahua, Mexico, would today call "el Chuco." He went to school in this border city before excelling at Texas Western (which later became the University of Texas at El Paso), a chronically underserved institution of higher learning where he met his wife. He served in the military in Germany, before he and his wife and children made it back home.

His voice cracks. I see his eyes fill with tears. I feel him breaking down before me. "He killed the town I know and love . . . I can't understand . . . We always now look for the exits when we go to the store."

His voice trails off.

Guillermo Glen, an eyewitness to the shooting and a community activist most recently engaged in challenging the underfunding of public schools in the impoverished Mexican barrios of El Paso, says, "I wasn't shocked." Another pause; he, too, must collect himself, before intoning, "Days before the mass execution at the Walmart, Donald Trump Jr., the President Trump's son, Steve Bannon, and others were in El Paso fundraising on the promise of the wall." Trump Jr. was a special guest at what organizers dubbed "The Symposium at the Wall." It had been organized by a group that raised millions to build a border barrier on private land.

Glen had stopped at that Walmart on that Saturday morning. It became a day that he was condemned to remember. He continues: "Crusius [the killer] was methodical. He had chosen his rifle, down to the kind of shells he was using." Indeed, the killer had purchased online a GP WASR-10 semiautomatic rifle. It was a Romanian-made firearm, a variant of the AK-47 assault rifle, according to the US government, which he purchased on or about June 19, 2019. He also purchased 1,000 rounds of 7.62-by-39-millimeter hollow-point ammunition on or about the same day.

Glen reports that the killer wore dark clothes.

He donned ear protection and safety glasses.

"He stalked his victims, chasing them down the aisles."

The killer reportedly smirked as he shot, maimed, and killed. Chris Grant, who was wounded in the attack, "targeting Hispanic people and letting white and Black shoppers go by."[5] Patrick Crusius killed twenty-two people. He wounded some twenty-seven others. Thirteen of them were citizens of the United States; seven were citizens of Mexico; two were from Germany. Rumors surfaced in the wake of the shooting that several injured people who lacked the multiple and growing privileges of citizenship refused to go to emergency rooms. They feared detention and deportation.

In police custody following the attack, the perpetrator explained that his goal was "to kill as many Mexicans as possible."[6]

He had authored a xenophobic, anti-immigrant manifesto, posting it online just nineteen minutes before the assault began. Titled "The Inconvenient Truth," the document opens by stating, "This attack is a response to the Hispanic invasion of Texas. They are the instigators, not me. I am simply defending my country from cultural and ethnic replacement brought on by the invasion." In the manifesto, the killer also avowed his support of the Christchurch shooting, when another white nationalist carried out two attacks at mosques in Christchurch, New Zealand, on March 15, 2019, killing fifty-one people and injuring another forty-nine. Taken together, these terrorist events fix white nationalism as part of what Aisha M. Beliso–De Jesús and Jemima Pierre refer to as "the global system of white supremacy."[7] The system supersedes borders and speaks to the centrality of international boundaries in white nationalist thought.

The mass shooting of August 3, 2019, demands a reckoning. It must be situated in a recent and vicious amplification of preexisting US-Mexico border and immigration policy, how it fuels a nihilistic and violent will to power.

■ Border-Crossing Rage

> If you ask an older Ilongot man of northern Luzon, Philippines, why he cuts off human heads, his answer is brief, and one on which no anthropologist can readily elaborate: He says that rage, born of grief, impels him to kill his fellow human beings. He claims that he needs a place "to carry his anger." The act of severing and tossing away the victim's head enables him, he says, to vent and, he hopes, throw away the anger of his bereavement.

So writes Renato Rosaldo in "Grief and a Headhunter's Rage: On the Cultural Force of Emotions,"[8] a piece that helped set the tone for a certain kind of reflexive anthropology. This essay would later become the introduction to Rosaldo's *Culture and Truth: The Remaking of Social Analysis*, a book that, among other things, brought questions of borders, identity, flows, and emotional force to the forefront of anthropology in the late 1980s.[9] "Grief and a Headhunter's Rage" famously describes how this anthropologist struggled to grasp the most salient cultural practice of the Ilongot of the Philippines, their headhunting. They told Rosaldo that they practiced headhunting to release the rage created from a devastating loss. He kept trying to push the analysis deeper.

It took some fourteen years—and a major personal tragedy—before Rosaldo could fully appreciate the Ilongot explanation. What had happened was that when they returned to the Philippines for more fieldwork, his partner and fellow anthropologist Michelle Zimbalist Rosaldo plummeted to her death from a cliff. Bereft and pained, Rosaldo was consumed with rage and despair. This tragedy and its complex reverberations spurred his breaking with certain conventions in the "white public space" that is anthropology.[10] Rosaldo turned to an alternative canon in *Culture and Truth*. He invoked the works of Sandra Cisneros and certain Chicano intellectuals, positioning the former as breaking with a nostalgia for a hetero-patriarchal, ethno-nationalist unity and turning to the border as a site of multiple and complex encounters and crossings, a space of heterogeneity, if not possibility.[11]

"Grief and a Headhunter's Rage" was one of the groundbreaking works in what was once called—if not summarily dismissed as—postmodern anthropology. Hardly a singular movement but more of a constellation of forces in anthropology and related disciplines, postdisciplines, and the arts, postmodernism underscored a variety of questions about knowledge production that included certainty, authorship, relativism, and the suggestion that all observers were situated, thus rendering true what Rosaldo called "the positioned subject" and what others would call "positionality," challenging certain strains of positivism in anthropology and allied disciplines. Progress, capital, and science all were interrogated as stories that people ensconced in hegemonic positions told themselves about knowledge from neutral, if not neutralizing, Archimedean coordinates. Rosaldo called for a reorientation of modern anthropology and its disciplinary regimes, away from its dominant emphasis on the quest for rational, deep, structural patterns, and particularly for a shift of the discipline's demands for detachment, for a dislocation of its prohibitions on affective links to the people anthropologists studied, those they observed and spent years of their lives working with, living with, and learning from.

Faye Harrison, the editor of and a contributor to the pathbreaking volume of essays *Decolonizing Anthropology: Moving Further toward an Anthropology for Liberation*, situated the book differently.[12] Following her and her book's call to advance an agenda in which the discipline becomes an instrument for anti-racist advocacy and progressive social change, she recognized the Rosaldo book as an early attempt to decolonize the discipline.[13]

Rosaldo's grief turning into rage may now, some thirty years later, produce a misrecognition. Grief, rage, and similar emotional forces, when affected by the wrong kind of bodies, provokes those entrenched in dominant hegemonic positions. The limits of my heteronormative living as a cis-gender Latinx man working in the academy compel me to recognize that such sentiments broach the hot-headed macho, a man ostensibly consumed by irresponsible, dangerous, corporeal urges and other passions such as lust and envy.[14] Such invocations disrupt "the cool rationality of the inwardly turned subjection imagined by Foucault and his followers . . . [refusing] any characterization of docility."[15] Such characterizations approach the "rapists" and "bad hombres" who have found their way into charged racist, xenophobic political discourse today. They fortify at once the ongoing militarized border policing and the carceral turn in immigration proceedings.

Rosaldo's embrace of the emotional force of rage and sadness turns me to a related body of theoretical writings, the border-crossing pedagogies of women of color feminisms. Audre Lorde's famous works on the uses of anger and the erotic, as well as the works of Cherríe Moraga and Gloria Anzaldúa, among other activist-scholars, mobilize anger productively.[16] They helped introduce intersectional analysis to anthropology, allied disciplines, and post- or anti-disciplinary fields of scholarship and made related interventions. Indeed, Bianca Williams of the #Black Lives Matter Syllabus Project explains that Lorde's "The Uses of Anger" helped channel her rage at the specificity of anti-Black police violence into political organizing:

> If I think back to identify the moment when the simmering anger spilled over into my belly, and I wanted to pull my hair out with frustration, cry deep pools of tears, scream at the top of my lungs, and run into the streets to ask people, What the heck is going on? . . . It was then that I slowly gave myself over to the anger, day by day trying to figure out how this well-stocked arsenal could help me do something productive, while recognizing that it also had the potential to eat me alive.[17]

Dignified rage, *la digna rabia*, crosses northward from southern Mexico. The term describes how Indigenous communities and Zapatista-aligned intellectuals have been fighting for dignity through five hundred years of resistance. It shows how this movement in the land of hope and sorrow that is Chiapas inspires people beyond Mexico, beyond international boundaries.[18] As Mariana Mora describes it, once, while doing fieldwork on Zapatismo in Chiapas, an Indigenous woman overheard her discussing dispossession and oppression, and interjected, "*Da rabia* [it gives us rage]. We could see with our own eyes how those lands were for just a few families [of ranchers] and we couldn't get land for our children."[19]

Border Crossings

In Rosaldo's hands, borders became more than stages, sites, or spectacles of state violence and exclusion. They reflected more than routine bureaucratic administration of state power, or the regulation of human and nonhuman flows, which borders in everyday life largely are.

Borders bore theory. Borders and, notably, their crossing became critical apparatuses for mediating identities and mobilities. They augured deep contemplations on reflexivity in the discipline and a concomitant flattening of ethnographic authority. Borders were sites of complex, intersubjective encounters of self and other, and particularly "sites of creative cultural production."[20] Culture had to be put into motion, and borders made up the key analytical locale for consideration of what that meant.

Notably, Rosaldo spent some of his youth in the border region. His familiarity with the routine crossings of the US-Mexico divide perhaps informs such theorizations. Borders as sites of regular crossings, certain moving subjects and other mobile kinds of life that cross international boundaries threaten dominant positions. They threaten those inculcated in the hardened borders of today, to the point that certain communities on less prominent international boundaries strive to mask their fluidity.[21] Policed, if not militarized, boundaries define too many borders today. Weaponized environs and killer terrains—scorching deserts, deep oceans—vigilantism, privatized brutal economies, all speak to the vulnerability of those crossing borders without rights, as recent work has made clear.

But can analytics help us grieve?

What do I remember now? The chiles rellenos on homemade tortillas, the horror of the shooting, my grandparent's onetime embrace, family separation, my family's large and warm get-togethers, or the ongoing and death-causing militarization of border law enforcement? I grieve and I rage. When people who have made the calculation to abandon their homes and to brave the long and dangerous voyage north only to be subjected to a subsequent hostile reception by US officialdom, including mass detention and possibly the taking of children, along with the latest episode of right-wing populist violence at the border, their seeking refuge at the contemporary border demands that I engage certain traditions, such as Rosaldo's and similarly positioned scholars in the discipline.[22]

■ Border Crossers

People who seek asylum or other kinds of refuge unsettle those already struggling in an increasingly moribund neoliberalism. They animate calls for totalitarian practices of containment, control, and confinement bordering on death, a legacy of the plenary powers of immigration law that articulates with practices and policies of border militarization, provoking settler paranoias and violent white and white-identified wills to power.

The new denizens who arrive at the US-Mexico border and other official crossings across the globe generate feelings of anger, sadness, love, hate, pleasure, and, for some, perhaps fugitive imaginings of borderless worlds and abolitionist possibilities.[23] The new denizens press on detached accounts of life.

The shifting politics of death and life that infiltrate contemporary border crossings from south of the border to the United States capture new struggles to recognize asylum seekers, refugees, and other "border figures" who slip in between these key legal categories and beyond contemporary analytics.[24] Such affective social energies reverberate in immigration courts, at the US-Mexico border, and within certain corridors of the discipline itself.[25] Monstrous forces respond, wielding totalitarian powers of incarceration, murky racial exceptions to constitutional law and to rights that immigration law contains, and fomenting mob violence, the last integral to settler rule. Increasingly migrations to the US-Mexico border are for security. People are fleeing persecution or large environmental calamity, representing a departure from the ebbs and flows of large-scale importation and frequent deportations of migrant labor of yesterday.[26]

Such life beyond borders produces reprisals which illustrate that white supremacy is far more than a matter of prejudice. It is a global system that demands to be named, analyzed, and confronted. It is a global system that kills, either gradually, by the social inheritances of disease, or because victims are exposed to pernicious wielders of structural power and related regimes of dispossession, or, far more horrifically, when officers of the state shoot or choke away Black life.

Those crossing the US-Mexico border, and those crossing from Central American countries into the seemingly ever-thickening border that Mexico has become, increasingly escape undeclared wars, environmental decimations, and other pernicious forces. They encounter what certain orders of the dispossessed in the US-Mexico border region have experienced over the past thirty years, a hardened border enforcement fluent in military tactics, strategy, and equipment.[27] This border regime has forced undocumented border crossers to adopt increasingly precarious strategies that result in such abject decisions as crossing through sewer tunnels below the international boundary or through the "killing deserts."[28]

Terms such as "migrant," "immigrant," and "push and pull factors" mask a growing abandonment of settler states. This abandonment plays out in asylum proceedings and the draconian efforts of containment at and across international boundaries and checkpoints. The rise in the number of people seeking refuge across the globe speaks to it, as does the global resurgence of right-wing populism. Current arrangements only amplify the long-standing caging and deporting of bodies that refuse to stay in place. People on the move contend with the suspicion that they were migrating for a better way of life. These lives in flight are too often read as economic immigrants, an effect of the alienations and ideologies of contemporary racial capitalism.

People from Africa and the Middle East, Cuba, Honduras, El Salvador, Nicaragua, Guatemala, Mexico, and elsewhere abandon home for other countries in search of safety, security, and solemnity, and appear at the US-Mexico border. Ruthless privatized sovereigns, narco-traffickers, human traffickers, and their allies in the governing bureaucracies of Mexico, the Northern Triangle, and related circuits of empire sever heads and limbs on a scale much larger than the Ilongot. Their mammoth ill-gotten gains allow them to exercise control over large swaths of Mexico and the Northern Triangle. Rich anthropologies of contemporary Mexico and the Northern Triangle capture the power of these "dark" sovereigns, their origins, and these countries' depiction as sites of the monstrous and the macabre,[29] inextricably linked to the dispossessions of the settler colonial underpinnings of racial capitalism.[30]

Here, the shortcomings of the legal binary opposition made between immigrant and asylum seeker—the latter seen as subject to political violence and persecution, and the former as exercising an economic, rational choice made available to them by liberal governmentality—become clear. The binary is central to the ways in which those fleeing to the United States are being perceived and received when they present themselves to the border authorities. Asylum seekers, immigrants, and other "border figures" remind us that the thick borders of humanity often reinforce state power.

That is to say, the conjunction of the massacre in El Paso with what has become the rule of border and migration portends to more than what another anthropologist has poignantly referred to as the "Latino Threat," or the pervasive sense that Latinxs are unlike other immigrants.[31] It is the settler core that demands the caging, if not the killing, of these unregulated and increasingly mass movements challenging much of the Global North.[32] In modern liberal democracies, that which was originally excluded from politics—certain kinds of exception, that which stands outside the law—may confirm the law. Such a reckoning with life, no matter how bare, demands a deep, critical engagement with the histories of enslavement and colonialism.

Border crossers provoke those enraptured by nativist mythology. Borders tell of empire and race. They tell of blood and soil in certain modern vicious imaginaries. And they can tell of more.

Movements of the critically vulnerable and precariously positioned populations usher in alternatives. They demand a recalibration of expectation about our contemporary mode of living in place. Excessive movement provokes deep unease, disruption, and, perhaps, foreshadows a coming political community. Neopopulist-qua-settler violence and the violence of immigration policy index how certain people on the move unsettle those who are entrenched in a world that once was. Such movements usher in a paranoid, violent, nihilistic will to power.

To bear witness on behalf of those who refuse or, more precisely, attempt to refuse the confinements that international boundaries represent is to break with the long-standing tension between resistance and accommodation. Their movements are indeterminate; they are often illegible, complex, and historically and culturally specific. It is they who live in the future; it is we who, by living in the stasis of polities and on the wrong side of global apartheid,[33] engender the violent schisms that borders have become and the concomitant wills to power that they charge.

We live in the fixity of citizenship and its proliferating walls and cage.[34] *We are anachronisms. They live the terrifying effects of cages, walls, and other containments.*

This order of border crossers effect these new kinds of flows on their persons. They seek refuge, either formally through requests for asylum or by entering the United States clandestinely. Their cracked voices and their often-gendered silences at ports of entry and in immigration courts across the United States tell of the terrifying normalcy of political persecution and corruption that the drug wars south of the border produce.

Even those who surrender themselves to the US authorities, as asylum seekers often do, encounter militarized policing practices at the border often carried out by US Latinos, veterans of military interventions on behalf of the US empire abroad. After deployment and their return to the United States, enter law enforcement, a job in which they can make a good living and have better benefits than most other veterans have. One of them stiffens before me as he details his service in Iraq. He says of the border fencing: "It's certainly not insurmountable. It's certainly not uncrossable. To jump over it could hurt. It would hurt bad." With a pistol in his holster and an automatic rifle in the back of his truck he says: "I'll pick people up who have climbed and jumped down it. They'll have broken bones. Crushed ankles, messed-up knees."

Would-be border fence jumpers land on desert rock and hot terrain, or what "border people,"[35] as I once was, call *caliche*. *Caliche* has become part of the US government's arsenal, the tactical infrastructure of clandestine boundary punishment. It caused untold migrant suffering and slow death in the attempts to avoid apprehension by the Border Patrol[36] and is part of the treacherous geographies, including the "killing deserts," that I have long documented and analyzed.[37]

Crossing them has become part of their flight from this terrible normalcy of political persecution, corruption, and other maladies created by the drug wars, or the latest turn in the regimes of dispossession. The rapists and bad hombres of the present moment are those who behead and dismember human beings and enflesh the macabre spectacles of the drug war and its privatized hetero-patriarchal sovereignties and collude with the logics of US empire. Or crossing the deserts has become part of their flight from the far more banal snuffing out of a resistant way of life, the drying up of collective farms, the collapsing of markets, or, still for some, the pursuit of a better way of life.[38]

Those new crossers all too often bring only the clothes on their back, soiled from hard labor and the exertions of suddenly abandoning their homes. As I would learn from attorneys and activists with whom I collaborated in El Paso, Nogales, Chicago, and elsewhere, and as I sometimes must explain in immigration courts, many of these new crossers speak nonstandard Spanish, if they speak the dominant language of their homelands at all. Such racio-linguistic difference becomes instrumental both in the containment and in their lines of flight: many are Indigenous.[39] They confront hardening actual and ideological walls, militarized policing, and racial states of emergency and exceptions, all emblematic of a politics of containment and a deeply differentiating anxiety affecting migrants and the migrant-resembling alike.

Back to the Border

I return to Renato Rosaldo, back to his writing on the Ilongot, back to cultures and truths, back to his work on headhunting, back to grappling with grief and my border crossing rage, and back to the pedagogies argued for in women of color feminisms. Back to his call to recognize the force of emotions along lines of difference. It echoes of those minority traditions that struggle against the tyranny of the new normal, against the complex conjunctions of racial capitalism and hetero-patriarchal domination, evident at the US-Mexico border and elsewhere in the globe.

> "Ana" is one example. She sought refuge. She tells how she moved her beauty salon to El Paso after "they assaulted us; they shot at us. And one time they stole all my documents and the documents of my little girl for school. It seemed that they knew all our movements. It was a period filled with much pain, of many deaths, because at every turn there were murders. We experienced it—I lived through various shootings. When I was with our courier, a coworker, we were caught in various street shootings."[40]

She recounts how men—they were always men—well dressed and well spoken, would enter her beauty shop in Mexico. During our conversation, she invoked *los bienvestidos*, a term (heard often during my fieldwork) for the well-heeled and well-dressed figure, inextricably linked to the drug war and its politics of dispossession and expropriation in Mexico, perhaps a spectral instantiation of racial capitalism at work. She told me, as her eyes pooled with tears, that she was thinking "I want to live" when a knife was put on her ribs.

When those who appeared as *bienvestidos* started to extort and threaten her more regularly, she decided to abandon her home. Eventually, she and her two children fled northward, to the border, and eventually settled in El Paso, where she is now trying to become a citizen.

Ana is not an asylum seeker, at least not formally so. She explains that what caused her to leave her home was "panic, or fear [a nervous laugh]. I think you can call it panic because it arose from all the fear. And we all experienced it; I don't think there is anyone in Juárez that didn't experience it."

It was common knowledge among those from Mexico in her circles that to be awarded asylum was exceedingly difficult. Indeed, most people who fled Mexico for the United States whom I spoke to did not consider seeking asylum, thus capturing different orders of border-crossing experiences. They were aware of the official resistance to Mexicans being taken seriously as asylum seekers. Many who had the required resources would acquire border-crossing cards in Mexico and make their way north.

"Ana" did this. She crossed the international boundary, seeking refuge for her and her family. She rebuilt her life and started a business. She is now raising her daughters in El Paso, where the militarized boundary gives her a sense of solemnity and security as she maneuvers toward citizenship for her and her family.

On Unsettling Border Crossers

The burned edges of settler colonialism smolder within liberal democratic societies. They infringe on the civil liberties, freedoms, and expanding categories of internal and external enemies. They must. They teeter between domains of war and domains of peace, inciting agents of white supremacy and exemplifying how integral it is to contemporary rule.[41]

Those trying to cross the southern border of the United States are forced to abandon their homes. They seek work and dignity, pleasure and solidarity, and freedom with all its vexed complications for their loved ones and themselves, entangled though they are with the pressures and limits of an always-compromising, always-colonialist present. These crossings unsettle those who lack peripheral vision or Du Boisian double-consciousness,[42] those vested in a cohesive imagined community versus those all too familiar with the complexities of the contradictory, transformative potentiality of populations on the move, and what they portend, particularly as represented in borders and their crossings.[43] Those not versed in the routines and regularities of such crossings or other kinds of diasporic ways of being charge racial emergencies. They inflame totalitarian-like technologies of containment, and sometimes seize on vicious extralegal wills to power, including horrendous purges. The mass execution that occurred in my hometown, the separation of families, the incarceration of children and adult migrants, continued anti-Black police violence, and the unremarkable centrality of militarized boundary policing, all fuel my grief and my border-crossing rage. White supremacist currents informing border and immigration policy here and across much of the globe and the terrifying prospect of blood-and-soil politics as racial border politics spawn my (and I am sure others') fraught reckonings with borders, their complex crossings, and the racial violence they portend.

A few days after the shooting, federal agents captured approximately 680 migrant workers from seven poultry plants across the state of Mississippi. The raid, notably, occurred hours before President Trump was scheduled to visit El Paso to commemorate the victims of the massacre, although they were had been planned months before. The raid ripped apart migrant communities. It was one of the largest workplace raids in history. The raid sowed financial insecurity. It terrorized the migrant community. The action separated children from their parents and other caregivers.[44]

On my fifth attempt to call my parents, my mom answered. Her voice quivered. My father hardly spoke to me, mumbling that they "were fine." They were on the highway, not far from the tragic scene of the shooting. My parents were trying to get home.

I call out the dead. I name those murdered:

Jordan Achondo. She died shielding her two-month-old son, who was found with her blood on him. Her husband, Andre Pablo Achondo, was also killed in the attack.
Maribel Campos
Arturo Benavidez
Andre Pablo Anchondo
Javier Amir Rodriguez
David Alvah Johnson
Sara Ester Regalado Moriel

Angelina Silva Englisbee
Adolfo Cerros Hernandez
Juan de Dios Velázquez Chairez
Gloria Irma Márquez
Maria Flores
María Eugenia Legarreta Rothe
Raul Flores
Jorge Calvillo Garcia
Alexander Gerhard Hoffman
Elsa Mendoza de la Mora
Luis Alfonzo Juarez
Ivan Filiberto Manzano
Margie Reckard
Leonardo Campos Jr.
Teresa Sanchez
Guillermo "Memo" Garcia

I grieve for them.

I also grieve for the others who were wounded, their friends, and their families. I grieve for all who are afflicted by the global structures of white supremacy.

I grieve for the thousands of migrants who have died and the thousands of others who have disappeared in the beautiful deserts that have been politically transformed into killer environs. I mourn the families whose children are taken, and those forced to make the tough choice of sending their children across borders, alone and vulnerable.

And I bear a dignified border-crossing rage.

■ ON THE BANALITY OF CROSSING

When policy makers, scholars, and other players instrumental to the US security establishment discuss "the border," they refer to the international boundary between the United States and Mexico, not the US-Canadian border or the territorial waters of the United States. Such sensibilities are inextricably linked to a profound sense that this southern boundary of the United States is out of control. Walls now reach to the heavens, and tunnels approach hell. Mexican border cities become sites of anxious waiting, for minutes, hours, days, weeks, months, years, decades, for a return to normalcy or a turn to a different order of crossing.

Policy makers and their allies have persuaded significant portions of the citizenry in much of the world that border regions must be sites of exclusion, masked in rhetoric taken as postracial. The violence of capture, of incarceration qua detention of the dispossessed, of family separation as well as the taking of children from other kinds of caring ones, and of expulsion has become routine. Policy makers, certain traditions in scholarship, and revanchist elements in US society have produced international boundaries in our fraught political imaginaries as sites for caging difference, for banning the unwanted, for sorting out the undeserving, for divvying up those imagined as embodying either danger or retrograde traditions and antimodern cultures. The wrong side of the contradiction stymies those caught in the purgatory that the border has become versus those who have the resources to pass through, fly over, or digitally reconstitute themselves on either side of this and other international boundaries.

The southern border of the United States severs the instrumental role US policy plays in the generation and government of human movement and populations made mobile. Far more severe than a wall, the border becomes a screen where the dispossessed and other kinds of people crossing it become distorted projections, barbarians at the gate. They are cast as crossing to steal, pander, or sell drugs or subjected to other gross distortions.

The centrality of the southern border crystallizes the material effects of dominant anxieties about difference and other socially produced inequalities with a vibrant racial nationalism that ricochets, locally, nationally, and globally. All too often in the West, the fortification of international boundaries becomes a silent accomplice in a revanchist politics of white nationalism and its related orthodoxies. It circumscribes the mobility of the dispossessed, thickens the walls, reinforces the cages of the nation-state and their long, long, reach, into all orders of law enforcement, from federal forces such as the Drug Enforcement Agency, Customs and Border Protection, Immigration and Customs Enforcement, to city police and county sheriffs.

These processes capture part of the dramatic transformation of the US-Mexico border over the past thirty years. They position those lacking certain privileges of US citizenship or similar status as life exposed, as worthy of detention or losing children or other members of their community, or as deserving of torture or practices that approach it. They are disposable.

Borders have become walls and cages. They cage our political and academic politicized imaginaries: a broken distortion of a lived reality. They fuel a vile nationalist paranoia, a rapacious, seething violent will to power with brutal, sometimes deadly consequences, which border enforcement charges. Across the globe, whether in certain areas of southern Mexico, in

Europe, or at the US-Mexico border, humans bear the stigma of having crossed international boundaries, either recently or historically, or those who resemble them, in ways orchestrated largely by nonborder people.

Such transformations demand critical reflection on the vicissitudes of dominant positions. They invite contemplation of how citizens of the Global North have made border enforcement integral to daily life, how such practices articulate with the ever-drying kindling of the global environment, sucking away its life-giving properties, to the point of combustion. Such imaginaries fan the resurgent will to power that is white nationalism, evident at borders, in the alt-right, and among those similarly positioned.

Everyday life, a domain central to anthropological thought and study and to the discipline's methods of ethnography, in actually existing border regions tells something different. The overwhelming majority of crossings at borders prove harmless. They are routine. The banality of US-Mexico border crossings and of those elsewhere in the world call into question the homogenous, sealed, imagined communities that anthropologists theorized as the nation long ago. It is an image in which generations of nonborder people, along with others lacking the experience of diaspora and related orders of border crossing, have been inculcated. Borders should be sealed. They should be hard. They should be policed.

Those of us from actually existing border regions, with their deep history of routine border crossings, know that this has not always been the case. Borders don't have to be hard. They don't have to be militarized.

Borders signify so much more than killing deserts, caged children, family separation, migrant encampments. Borders do not need to be the sites that approach torture. They don't need to be central in the campaigns of ethno-nationalism or the dreams of vindictive sovereigns and their ruthless followers.

International borders do far more than stop crossings. They do far more than slow such crossings. They do far more than contain the unwanted other. The borders of today ban not just migrants, refugees, asylum seekers, and other would-be border crossers. People from North Africa and the Middle East, Cuba, central Africa, Honduras, El Salvador, Nicaragua, Mexico, and elsewhere come to them.

Borders, as lived experiences, not paranoid nightmares, are sites of complex encounters. They can have been sites of mutual aid, of peoples from across the globe commingling, living, of affective and effective possibilities. They can be places where a radical humaneness is already always happening, or where human and nonhuman life of all sorts lives. The border remains full of life.

And beauty.

I can remember a crisp floral fragrance after a cool rain on a hot desert day in El Paso. Pockets of a crisp scent of flowers in the hot desert air would blossom. They would fill our lungs with the particles of desert flower.

"The monsoons . . ." my father would say seemingly every year, peering into the valley from the hills where we lived, when the thunder first cracked the sky that had turned suddenly gray, chasing away the high white clouds that dotted the expansive blue. We could see the rain mist hovering over our home and the region, including the other side of the border, and the bright lightning flashing on both sides of the border.

Below, we could see the valley nestled next to the Rio Grande. Children would swim in it. They would play in the watery boundary, cooling themselves off, before it became a fixation.

This big river became a border officially in 1848, when Mexico lost at least half of its territory to the United States. But the river refused to honor the *man-made* boundary. It would shift course to the consternation of statesmen and dignitaries. It demanded an international conference and diplomatic meetings and eventually a new treaty that demarcated on a map this international boundary.

Wildlife defies the boundary. Birds fly over it, to the north and to the south. Lizards climb over or bury under the walls, the fences, the armed guards, the buried sensors, the cameras. Jackrabbits and other animals burrow under them. Cacti and other plant roots reach deep under the terrain. They entangle below the border. The soil at the boundary blows across and away.

A border should be crossed.

People would. They would cross it. They would cross the border every day. They still do.

People would cross into El Paso. They would cross into Ciudad Juárez.

Farther west, they would cross, from Nogales, Arizona, to Nogales, Sonora, or vice versa. Older generations from this region referred to them as *ambos Nogales*, or "both Nogaleses," in this community, some sixty miles to the south of Tucson, where the only thing dividing the two communities is a wall that the border has become.

Farther west are scenes of a different border. Alex Rodriguez, a visionary filmmaker, in part 1 of the Border Trilogy captures families picnicking at the international boundary, along the coast of the United States. The film shows them reaching through holes of the fence. Individuals contort their torsos, to touch, to hold hands, to love each other, in spite of what the international boundary has become. The audience never witnesses the authorities, but the border is clearly patrolled.

I can remember the smell of the tortillas my mother would bring home from some of her trips to Ciudad Juárez, Chihuahua, Mexico. They weren't the corn tortillas of southern Mexico, which I've since learned to love. They were rich flour tortillas. You could of course get great tortillas in El Paso, on the US side of the international boundary, or someone in the family could make them. I recognize now that rich taste that I long for is probably *manteca*, the rich animal fat. The tortillas from Juárez tasted better.

As did other food. When my mother's parents or her sisters, my aunts, all of whom were originally from El Paso, would visit, we would head south. We would pile into a car and head into Ciudad Juárez to eat, moving against the northward flow of brown laborers heading to El Paso or elsewhere close to work, before returning to their homes in Mexico at night. My family and I would eat tacos, enchiladas, burritos, sometimes steak and fish. We would then indulge in sopapillas, a pillowy fry bread.

People cross borders. Every day.

At all hours.

People would cross the border to work.

They would cross it to shop.

They would cross it to go to school, to go see family, to see a doctor or a dentist, or to get inexpensive medication.

They would go see lovers or cross the border to get married.

I used to cross the border.

Every day.

Friends and families would cross it.

Acquaintances. I know that thousands upon thousands upon thousands of people cross the border every day. Officially and unofficially.

I know. I saw. I witnessed.

Crossing borders and reinforcing borders stir memories, trajectories, currents, and competing dispositions toward a past and a different future.[1]

Long-standing precedents such as in the regular crossings of the US-Mexico border unsettle nativist claims. They reveal how alternative arrangements remain possible. They challenge the imposition of borders as sites of exclusion and policing, integral to racial nationalism generally, and white ethno-nationalism specifically, by showing how such fixations can be eclipsed. Border people and Indigenous peoples bear knowledges that question the imagined communities of a cohesive nation, one integral to dominant strains of ethno-nationalism at the US-Mexico border as well as elsewhere in the globe.

Cuban bodegas, flags, and restaurants now dot Ciudad Juárez. Migrant hostels and camps teem with people from Guatemala, Honduras, and El Salvador, among other places. They await their turns to vie for refuge. Their newfound visibility unsettles those deeply invested in stasis. It unsettles those who favor the status quo. The dispossessed presence challenges the unequal privileges that border crossings and accompanying accidents of birth represent.

Reckoning with the banality of border crossing may douse ethnonationalist flames. Border crossings are commonplace.[2] The daily, the quotidian movements across the international borders that people who dwell in the US-Mexico border region know and experience firsthand call into question the mammoth reconfiguration of US border enforcement strategies. Life and all its kinetic energies seep beyond them. Still.

■ Lunch.

Our stomachs rumbling, we hopped on the interstate and drove for a few minutes, then parked, right next to the bridge that crosses over the international boundary.

We would take the bridge over the river, walking against traffic flows, as the rows and rows and row of cars sat, waiting their turn to enter the United States after inspection.[3]

To work.

To shop.

To eat.

To see friends, family, lovers.

To cross borders inflames those invested in their ordering.

From a hill in El Paso, or Nogales, Arizona, or elsewhere along the long divide between the United States and Mexico, one can look over, across the wall, or over the fence, or across the river, and peer into Mexico.

Such daily movements of border people may unsettle. They may open up possibility.

They call into question life in states and related fixations. Border people who live at international boundaries hold unrecognized, illegible knowledges that include border fictions. They witness them. They feel them. They watch the pull of social life, how it gradually deteriorates differences over generations. Their literal movements back and forth, and back and forth, across this international boundary, every day, their ties across borders, call into question conventions, the deep common sense of national cohesion that white ethno-nationalism espouses. They call into question the legal and extralegal reinforcement that assembles the border, thickening its experience, beyond its immediate crossing.

My friend "Ronnie" would get up early in the morning deep in Ciudad Juárez. She would spend an hour getting ready for her commute across the bridge. She'd have breakfast, get dressed, and "do" her hair, she would explain, as she touched her long black locks. She'd hop on a bus or a *pesero*, take it to within a few blocks south of the international port of entry. She would then head north, where she was sometimes compelled to present a document, and almost always—a few times she called me for the homework assignment from our history class at the University of Texas at El Paso because they wouldn't let her cross—she would be allowed to cross into the United States. She'd then catch another bus and show up at UTEP.

Ronnie and other border people bear the knowledge that people cross this international border every day, as elsewhere around the globe, and sometimes many times per day.

We would meet friends in downtown El Paso. We would snake our way through the crowds and head up and over the bridge, over the Rio Grande. We would have a quick meal, typically Mexican food, but the Chinese food was also quite good. We would go to a poetry reading or to an art show. We would be in Ciudad Juárez for a few hours, if that. Then we would make our way back to the port of entry, our bellies full, and make the short walk up the bridge and back over the Rio Grande.

Occasionally, a border guard would ask us our business and request our identification. *Passports weren't required.*

Then.

When I ran a nonprofit corporation in Nogales, Sonora, in the late 1990s that addressed an array of social problems that an impoverished group of young people experienced, I would cross the international boundary through the port of entry several times every day.

People cross the international boundary between the United States and Mexico.

They cross it every day.

Every day.

To see an aunt, an uncle, a grandparent.

To go to school.

To see a doctor.

To see a dentist.

To see a *curandera*.

To buy Coca Cola made with real cane sugar.

To have lunch.

To pick up salsa.

To go for a walk, down the avenidas.

To shop.

To sell.

To go home after a long day of work.

To simply be.

These are uneventful crossings.

This international boundary is crossed thousands upon thousands upon thousands of times.

We would be hungry, thirsty, or simply bored, and after driving a few miles, we would make our way over the international boundary and wind up at Fred's for a sandwich, at Shangri La, or at the market. In the banality of such practices, possibilities of living with borders differently and differentially, both long-standing and emergent, flicker. The memories of a different border, a different order of crossing, in an era of a different kind of enforcement, these knowledges call into question if not into refusal what the border for the wretched has become.

On a hot day in summer 2019, I ask a middle-aged driver, as I ask everybody whom I meet for the first time in El Paso, where he is from. This forty-something man explains he was born and raised in Juárez. His crow's feet tighten. He crossed the international boundary in the 1990s before, he explains, it hardened. "Aquí y allá," he tells me. He is from here and from there, a reference that many people with deep roots in the region increasingly severed by the hardening international boundary understand, appreciate, and live.

I ask the same of the young server by day and border activist by night. She smiles and tells me she's from both, though she is originally from Mexico City. She is studying for a degree in finance at the University of Texas at El Paso. She lives in El Paso now. But crossing is difficult now. It took her three hours to get to work in El Paso this morning. It may take her another three hours to get back. Traffic now crawls over the bridge. She tells me that some people she knows blame the new arrivals: the Central Americans, Cubans, and others who live this purgatory. She is considering renting an apartment so she can stay in the United States a few nights a week.

Thousands still cross it every day, on their way to school, shop, or work. They have the means and the appropriate documentation.

The movements of people who cross it matter-of-factly and those who cross it irregularly invite considerations of different ways. They unsettle. Diana Martinez, author of the powerful interlude in this book, is a key member of the Witness Tornillo Team, the organization that contested the caging of children. As she explained the organization's work, she told me that she has an uncle and other family members who live in Ciudad Juárez.

A world without the jagged edges that borders have become douse white nationalist flames. It inspires the imaginaries of luminaries, of artists, writers, and dreamers. Those bearing knowledge of the border of yesterday and perhaps tomorrow, those who dwell there, who are of the border and its lands, and some who are of the international boundary today, know that the international boundaries can be regularly crossed. Those who park and walk over the long winding bridge, or who sit in the long lines awaiting their turn to get to the other side, know of the tremendous political fiction that certain dominant positions hold regarding impermeable borders.

With perhaps the notable exception of totalitarian states, people on the move defy what border guards and border walls portend. And in even the more banal way, the everyday life of people who dwell at borders, reveal their ends, in the expression of being from here and there.

Borders shake at their foundations. Movements across them gesture to possible futures. They unsettle.

Populations bear borders across their backs. They bear them when they utter different languages, or when they wear different kinds of dress, when they cross the edges of racial nationalism.

Mass human mobility has often been linked to processes of violence, from the transatlantic slave trade to asylum seekers fleeing genocide and war throughout modern history. The effects of policing, militarization, and racism are particularly salient in spaces associated with migration, such as border regions, factory work zones, and immigrant enclaves. "Undocumented" people have been funneled into increasingly dangerous, clandestine routes.[4] Their very existence as people moving irregularly render them vulnerable to different orders of violence, including enslavement, human trafficking, detention camps, and kidnapping. Whether state, criminal, or broader scales of violence endemic to racial, class, and gender difference, the legal and extralegal government of borders interweave.

But, life exceeds borders.

These knowledges upset racial nationalists, conventions of immigration law, and practitioners of border governance alike.

Borders veer to porousness. They portend crossings.

People cross. And they cross. And they cross again.

Humans move. They inspire alternative representations in art and popular music. Cross-border movements infuse alternative kin relations, geographies, desires, and economies. These dynamics render the US-Mexico border material and imaginary. It is both utopian and dystopian. It is militarized and peaceful; organized and chaotic; masculine and feminine; it is straightening and queering; it is sometimes white, sometimes brown, and always other; it is where untold wealth and regimes of impoverishment collide.

The resurgence of detention, the criminalization of asylum, and practices that approach torture of certain kinds of border crossers, all speak to how the mass movement of human groups challenges international boundaries, exposing their rickety infrastructures. Resurgent right-wing populism in the West and the totalitarian efforts at containment, caging, and deporting of human beings for refusing to stay in place have normalized large-scale tactics of state terror, violence, and other manipulations once seen as exceptional.[5]

Borders are instrumental in the grammars of freedom. The mass caging of civilians, family separation, and other practices of migrant torture tell of a refusal to stay, to live the present as it is, with its borders, its walls, its cages.

Migrants, refugees, and other denizens seek a better world. They seek dignity for their families and themselves. Life surges beyond economic immigrant–versus-asylum categories superimposed on their lives by our laws.

They struggle to birth a world without borders, despite the resurgent ethno-nationalism that has seized contemporary thinking and liberal government in the United States and across much of the globe. Often seen as a mysterious fringe, this ethno-nationalism actually constitutes a crystallization of dominant emotions in law and policy today that seeks to order, stabilize, and secure borders.

Certain kind of border crossers and their movements refuse power's design, the unfreedom of capture, of staying, of settling where they belong. They move in counterpurpose to power, assuming it, revealing the cracks in the totalitarian aspirations of liberal democracies and their xenophobic demagogues.

Hardened borders must be recognized as far more than an exercise in new policing tactics, criminalization, and migrant death. Immigrants, young and old, and men, women, and children risk life and limb in order to evade the Border Patrol, vigilantes, and other agents of securitization. Walls and related law enforcement practices at the border have been instrumental in the deaths and caging of certain kinds of border crossers. Border Patrol helicopters, armed agents, officers on horseback, bikes, and in ATVs, barbed wire, watch towers, drones and biometric sensors, military tactics and strategy have become fundamental to the hardening of the border and it's accompanying social relations. Terrorists, drug lords, and other nightmarish figures fuel calls for greater and greater border security measures and augment preexisting orthodoxies.

All of this contrasts with the thousands who continue to cross the international boundary every day to work, go to school, go shopping, and see family and friends. All of this contrasts with those climbing over—or tunneling under—the new border enforcement regimes, or presenting themselves to the authorities to claim that their experiences are deserving of refuge. Migrants and other kinds of border crossers begin to reclaim their lives. Border crossers and their allies find new ways to love, parent, and collaborate beyond and around borders. Their daily refusals contribute to the slow death of the immigrant-refugee binary and the accompanying, far more discursively pervasive binaries about good and bad immigrants.[6]

And the wretched at our borders, including those who are Joaquin Dead and whose very lives interrupt the gendered, sexual, and racial orders that hardened borders would entrench, beckon a different future.[7] It coalesces with the ordinariness of border crossings to remind us that although the US-Mexico and other borders are normalized, they represent the afterlives of settler colonialism.

Borders are the ruins of a fundamental dispossession. They are the boundaries of stolen lands once held by Indigenous people.

What if we were to go forward to a time when borders were meant to be crossed? What if we were to go back to the time when border guards helped people cross? What if we were to go back to a future when the border is organized to treat vulnerable lives as precious and not disposable? What if we were to go back to a future when asylum isn't criminalized and migrant detention and mass expulsion are not rendered a norm?

What if we were to demilitarize the border patrol, so crossings are taken not as dramatic scenes of defiance but banal practices of humans seeking work, pleasure, even refuge?

What if the deep investment in securing the border went to education and the welfare of citizens and noncitizens?

What if borders are meant to be crossed?

AFTERWORD
Rifling in the Unsettling Present

What happened in my hometown of El Paso on August 3, 2019—at the Walmart not far from where my grandparents used to live and not far from one of the busiest ports of entry in the world—ricochets through space and time. Similar horrors are evident in the shooting in Buffalo, New York, where ten Black people were killed and three injured, where much of the shooting was livestreamed on May 14, 2022, and where the killer wrote a manifesto espousing his support of Great Replacement theory. The El Paso massacre and its white nationalist currents ricochet even more complexly in the mass shooting of nineteen schoolchildren and two adults in Uvalde, Texas, perpetrated by a young man who grew up in Uvalde and was likely Hispanic.[1]

These episodes—all involving rifles—speak to the smoldering legacy of settler colonialism and associated complexities. Political demagogues and those wrought in the foundational myths of settler colonialism seize on its nativist and related ethnonationalist policies and projections. These are intimately tied to orthodox notions of gender and sexual relations. Settler colonial myths lend themselves to *Great Replacement*–informed violence that proves to be inextricably linked with the grotesque consolidation of wealth and power into fewer and fewer hands. Indeed, Uvalde, Buffalo, and El Paso underscore how certain kinds of human life have become so extraordinarily dehumanized, so mired in relations with law and those who enforce it, that their killing becomes sadly predictable. They become situated institutionally, legally, and historically in the asymmetries of our economy as disposable.

These episodes point to a volatility among certain orders of aggrieved masculinity, for whom rifles and other kinds of weapons have prominence and bestow it as well. This is particularly the case for threats to an imagined mythical homeland and to relations of private property and other relations perceived as under duress. These episodes point to a time when vigilantism protected the homestead from Indigenous and other populations understood as intruders, as threats to a then emergent order where white heterosexual masculinity was becoming dominant.

But these episodes of horrendous violence, where rifles are intimately tied to settler colonial violence, may tell us something different. Perhaps the dominant ways of experiencing the world are losing their grip. Perhaps the efforts of groups on the ground, such as those engaged in struggles for immigrant rights, Black Lives Matter, and Indigenous rights, have set the stage for the coming of a better world, one where unsettling violence is no longer a normative symptom of a new struggling to be born.

SELECTED INTERVIEWS AND TESTIMONIES

■ Statement of Barbara Hines, JD

July 27, 2015

I would like to thank the Democratic Progressive Caucus, the House Judiciary Democrats, the Congressional Hispanic Caucus, the Congressional Asian Pacific American Caucus, the Congressional Black Caucus, and members of Congress for the opportunity to provide a statement regarding the detention of Central American mothers and children fleeing severe violence and persecution in their home countries.

I am currently a Senior Fellow at the Emerson Collective. I am also a coordinating member of the RAICES / Karnes Pro Bono Project.[1] Until last December, I was a Clinical Professor of Law at the University of Texas School of Law and the co-director of the immigration clinic there. I have been involved in litigation and advocacy to end the detention of families since 2006 when the Department of Homeland Security (DHS) opened the T. Don Hutto family detention facility in Taylor, Texas. I was co-counsel in the litigation that resulted in the closing of the Hutto facility. Since the re-establishment of family detention last summer, I have focused on the direct representation of women and children at the Karnes detention center, as well as local and national advocacy and litigation to end this shortsighted practice. Based on my experiences, I am convinced that there is no humane, moral or legal way to detain families, particularly in large, secure facilities operated by private for-profit prison companies.[2]

The Failed Experiment at the T. Don Hutto Detention Center

In 2006, DHS, under the Bush administration, detained over 500 mothers, fathers, and children, many of whom were asylum seekers, at the T. Don Hutto detention center, a former medium security prison, operated by the Corrections Corporation of America (CCA). The facility was not licensed under any Texas child welfare law or regulation. Families were subjected to deplorable conditions and a penal-like regime; children and their parents wore prison uniforms, had no free movement within the jail, were subjected to multiple daily prison counts, and prohibited from having toys and writing implements in their cells.[3] Until ensuing media attention and litigation, CCA provided only one hour of education per day. The image of a three-month-old Iraqi baby in a prison uniform remains with me today. She spent six months of her young life at Hutto until she and her parents were granted asylum.[4]

In 2007, the American Civil Liberties Union, the University of Texas Immigration Clinic, and the former law firm of LeBouef, Lamb, Green and McRae sued to enforce the *Flores* settlement.[5] *Flores* favors the release of immigrant children and requires that if immigrant children are detained, they must be housed in the least-restrictive alternative setting in a facility that is licensed under state law.[6] The parties in the Hutto litigation reached a settlement that lasted for two years. In August 2009, as the expiration of the settlement approached, DHS, under President Obama's newly elected administration, made the legally correct and humane decision to end family detention, except for a small, 90-bed facility in a former nursing home in Berks County, Pennsylvania.[7] Generally, as was the practice before 2006, families were released into the community to pursue their immigration cases.[8]

The failed Hutto experiment is relevant to frame today's debate. The Obama administration previously recognized that there is simply no humane way to detain families. The deleterious effects of detention on children and their mothers and the complaints that were reported at Hutto of inadequate medical care, weight loss, inedible food, threats of separation as a disciplinary tool, and more are remarkably similar to conditions and complaints at today's detention centers.

It is lamentable that the current administration, which ended family detention in 2009, has now expanded the incarceration of vulnerable mothers and children to unprecedented levels.

Family Detention 2014

In June 2014, after an increase in the number of Central American children and families fleeing horrific conditions in the Northern Triangle,[9] DHS implemented the most punitive response possible to this humanitarian crisis. In spite of evidence to the contrary, OHS characterized mothers and children as illegal border crossers without valid refugee claims.[10] OHS reinstituted family detention and this time around, insisted that all families should be detained without any individualized consideration of the need to detain.

In its escalation of family detention, OHS has ignored its domestic and international obligations to protect families seeking refuge in the United States. In fact, asylum applicants cannot apply for asylum in their home countries.[11] Furthermore, contrary to OHS's contentions, the vast majority of the families have credible asylum claims and many have won their asylum cases on the merits.[12] Yet, even in light of these facts, DHS, until very recently, continued to argue that mothers and children, the most vulnerable of all migrants, should be detained without the possibility of release.

The former Artesia detention center and the current Karnes and Dilley centers are located in remote rural areas which, as discussed below, present a significant impediment to pro bono legal representation. The Karnes detention center, operated by the GEO corporation, is located in the small town of Karnes City, Texas, approximately one hour from San Antonio, Texas, and two hours from Austin, Texas. Karnes currently has capacity to house 532 mothers and children, with plans to expand to almost 1,200 beds. The Dilley detention center, operated by CCA, in an even smaller community in Dilley, Texas, is located more than one hour from San Antonio, Texas, and more than two hours from Austin, Texas. Dilley has capacity for 2,400 mothers and children. It is most disturbing that DHS awarded another contract for the care of families to CCA, the very entity that designed the penal-like regime at Hutto.

Neither the Karnes nor the Dilley facility is licensed to house children under child welfare standards in the state of Texas.[13] A lack of a licensing means that there is no independent oversight, binding child welfare standards, or child care expertise to ensure children's safety and well-being. Guards do not have training in addressing either the needs of mothers and children seeking asylum or trauma survivors.[14] Women have no control over their children's lives. Both facilities are secure lockdown detention centers run on a rigid schedule, including meal times, wake-up and lights-out times, and multiple body counts and room checks during the day and night.

Bond and Release Practices

In addition to its rapid expansion of family detention in June 2014, DHS simultaneously instituted an across-the-board no-release policy for women and children, claiming that such a policy would send a message of deterrence to other Central Americans fleeing violence in the Northern Triangle. DHS characterized its policy as an "an aggressive deterrence strategy focused on the removal and repatriation of recent border crossers."[15] Thus, ICE placed families into expedited proceedings that require mandatory detention until a screening interview could be held. Then, even after detained women passed their credible fear interviews establishing eligibility to pursue their asylum cases, ICE refused to conduct individualized determinations of flight risk or danger to the community. This practice violates long-standing principles of civil detention that require an individualized evaluation to determine whether detention is necessary in the first place. ICE's policy of no-bond applies only to women and children. Central American fathers traveling with their children are generally released at the border and single Central American women, although initially detained, are granted bond by ICE after passing the credible fear interviews.

Before the immigration courts, ICE lawyers aggressively opposed all requests for redetermination of custody to secure release of mothers and children on reasonable conditions or upon payment of a monetary bond. ICE relied on the inapposite post-9/11 decision of the Attorney General in *Matter of D–J–*, and argued that all women and children posed national security risks and that their migration diverted DHS resources needed for immigration enforcement.[16] ICE's intransigence regarding the release of women resulted in families being detained for longer periods of time until they were able to secure pro bona counsel, appear for a hearing before the immigration court, and pay the bond amount.

In February 2015, in response to a class-action lawsuit filed by the American Civil Liberties Union, the University of Texas Law School, and the law firm of Covington and Burling, the federal court in *R–I–L–R–* issued a preliminary injunction prohibiting the use of deterrence as a rationale for detention of families or a factor in required, individualized custody determinations. The court also recognized that deterrence was likely to be ineffective to address national security threats.[17]

Although after the court decision, DHS agreed to discontinue the use of deterrence as a factor in custody decisions, it has continued to insist that it could be entitled to use deterrence in the future. Moreover, its release policies are still neither consistent nor individualized. Simply said, the government has not adopted any process, such as a robust case management system, to ensure that children and their mothers are detained only if there is reason to believe that they will not appear for their proceedings to pursue their asylum claims. Initially after the court ruling, DHS set bonds ranging from $7,500 to $10,000 for all mothers and children at Karnes, but still failed to make individualized release decisions. Consequently, most women were forced to remain in detention awaiting a court hearing to seek reduction of bond. After Secretary [of Homeland Security Jeh] Johnson's initial announcement that the length of detention for families would be reduced, some Karnes bonds were set at slightly lower amounts, in the range of $3,000 to $7,500. However, in my experience at Karnes, the amount of bonds for similar cases varies dramatically and depends not on the family's individual circumstances, but rather on the ICE officer making the determination. Additionally, many women in family detention centers are unable to pay such high bond amounts.

Ankle Monitors

After Secretary Johnson's June 24, 2015, announcement that families who passed the credible fear interview would not longer be detained,[18] ICE's policy changed again. Since then, scores of women have been released from Karnes and Dilley with ankle monitors. While ankle monitors may appear to be a facile solution to end family detention, the use of these devices raises important policy questions.

First, ICE's blanket use of ankle monitors still fails to provide an individualized custody determination. All women are placed on these devices, regardless of the need to detain or flight risk. In fact, most families have close relatives in the US who can provide support and shelter for them and strong incentives to appear for the hearings so that there is no need to impose onerous conditions on release at all. For those that do require some additional level of monitoring after release, there are a myriad of more reasonable alternatives to ensure that women appear for their court hearings such as regular reporting dates.[19] Furthermore, studies show that asylum seekers on supervised release have a high appearance rate and that legal representation is a very significant factor to ensure compliance.[20]

Second, ICE has used coercive tactics to induce women to accept ankle monitors even if an immigration judge might release her on an order of recognizance or even a low bond. For example, in one recent case that I supervised through the RAICES / Karnes Pro Bona Project, the immigration judge ordered our client released on an order of recognizance and set no other conditions. However, ICE placed her on an ankle monitor when she was released from Karnes. We were forced to file an emergency motion before the immigration court in order to obtain a ruling ordering ICE to remove the monitor.[21] Even after that, her father, with whom she reunited in another city, received numerous automated phone calls stating that, according to GPS monitoring, his daughter was not in compliance. In another case, ICE set an exorbitantly high bond of $10,000 for a Karnes mother in "withholding only" proceedings who had been detained for months.[22] After the RAICES bond fund[23] assisted in posting her bond,[24] ICE put her on an ankle monitor before releasing her. After extensive advocacy by her lawyer, ICE agreed to remove the device.

Third, ankle monitors are cumbersome, painful, and stigmatize mothers and children. Another client, whose husband is a lawful permanent resident residing in the San Antonio area, was placed on an ankle monitor. Her ankle began to swell because the device had been too tightly secured. She was forced to endure this painful swelling until her first reporting appointment, when the contractor loosened the device. Her young daughter reports that she feels ashamed as she walks out of her home and perceives that people are staring at her mother. In another case, I counseled a woman at the bus station as she waited to depart from San Antonio. Her first question, as she began to cry, was when or how her ankle monitor could be removed. She told me that in her country, "grilletes" (shackles) are only used for criminals. She was also panicked about how she would be able charge the device on her bus trip across the country.

Impediments to Access to Counsel and Pro Bono Legal Services

Most women at Karnes and Dilley cannot afford to hire private counsel and, instead, depend on pro bona counsel.[25] The RAICES / Karnes Pro Bono Project provides legal services at Karnes, while the CARA project (CLINIC, RAICES, and AILA/AIC) provides legal services at Dilley. Lawyers for this vulnerable population of asylum seekers are essential and outcome determinative. According to a recent study by Syracuse University's Transactional Records Access Clearinghouse (TRAC), women and their children requesting asylum are seventeen times more likely to win their asylum cases if they have legal representation.[26] Another study concluded that legal representation is "the single most important factor affecting the outcome of an asylum-seeker's case."[27]

The location of these facilities in rural Texas and the sheer number of detained women and children makes pro bona representation extremely challenging, despite the extraordinary efforts of volunteer lawyers at Karnes and Dilley. Unfortunately, based on my experience at Karnes, the task of pro bona lawyering has been made more difficult because of ICE's and GEO's unreasonable barriers to access to counsel and their ever-changing policies. Attorneys, students, and legal assistants cannot adequately prepare for visitation when the "rules" for such visitation are subject to frequent and unexplained modifications. Volunteer lawyers and the RAICES/Karnes coordinating team have spent inordinate amounts of effort and time navigating issues relating to access, clearances, and the use of electronic devices. All of these obstacles impede the provision of pro bona legal assistance and waste valuable attorney time.[28]

Unnecessary Clearance Procedures and Interference with the AttorneyClient Relationship

ICE has insisted on clearances for paralegals, legal assistants, and law students to enter Karnes, although the Family Residential Standards do not require such clearances. According to these standards, legal assistants may enter a family detention center upon presentation of a letter from a legal representative under whom she is working.[29] Similarly, law students, practicing under the regulations of the Executive Office of Immigration Review (EOIR), are considered "attorneys" and, like legal assistants, require no prior clearance to enter a family detention center.[30]

In addition, ICE's rules are not clearly communicated to staff. For example, on one occasion GEO officials told University of Texas law students that they could not enter Karnes without a supervising attorney, even though they had already been cleared for admittance to the facility and had visited without a supervisor on multiple previous occasions.

ICE officials have also improperly inquired as to the specific nature of legal visits, another violation of the Family Residential Standards. In seeking clearance for University of Texas law students and law students from another immigration clinic, an ICE official requested information regarding the purpose of the legal visit. Shortly after the hunger strike at Karnes, ICE officials entered the attorney visitation area and demanded that a RAICES attorney disclose to them the purpose of his legal visit. These practices contravene the Family Residential Standards, which state that "legal representatives and legal assistants may not be required to state the legal subject matter of the visit."[31] In April and May 2015, I sent a series of emails to ICE officials at Karnes and at the San Antonio Field Office, questioning the need for clearances under the Family Residential Standards and challenging ICE's queries about the nature of legal visits as a condition of clearance. I received no response whatsoever to multiple emails.

Obtaining timely clearances has been an ongoing and time-consuming obstacle at Karnes. After months of complaints going all the way up to the White House staff, clearances are now being approved more expeditiously.[32] Nevertheless, the requirement of such clearances clearly contravenes the Family Residential Standards and compliance with the process diverts needed pro bono resources away from families who need legal representation.

GEO staff have also imposed arbitrary rules regarding ingress and egress to the facility. For example, law students and their supervising attorneys from Elon University on an alternative spring break trip to Karnes were prohibited from bringing any food or water into the visitation area. GEO informed them that if they left the facility, they would not be able to reenter that day. The team spent eleven hours without food or water in order to finish their legal work. In a similar situation, University of Texas law students were effectively denied the option to get lunch when they were told they would be unable to return the same day if they left the facility even briefly. While this situation has since been remedied through

DHS headquarters, it is yet one more example of the problems of detaining families in correctional type facilities.

In addition, since the hunger strike, one ICE official in San Antonio has made numerous derogatory comments to other lawyers regarding RAICES, which impedes our project's ability to recruit pro bono lawyers.

Banning of Legal Assistants

In August 2014, Virginia Raymond, an active volunteer attorney, requested clearance for her paralegal, Victoria Rossi. ICE mistakenly cleared Ms. Rossi as an interpreter, but neither ICE nor Ms. Raymond noticed the error. Ms. Rossi visited Karnes as Ms. Raymond's legal assistant for many months. On February 2, 2015, the *Texas Observer* published an article by Ms. Rossi that was highly critical of Karnes and family detention.[33] After publication of the article, ICE denied her further access into the facility, claiming that she was entering Karnes as an interpreter but was working as a paralegal. Ms. Raymond submitted a new request for a clearance for Ms. Rossi as a paralegal, but ICE denied the request without providing reasons for the denial or any appeal mechanism.[34]

Johana De Leon, a legal assistant at RAICES, is actively involved in the coordination and legal work of the RAICES / Karnes Pro Bono Project. Until March 2015, she spent several days a week at Karnes conducting intakes, preparing women for credible fear interviews, and obtaining documents and signatures for volunteer lawyers who were unable to travel to Karnes. Because Ms. De Leon was at Karnes so frequently, she developed a relationship of trust with many of the women who had been locked up for many months. When 78 women signed a letter protesting their lengthy detention and conditions at Karnes, RAICES made the letter available to the media. After a smaller number of women began a hunger strike, Deborah Achim, the San Antonio Field Office Director for Enforcement and Removal Operations, contacted the director of RAICES to accuse Ms. De Leon of being responsible for both the letter and the hunger strike and to prohibit her from entering the facility. Ms. Achim has never substantiated these allegations, which Ms. De Leon denies, and has not provided anything in writing regarding the banning of Ms. De Leon or an appeal mechanism. Ms. De Leon has not been allowed back into Karnes since that time and recently, ICE denied her new request for clearance. Her inability to counsel women at Karnes has significantly impeded the work of the Pro Bono Project.[35]

Prohibition of Laptops, Cell Phones, and Other Devices

Since the opening of Karnes in August 2014, the RAICES / Karnes Pro Bono Project has attempted to negotiate the use of electronic devices at the facility.

Despite agreements with the San Antonio Field Office, bringing in a laptop, hot spot, or cell phone has been a consistent challenge, depending on which ICE or GEO staff person is on duty on a particular day. Frequently, pro bona volunteers were denied the ability to take their devices into Karnes, causing significant delays and inefficiency in legal representation and counseling. Through constant pressure and negotiations with DHS headquarters, finally in late spring 2015, after more than nine months of varying rules, ICE adopted a standard procedure that allows pro bona volunteers to use laptops and hot spots at Karnes. However, cell phones are still not permitted, which makes access to language lines for interpreters of indigenous languages extremely difficult. If Karnes is truly a civil, family-friendly residential center, there is no justification for such arbitrary policies that thwart the delivery of pro bona services.

Conditions of Detention

It is important to note from the outset that cosmetic and superficial changes to detention facilities do not diminish the profound impact of detention on families. While mothers and children no longer wear prison garb and toys are available at the Dilley and Karnes detention centers, the underlying tragedy is the fact that these asylum seekers are locked up. While other speakers at this forum will focus on negatives effects of detention on the mental and physical health of mothers and children, I would like to highlight a few examples and cases in which I have been involved.

Medical Conditions and Isolation

Much has been written about the dire medical conditions at both the Karnes and Dilley detention centers.[36] The vaccination of 250 children with adult dosages of hepatitis A [vaccine] is an unfortunate and dangerous example. On the day of the vaccination incident, I met with a mother at Dilley, whose abusive, gang-member domestic partner had kidnapped her and broken her fingers. She removed the cast from her fingers during her flight from her home country because the cast impeded her ability to carry her son on the journey to the U.S. When she sought medical care at Dilley for the pain in her hand, she was forced to wait for hours to see medical personnel, received no treatment, and was repeatedly told to drink water for the pain. This mother, visibly upset, reported to me that her son had been vaccinated that morning and that he was feverish, had no appetite, and was in pain when he walked. As she instructed her young son to show me the injection marks on his legs, his eyes welled up with tears. The next day I learned that he was one of the 250 children who were forcibly over-vaccinated.[37]

This perilous incident is not an isolated one. In fact, substandard medical care has been a recurrent theme since family detention began again last summer. One of the first cases, handled by a volunteer attorney with the RAICES / Karnes Pro Bono Project in August 2014, involved seven-year-old Nayeli Bermudez Beltran, who suffered from a brain tumor. During her stay at Karnes, she received absolutely no medical care and was only released from detention because of advocacy and media pressure.[38] Unfortunately, almost one year later, ICE, CCA, and GEO have not improved their medical care system. Inadequate medical care for children and mothers is yet one more reason why family detention is not sustainable.

Medical Isolation

I am also gravely concerned about the use of medical facilities for punishment and isolation at Karnes. In March 2015, 78 women signed a letter protesting conditions of detention and a smaller number initiated a hunger fast. ICE retaliated against three women and their children whom agency believed were the instigators of peaceful, constitutionally protected activities and placed them in isolation in the medical facilities at Karnes.[39]

Likewise, two women at Karnes who, in desperation, attempted suicide or self-harm were improperly isolated from both their attorneys and their children in the medical area. In the first case, in early June 2015, a nineteen-year-old mother who had been detained for more than seven months attempted suicide. She was placed in medical isolation, threatened, and separated from her four-year-old son.

During the five days that she was isolated, guards at Karnes "cared" for her child. Attorneys who had agreed to take over her case on a pro bona basis were prohibited from speaking to her directly, and she was removed before her attorneys could file a motion to reopen her removal proceedings.[40] Again, in late June 2015, another young mother cut herself with a razor after she learned that ICE had raised her bond to $8,500. She too was separated for four days from her five-year-old daughter who was left with GEO guards until her release back into the general population.

Lawyers from the RAICES / Karnes Pro Bono Project were denied access to the client and could only speak with her via telephone, which severely impeded their ability to adequately represent her. The client complained of mistreatment by GEO and medical staff and the stress and anxiety of separation from her child while in isolation.[41]

The *Flores* Decision

On July, 24, 2015, Judge Dolly Gee ruled in the *Flores* enforcement suit that DHS's family detention policy is ill-conceived, illegal, and a violation of the *Flores* settlement.[42] The court held that the *Flores* agreement encompasses accompanied as well as unaccompanied children, as did the judge in the Hutto litigation in 2007.

According to her decision, children may not be housed in secure, unlicensed facilities. Like the court in *R–I–L–R–*, Judge Gee found that the no-bond, deterrence rationale is impermissible because it contravenes the *Flores* settlement's preference for the release of children. Finally, parents should be released with their children, unless after an individualized determination, they present a significant flight risk or threat to others or to national security and such risk or threat cannot be mitigated by bond or other conditions of release. The decision gives the government until August 3, 2015, to show cause why the order should not be entered and implemented within 90 days. The court's decision is a vindication of arguments that have been made by lawyers, advocates, and members of Congress who have voiced their consistent opposition to family detention.

Conclusion

More than one year after the unprecedented escalation of family detention, the evidence overwhelmingly demonstrates that locking up mothers and children is unworkable, inhumane, and illegal. The millions of dollars spent on family detention should be used to develop community-based case management systems, to facilitate access to pro bona counsel, and to welcome asylum seekers into our communities. As Judge Gee clearly stated in her recent order, keeping children and their mothers detained at Karnes, Berks, and Dilley violates the law.

1. RAICES is a nonprofit organization in San Antonio, Texas, that provides legal services to immigrants. See http://raicestexas.org.

2. The T. Don Hutto family detention center was operated by the Corrections Corporation of America (CCA). The Karnes detention center is operated by the GEO Corporation, while the Dilley center is operated by CCA.

3. Unlike the current family detention system that targets only mothers and children, at that time, fathers were also detained at Hutto.

4. http://www.newyorker.com/magazine/2008/03/03/the-lost-children.

5. In Re Hutto Family Detention Center, A-07-CA-164-SS (W.D. Tex. 2007), available at https:/ /www.aclu.org/sites/default/files/field_document/hutto_settlement.pdf.

6. Flores v. Reno, available at https://www.aclu.org/sites/default/files/assets/flores_settlement_final_plus_extension_of_settlement011797.pdf; now Flores v. Johnson, CV-85-4544 (DMG) (C.D. Cal. 2015). See discussion, *infra,* regarding the *Flores* settlement.

7. Congress noted that the Berks facility was "more homelike" than Hutto, but that it still violated the *Flores* settlement. House Committee on Appropriations, DHS appropriations bill, 2007: report together with additional views to accompany H.R. 5441, 109th Cong., 2nd sess., 2006, H. Rep. 109-476. Since 2014, Berks has expanded its capacity, and families there have been subjected to prolonged detention under ICE's no-release policy. Advocates and lawyers report the same detrimental and inhumane conditions at Berks as Karnes and Dilley. http://www.humanrightsfirst.org/press-release/human-rights-first-tours-berks-family-detentionfacility.

8. Declaration of Barbara Hines, filed in RILR v. Johnson, CA-15-11 (JEB) (D.D.C. 2015).

9. El Salvador, Guatemala, and Honduras.

10. http://www.dhs.gov/news/2014/06/20/fact-sheet-artesia-temporary-facility-adults-childrenexpedited-removal.

11. "Any alien who is physically present in the United States or who arrives in the United States (whether or not at a designated port of arrival . . .) irrespective of such alien's status, may apply for asylum in accordance with this section"; INA § 208(a). "The term refugee means . . . any person who is outside any country of such person's nationality or, in the case of a person having no nationality, is outside any country in which such person last habitually resided, and who is unable or unwilling to return to, and is unable or unwilling to avail himself or herself of the protection of that country"; INA § 101(a)(42)(A).

12. More than 87.9 percent of the families have passed the credible fear interview, the threshold review to establish asylum eligibility. http://www.humanrightsfirst.org/sites/default/files/hrf-oneyr-family-detention-report.pdf; http://www.uscis.gov/sites/default/files/USCIS/Outreach/PED-CF RF-familiy-facilities-FY2015Q2.pdf.

13. In May 2015, almost six months after opening, Dilley received a Temporary Shelter Program license, which allows it to "care" for 24 children during the day for short periods of time, for example, while their mothers are in court or at the medical facility. http://ncronline.org/news/politics/detention-center-receives-child-care-license-state-texas.

14. Memorandum in Support of Motion to Enforce Settlement of Class Action, Flores v. Johnson, Case 2:85-cv-04544-RJK (C.D. Cal. 2015); http://www.expressnews.com/news/local/article/Activistscomplain-about-conditions-in-Dilley-6016044.php.

15. U.S. Dep't of Homeland Sec., Statement by Secretary of Homeland Security Jeh Johnson Before the Senate Committee on Appropriations, June 10, 2014, available at http://www.dhs.gov/news/2014/07/10/statement-secretary-homeland-security-jeh-johnson-senate-committee-appropriations.

16. 23 I&N Dec. 572 (A.G. 2003). See Immigration Court Declaration of Philip T. Miller, ICE Assistant Director of Field Operations for Enforcement and Removal Operations ("Miller Decl."), at 55 (Aug. 7, 2014), available at http://www.aila.org/content/default.aspx?docid=4991O; Immigration Court Declaration of Traci A. Lembke, ICE Assistant Director over Investigation Programs for HSI and ICE ("Lembke Decl."), at 60 (Aug. 7, 2014) ("[i]mplementing a 'no bond' or 'high bond' policy would help . . . by deterring further mass migration").

17. Order and Memorandum, RILR v. Johnson, Civil Action No. 1:15-cv-00011 (Feb. 20, 2015), available at https://www.aclu.org/cases/rilr-v-johnson.

18. http://www.dhs.gov/news/2015/06/24/statement-secretary-jeh-c-johnson-family-residential-centers.

19. http://immigrationpolicy.org/special-reports/humane-approach-can-work-effectiveness-alternatives-detention-asylum-seekers.

20. *Id.*

21. http://www.lexisnexis.com/legalnewsroom/immigration/b/newsheadlines/archive/2015/07/03/celebrating-freedom-from-ankle-bracelets-detention-from-karnes.aspx.

22. Women who have been previously deported are not eligible for asylum and may only apply for withholding of removal. INA § 241(b)(3)(B).

23. The RAICES bond fund solicits donations to pay bonds of women at Karnes and Dilley whose families cannot afford the bond amount. It is an example of the extraordinary community response to the unjust detention of mothers and children. http://www.raicestexas.org/pages/bondfund.

24. http://immigrationpolicy.org/special-reports/humane-approach-can-work-effectiveness-alternatives-detention-asylum-seekers.

25. Because I work at the Texas detention centers, my direct knowledge of access to counsel and conditions at Berks is more limited.

26. http://trac.syr.edu/immigration/reports/377/.

27. Jaya Ramji-Nogales, Andrew I. Schoenholtz, and Phillip G. Schrag, *Refugee Roulette: Disparities in Asylum Adjudication*, 60 STAN. L. REV. 295, 340 (2007), available at https://www.acslaw.org/files/RefugeeRoulette.pdf.

28. See generally, S. Schulman to S. Saldana, "Re: Access for Pro Bono Volunteers at Karnes, Dilley and Berks Family Detention Centers," Apr. 20, 2015, on file with author.

29. Family Residential Standards, Visitation, Sec. V, if10(c)(2).

30. *Id.*, Sec. V, if10(c)(1).

31. *Id.*, Sec. V, if10(d).

32. Letter from S. Schulman to S. Saldana, *"Re: Access for Pro Bono Volunteers at Karnes, Dilley and Berks Family Detention Centers,"* Apr. 20, 2015, on file with author.

33. http://www.texasobserver.org/seeking-asylum-karnes-city/.

34. Flores v. Holder, 2:85-cv-04544 (C.D. Cal.), Doc. 140, Declaration of Victoria Rossi, dated Apr. 22, 2015. See also Brad Tyer, *Paralegal Blocked from Karnes Detention Center after Observer Story,* TEXAS OBSERVER, March 27, 2015, available at http://www.texasobserver.org/paralegal-deniedaccess-to-karnes/.

35. Flores v. Holder, 2:85-cv-04544 (C.D. Cal.), Doc. 140, Declaration of Johana G. De Leon-Amendarez, Apr. 21, 2015. See also, Michael W. Macleod-Ball, Acting Director, ACLU Washington Legislative Office, to Sarah R. Saldana, Director, U.S. Immigration and Customs Enforcement (Apr. 17, 2015), available at http://endfamilydetention.com/aclu-letter-to-ice-director-sarah-saldana/.

36. http://www.expressnews.com/news/local/article/Activists-complain-about-conditions-in-Dilley-6016o4-4.php; https://womensrefugeecommission.org/images/zdocs/CRCL-Complaint-Psych-Impact-of-Family-Detention.pdf.

37. http://grassrootsleadership.org/releases/2015/07/attorney-describes-effects-vaccine-overdose-refugee-child-dilley-detention-camp; http://www.upi.com/Top_News/US/2015/07/09/250-detained-immigrant-children-given-overdose-of-vaccine-in-Texas/96814364-78936/; http://fusion.net/story/165837/dilley-detention-center-horror-stories-from-the-medical-ward/.

38. http://www.houstonchronicle.com/news/article/Feds-release-7-year-old-immigrant-girl-with-5732146.php.

39. http://www.colorlines.com/articles/why-mothers-are-strike-karnes-immigrant-detention-center; http://www.texasobserver.org/family-detention-freedom-of-speech/; Pineda Cruz, et al. v. Thompson, et al., C.N. A-15-CV-326 (W.D. Tex 2015).

40. http://www.mcclatchydc.com/news/immigration/article25186393.html.

41. Before her bond was raised, this client met with the Democratic congressional members who visited Karnes on June 22, 2015. Prior to the visit, she had been assured by ICE that she would be released on her own recognizance. Affidavit of client on file with RAICES / Karnes Pro Bono Project.

42. http://graphics8.nytimes.com/packages/pdf/us/FloresRuling.pdf; http://www.nytimes.com/2015/07/26/us/detained-immigrant-children-judge-dolly-gee ruling.html.

■ Father Robert Mosher Interview

Father Bob: So, basically, we want the detained migrant to feel that there are people who are worried about them outside the walls of their prison camps. Most recently, a fundraising effort to pay the bonds of detained migrants were given bonds, funded by the immigration judge or by [inaudible 00:00:24] has become a huge activity for us because of the generosity of people who are increasingly outraged by the president [inaudible 00:00:35] policies and practices, especially the separation of parents and children.

When we promote these funds by saying it helps to reunite families, that's the magic phrase that people are looking for. And we've had hundreds of thousands of dollars donated to our fund, with which we can pay between two and five thousand–dollar bonds, so along with other organizations, we don't always pay the whole bond.

Gilberto: The average bond in that area—

Father Bob: We figure it's up in that area, between seven and ten thousand dollars.

Gilberto: Okay.

Father Bob: Yeah. And they're getting paid, thanks to the generosity of people coming together, saying this separation of parents from their children just can't happen, we can't allow that. And it's such a relief, really, to see the anger of people, which sounds a little funny, but it's important to be angry about this and not to direct anger into destructive acts or hatred, but to channel this anger into constructive acts like releasing these people [inaudible 00:01:46], people really respond to that. So that's probably our major activity at the moment.

Father Bob: We always have monthly meetings of the entire group, but there's so much going on that we have subcommittee meetings as well. And sometimes they meet here in the [inaudible 00:02:05] center, other times we meet in a bar. El Paso seems to have a lot of bars with nice patios in which people can gather and have their own meetings. We've been able to do that as well.

And we don't have any official leadership. We take decisions by consensus and consulting each other on email, as well as the general lines of our [inaudible 00:02:32] and policies at the general meeting, they're recommended by different subcommittees and individuals, we debate them, we decide what to do. So far we haven't felt any need to have a president, vice president, secretary, or treasurer. We all just—we have opened up a bank account in a credit union, and on that we can make out checks for the bonds. Three of us are the signators for the bank account. So it's working very well so far; we haven't felt the need [for officers]. And indeed the group is rather allergic to any sort of authoritarian structure. We like taking decisions that way, in a consensual way.

Gilberto: Is it primarily laypeople?

Father Bob: Oh, yeah, it's not even a majority Catholic, I would say.

Gilberto: Okay.

Father Bob: It's a completely secular group of people from different backgrounds, some of them quite militant in their political activities, others who are just doing what they can, sometimes they're volunteers from Annunciation House. There's myself, and other, what shall we say, openly Catholic people. And others who have no particular religion or faith at all. We all come together, inspired by the idea [crosstalk 00:04:00] in solidarity with the contained migrant.

Gilberto: Right, and the injustices that are evident.

Father Bob: Yeah, what they're suffering. We've done really good work; we've even published a detailed report on the abuses that have been collected not just from El Paso processing center but from the other ones in the area.

Gilberto: Is that available online?

Father Bob: Yes.

Gilberto: Okay.

Father Bob: Yes, we have a webpage, and you'll be able to see the report we came out with. I don't know if we have any hard copies.

Gilberto: I prefer the online stuff anyways; I'll lose it.

Father Bob: Yeah, we printed a few copies in color, it looks really nice. But it's good—it's inspired other organizations to publish their own accounts, like in [inaudible 00:04:45] there's a group that has published their own investigation of abuses.

Gilberto: Do you think the abuses are extreme—[how] would you characterize them? How [inaudible 00:04:56] are the abuses—

Father Bob: Well, that's a relative term.

Gilberto: I know.

Father Bob: They are shocking, just on their own merit. There are some things like the quality of food, the sanitation of the place, the insects that infest some of these places. Some of them are really terrible. The food is badly cooked, sometimes not cooked at all, half frozen. But what most concerns us is the abuse by the guards; there have been numerous abuses [inaudible 00:05:31] that the people have described in detail in this report. It's pretty savage in these detention camps. You wouldn't think so, but when you visit, they are. I've been saying mass, twice a month as part of the chaplain's team for the Catholic detainees, and the guards are very friendly, and we're trying to promote cooperation with them in order to be able to minister [inaudible 00:05:58] to the detainees and set up conferences or confessions with them, and attend to their spiritual needs.

But the detailed descriptions of abuses show that they are taking place, and we've always known that some of the many ways—for instance, we consider solitary confinement, even in federal or county prisons, even in the case of people condemned for crimes, solitary confinement is something that shouldn't be used; it's like a form of torture. And to apply that to people who have committed no crimes at all but only the misdemeanor of being in a country that [inaudible 00:06:40] looking for refuge—we use solitary confinement against them, it's really reprehensible. That's just a few examples.

Gilberto: Right. And can you elaborate, [using solitary confinement with (inaudible 00:06:56)] migrants on what grounds?

Father Bob: Controlling unacceptable behavior, I guess; when people get unruly, the guards get threatened and decide to use this as a threat in order to impose what they regard as good behavior.

Gilberto: Okay. Can you describe to me the interior of the detention camp?

Father Bob: It's pretty plain; it doesn't require much capacity to describe it. It's cinder block walls, painted over. Cement floors, razor wire on top of all the walls, double-fencing around the enclosure: it looks like a prison. They have to wear color-coded overalls according to their degree of conformity, I guess you would say, although some of the overalls are coded to indicate past criminal activity. So they're a minority, but there are red, orange, and blue colors, and the blue ones are the people who have committed no crimes, have no criminal background, and are being held there because they're [inaudible 00:08:16].

And of course, there's the issue of private companies who need to fill 43,000 beds every night. They have a contract with the US government; it's a figure established quite randomly by Congress; there's really no reason why that number is so important, except that it's the number of beds that Congress has required to be filled [inaudible 00:08:45]. So that's why even people without any criminal history go into these detention camps [inaudible 00:08:54].

They're not that well organized in the sense that they could easily get a situation of overcrowding in these camps, like overbooking. So they sent the overflow to a federal prison or a county jail, where they're mixed in with the general public.

Gilberto: And you think the county jail or the federal prison is on par with a detention center?

Father Bob: Well, the treatment is the same—that's the crime, or the injustice, that's taking place. But to mix the populations as well is even more egregious, where you have migrants who have no criminal background being mixed with dangerous people who do need to be taken out of the public sphere for the public good and so they can recover a more humane way back into their lives, which is the purpose of the prison.

I think prisons are [inaudible 00:10:00] out of the public arena, and work life, [and inmates are] locked away and forgotten about, but to recover their humanity and eventually be reintegrated into society. But a great harm is done when you're mixing ordinary people who have never acted violently with this more violent population. It kind of undermines the whole reason for a prison.

Gilberto: Do you have a sense of the numbers of people being held in the El Paso area?

Father Bob: Well, the El Paso detention facility, called the processing center, holds about 2,000, and it's men and women in separate barracks. I don't know about the other facilities, probably well over 1,000 also in [inaudible 00:10:50] facility for immigrants, not to be confused with their correction facility, even though, I'm not sure, but a lot of migrants probably end up in the correction facility as well. There's a few others; other members of the DMSC [Detained Migrant Solidarity Committee] would know [inaudible 00:11:09] better than me.

Gilberto: Okay. When I walked in, you mentioned to me solidarity. Is there a relationship between solidarity movements of the '80s, and this DMSC.

Father Bob: Well, I suggested that name, the Detained Migrants Solidarity Committee, back when we were founded about four years ago, because it has such a resonance with me after living in Chile during the dictatorship. The Catholic Church actually established a human rights [inaudible 00:11:45] throughout the country, from North to South.

Gilberto: In Chile, you're talking about.

Father Bob: In Chile, during the dictatorship, every single diocese, eighteen or so dioceses in the country, the dioceses [inaudible 00:12:01] territory, and it's established by the Catholic Church, presided over by a bishop. They're usually located in major cities. In every one of these major cities, the Catholic Church established a human rights organization and decided to put it under its own wing in order for it to have some protection, and the right-wing military government, which had a certain respect for the institution of the Catholic Church, enough so that they never, in the seventeen years of [inaudible 00:12:31] dictatorship—they often threatened to—but never actually invaded those offices, the military forces, or confiscate[d] the files that were in them.

We were expecting them to eventually—those who worked with the [inaudible 00:12:49], it was called—we expected them to invade someday, which is why we kept copies of everything we had on file, outside of the country during the seventeen years.

Gilberto: So . . .

Father Bob: That was, I guess, my point, is that was an experience of solidarity that brought everyone together. Communists, socialists, Christian democrats, [inaudible 00:13:14] Catholics, and occupy the parishes and chapels and buildings of the Catholic Church as centers of refuge, of therapy, of legal assistance. Solidarity created such trust among the people who were opposed to [inaudible 00:13:32] dictatorship and who were victims of that dictatorship, that it was a great unifying force for the country in general.

And so when the idea came up to create an organization that acted on behalf of detained migrants, solidarity just came to mind as a wonderful experience of [inaudible 00:13:52] that I had seen work in Chile, in the sense of bringing people together around a common value that they could all share.

Gilberto: Right, and of course the local history of solidarity in the area is also in Tucson, and in Mexico and all that, and the [inaudible 00:14:07].

Father Bob: Yeah, I think I've heard of that. I can come back to the United States to visit our colleagues here, could see the sanctuary [inaudible 00:14:21] taking place in the seminaries and [inaudible 00:14:24].

Gilberto: Yeah. So [inaudible 00:14:28] linkages between terror in Chile and what migrants experience right now in the United States. Do you think it's . . . is it a fair comparison to say that—

Father Bob: I think that there is a lot of similarity. I would even go so far as to say [that] Trump is our [inaudible 00:14:51; Pinochet?] in many ways. Obviously he's not a military professional, [inaudible 00:14:57] and there's no violent military coup that brought Trump to power. But the oppressive actions of this administration, which have not been seen before; some of them are merely intensifications of things we have seen before. The separation of families has taken place before.

Obama used to be called the [inaudible 00:15:24; deporter?] in chief for good reason. But it's at a new level now, and there are parallels with the racism of Pinochet's regime, with the repressive measures, with the instances of torture, if you can consider the separation of parents and children as a form of torture, which I do consider. So general Pinochet was a difference in degree rather than kind.

Gilberto: Gotcha.

Father Bob: In many ways—not absolute on that. 'Cause again, Trump was elected, maybe not by the majority of voters but by the majority of electors anyway. And Pinochet never even received a single vote for anything.

Gilberto: Right.

Father Bob: Which was often pointed during his regime. And then he established [inaudible 00:16:26] we would say that Pinochet ran as the only candidate, and he still lost, [inaudible 00:16:34]. So I guess it's the whole anti-democratic [inaudible 00:16:40] of the regime here in the states that makes me think that my time in Chile was like a preparation for what's going on in my own country.

Gilberto: Right.

Father Bob: And it seems to be [inaudible 00:16:53] in the sense that, just as in Chile, we saw vastly different sectors of Chilean society, which was a problem for many years—how to maintain a single country with disparate political and social forces in the country. How they came together under tough oppressive circumstances is very similar to my experience [with] what's going on now and how people are coming together from a great diversity of [inaudible 00:17:22] in order to oppose the ideology and the [inaudible 00:17:27] of the president and administration.

Gilberto: You feel far more hopeful, [inaudible 00:17:31] that's good to hear.

Father Bob: It's quite positive. People are waking up, not just to the policies of the president's administration but also to some of the structural injustices. We see progressive political movements actually gaining new strength now in the country, offering a greater variety of political options to the American electorate in the future. It's very promising.

Gilberto: Yeah, [inaudible 00:17:58] radical socialist candidate in New York was out here, [inaudible 00:18:03] right?

Father Bob: Yes, that's right. Which probably turned the tide in her favor.

Gilberto: Right.

Father Bob: Just by visiting here.

Gilberto: Yeah.

Father Bob: Plus the Democrats are, I don't know, they seem helpless in the sense that they really have this shared complacency about their own party that works against them.

Gilberto: It's a generational shift, I feel. The younger ones are really acting right now [crosstalk 00:18:26].

Father Bob: True, and they're also more progressive.

Gilberto: Right, yeah, I agree [inaudible 00:18:32]. Can you tell me more about the everyday forms of solidarity you guys. . . . What do you guys do?

Father Bob: It's really lovely. We debate a lot and we disagree with each other a lot, but 90 percent is what we have in common. None of us can stand what's going on, what people are suffering these days, and we want to do something about it. Point it out, educate people, go out into the streets and demonstrate, and pay their bonds. It's a wonderful mix of pragmatism and idealism in something like this I really like.

Everyday solidarity is just having these meetings that go on for three or four hours, trying to debate the best things to do, what to avoid, what we want to do in the long run. These meetings just go on for hours and hours. I couldn't possibly go to all the different subcommittee meetings, [or] I'd wear myself out, because you do spend energy attending these meetings. But, again, this is what I saw happening in Chile. You had a regime where gatherings of three or four people were prohibited by law, in public, and where parishes and chapels became the only safe place where people could meet and debate.

You're seeing something very similar to what's taking place here. People thirst for that, especially when there are attempts to take it away from them. There's an air of, what should I say—urgency—about removing all restrictions and just meeting and talking and getting your voice out, because in Chile's case, it was being repressed in other places. And in the United States' case, it [has] probably been 'cause it hasn't been valued, that kind of debate and meeting and getting your voice out and discovering who you are by participating in these meetings. That met a very basic human need in Chile. You could see personalities just flourish after a few weeks of meetings in many cases. It was a beautiful thing to see how people who would come to a meeting, shy and quiet and not saying anything, sit in the back.

Over time, and not very long, maybe a few weeks even, [they would] begin to raise their voice and express an opinion. Before you know it, they're leading the meeting. The flourishing of personality shows that a very deep human need is being met. And, to a different degree, maybe less so here at these meetings. You see the same thing. You see people with leadership skills discover that they have those leadership skills and negotiating skills and debating skills, and seeing personalities flourish in these meetings too, which is really probably the most valuable thing that happens. We had so many meetings in Chile, we often said it doesn't really matter if we actually do anything at the meeting—it's the meeting itself that is the valuable experience.

And they would go on for hours and hours in Chile too, and I see the same thing here. They're not all that efficient, but they sure are inclusive and exciting leaders.

Gilberto: Sounds like it. So do you mind if I ask, what are the tensions really about? Tactics and . . .

Father Bob: Different things, whatever comes up. Like how do we define our mission? What are we really about? And then we'll come up with a mission statement as well as a vision statement. We'll try to use some of the tools that we find online for different group dynamics, ice breakers, but also how to achieve the goal that the group sets out for themselves, the steps, the resources, identifying them. There are many resources on the internet for how to organize [inaudible 00:22:57] or whatever ideal [inaudible 00:23:01] for itself, in a way that reflects the entire group's shared vision.

Gilberto: Right.

Father Bob: It develops in that sense, as an anthropologist would be interested in how certain traditions and a whole cultural way of being can come about within [inaudible 00:23:21] that almost creates a subculture within the American culture, especially over time.

Gilberto: Right.

Father Bob: A certain language, even a certain way of dressing.

Gilberto: And behaving and [crosstalk 00:23:36] imagining the world, right?

Father Bob: Different traditions begin to be established, a kind of collection of wisdom or . . .

Gilberto: Wisdom, a collective wisdom [crosstalk 00:23:51].

Father Bob: Collective wisdom, which used to be one of the older definitions of culture [crosstalk 00:23:57], words of wisdom of a group. Over time, we began to see how this accumulates so that past mistakes are not repeated.

Gilberto: Right. But it sounds—I hear you talk about it, I hear a real warmth. Is that the exhaustion that you get with many movements, right?

Father Bob: That's one of the things that gives me life and maintains my interest in—this group's interest in—supporting them. From a religious point of view, it's God at work [crosstalk 00:24:24], helping people to become more who they were always meant to be, and becoming instruments of the new reality that God has created the world to be. It's a very Christian perspective, but it goes back to Judaism of course. The proposals of the prophets to oppose injustice and create a new society.

Father Bob: Michael Harrington was always very good at pointing out the connection between the biblical roots of such injustice.

Gilberto: Can you share with me any stories of . . . of the people who are fleeing Latin America?

Father Bob: Or Central America, most of them are from Central America. Some of them are from Mexico, and they actually come from all over, we've had Chinese and Africans and Russians. But the great majority come from Central America, Honduras, El Salvador, [inaudible 00:25:28]—those names frequently come up.

I've been visiting a Honduran in the El Paso processing center for the past several Saturdays. She can only be visited by people from the public on certain days of the week—once a week, in fact, according to the first letter of her last name; I don't know if you know that.

Gilberto: No, I don't.

Father Bob: There are so many detainees that they assign each day of the week, alphabetically, to the first letter of your last name. So her last name begins with an *N*, and they don't allow prisoners with *N* to receive visitors until Saturday evening each week. So once a week I go to visit this woman, because she sent a letter here ask[ing] for help. She was separated from her nine-year-old son as soon as they were caught by the US Border Patrol and she asked for asylum.

She didn't present herself voluntarily at the bridge, which many asylum seekers do, so she only asked for asylum after she was caught coming into the country. So, in that sense, her case doesn't look good. But again, you have to respect that petition and investigate and let her have her day in court before a judge. So that much at least is working, although very slowly. She could be years in the detention camp before she gets to see a judge.

But the criminal or the unjust thing happening to her is this separation from her boy. And her boy, I think because she had said she had a family who would put them up in New Jersey, they shipped the boy, threw him up to New York, and he's being taken care of at a shelter there, run by the government, two thousand miles away from here. So that happened on May 15; she's been over two months now without seeing her son. And she just says there's no greater pain, and she hardly ever sleeps; she can't stop wondering about him.

She was able to speak to him on the phone once a week, and he recently turned ten, so she really felt it then. She said to me very plaintively, "I wish I could make him little again"; of course any mother knows what that's like, doing something for your child on the child's birthday. The pain these people feel over something so arbitrary and barbaric. It was the explicit intention of Jeff Sessions to [inaudible 00:28:20] to punish them for looking for refuge here, as if that were a crime.

And in the first place, it's, Do you want to make people suffer? To teach them a lesson by hurting them is not acceptable. It's not the [inaudible 00:28:42] of trying to [inaudible 00:28:44; instill?] in people a respect for the law, if that's what he's after. This is not a legitimate means of doing that. And to make people suffer for this supposed purpose of sending a message back to other people in their own home country is just a ridiculous notion and is immoral for that reason as well. To use pain to achieve some justifiable good end, because the pain itself, when you choose that as a means, that has its own end and that is the destruction of the human personality, of the human person.

In this case, the pain is so great that it creates a trauma for both the mother and the child. And you could see this. All I do is keep her company and listen to her as much as I can. And she just, she appreciates that because it gives her a chance to talk about what she's going through, and that's helpful for her, but she doesn't experience any resolution.

Gilberto: When you visit her, is [it] at a table that you're sitting?

Father Bob: It's in a prison setting. We're sitting in front of a glass partition; we're talking on these phone pieces to talk to each other. We're sitting down on these metal fixed stools. There's a table underneath the glass partition. Just like what you see in the movies.

Gilberto: Right, plexiglass.

Father Bob: As if this was a dangerous person.

Gilberto: Right.

Father Bob: Can't have any contact of any kind with people outside.

Gilberto: You said she wrote you. How do you think she found your group?

Father Bob: I think the lawyer who was helping her asked her to write. I suppose the lawyer was thinking of the DMSC, and this is the only address that the DMSC has because our general meetings always take place here. So probably [inaudible 00:30:55].

Gilberto: Okay. So there is an awareness among legal circles of your guys' efforts?

Father Bob: We're explicitly a member of the border immigration council.

Gilberto: Oh, you are?

Father Bob: Which brings together legal and grassroots organizations like us [inaudible 00:31:14] in an official capacity. We've had press conferences and statements.

Gilberto: And reports, as you mentioned.

Father Bob: Which we have launched with [inaudible 00:31:25].

Gilberto: When I walked in, you said to me, Ground Zero.

Father Bob: Yes. I think it works well. It's descriptive and it's also somewhat alliterative to say "ground zero" and "zero toleration."

Gilberto: Yeah, it works. I appreciate it myself. I imagine that the DMSC is in conversation with other, similar organizations across the world. Are you getting similar . . . [inaudible 00:32:01]?

Father Bob: Yeah, we actually belong to the Detention Watch Network.

Gilberto: Oh, okay.

Father Bob: Which is a national organization that provides us with all kinds of tools for running meetings, for investigation, and for being part of national campaigns for particular issues, like the treatment of transgender detainees [crosstalk 00:32:23]. Occasionally we'll hear about the suicide of someone in another part of the country, or the attempted suicide of another. We have national campaigns to bring those to public attention; we become part of that. So a local expression [inaudible 00:32:40].

Gilberto: Okay. Wow. So what else would you want to tell me that I should know? This is very compelling [inaudible 00:32:49], and I appreciate it very much. Is there anything in particular that I overlooked or that you want me to know?

Father Bob: No, that's probably all the major points, what I most value about the Detained Migrants Solidarity Committee. It's one of many instances of grassroots organizations that have sprung up, not since Trump became president but even before, when the Obama administration was also deporting great numbers of people and not really being very successful at protecting our Dreamers.

Gilberto: Right.

Father Bob: So, for the past, well, since I've been here, for the past seven years, I've seen many organizations spring out from ordinary students and Dreamers—[for example,] Occupy El Paso for a while—it's just a marvelous place for bringing people with shared values but different backgrounds together, to work in a concerted way.

I really love El Paso that way [crosstalk 00:33:51], and it reminds me so much of Chile in the 1980s when I was there.

Gilberto: That [inaudible 00:33:57] you made earlier on in this conversation was fantastic, it really made me [crosstalk 00:34:03].

Father Bob: I guess more for the effects than the actual origins.

Gilberto: Right, yeah.

Father Bob: I can see the same thing happening to people here, where they just overcome their fears, their [inaudible 00:34:14], and their differences and begin to make commitments and to stand up and to March and to attend meetings.

Gilberto: Right. I sense that growing and growing, [inaudible 00:34:31].

Father Bob: Yes.

Gilberto: Yeah.

Father Bob: This might be a bubble that we're in at the moment.

Gilberto: Right.

Father Bob: The hundreds of thousands of dollars in donations that we've gotten for the [inaudible 00:34:42], as we call it, for paying the bonds of teaching this many and being above all this [inaudible 00:34:51] people may forget about these great members who have been a few months, especially since it's no longer officially being [inaudible 00:34:59] that's going on at the moment.

Gilberto: Right. So the new policy will be a question of [inaudible 00:35:14] rather than separating—

Father Bob: Yes [crosstalk 00:35:17]. But somewhat less intense than actual[ly] separating the children from their parents. It used to be the kind of thing that would shock us so profoundly as a society. When the movie based on the book *Sophie's Choice* came out with Meryl Streep—

Gilberto: I never saw it.

Father Bob: This was the central dramatic element of the book, that you wouldn't even get to until you're very deep into the [inaudible 00:35:45] at the end. What was Sophie's secret was the whole thing, and Meryl Streep played the part of Sophie in the movie, and the movie, too, kept you going with, What was it that this character, this Polish woman who had been imprisoned in a concentration camp under Nazi-occupied Poland—what was her big secret? How was she so deeply marked by that experience that she kept getting into this destructive relationship with her boyfriend, and eventually, by the end of the book—spoiler alert—she takes her own life at the same time as her boyfriend.

Well, Sophie's choice refers to the fact that she had to choose, at one point, between her son and her daughter.

Gilberto: Oh, God.

Father Bob: Who was she going to take with her to the concentration camp? And the Nazi guard who was forcing her to make that choice was staring at her and forcing her to do it, and she chose her son, and her daughter was dragged away, screaming. The movie shows it in such an impactful way, as the girl is screaming, being dragged away, Meryl Streep's character, holding onto her son, also with [inaudible 00:37:06] as if she was the one [inaudible 00:37:09] in this very [inaudible 00:37:11].

That won the Academy Award; it was a huge thing [inaudible 00:37:16] were very celebrated.

Gilberto: I remember the buzz.

Father Bob: It was around 1980, 1979, maybe before. And now that's taking place all the time with thousands of kids, people coming to the border, asking for asylum, and being told, "We can only take three of you, so your child can't come in with you; you're going to have to leave that child behind."

Gilberto: I didn't know that was happening. So they're leaving the child at the border in Mexico?

Father Bob: They're told, that's the "choice" they're given, of course. I haven't seen a family that accepted it as a choice [crosstalk 00:37:53]; this is even before the separation of the children and their parents. They come up to the bridge or the gate, they ask for asylum, and they're often turned away by the [inaudible 00:38:04] officers, or they're told, We can take three people, and in your family you are five members, so two of you are going to have to stay.

There's Sophie's choice right there, the trauma: which children do I choose to bring with me?

Gilberto: So as far as you know, people have not made that choice; they said no.

Father Bob: They won't accept it, as far I can see; nobody's coming in to the states to separate their families [inaudible 00:38:36].

Gilberto: Right.

Father Bob: I've never heard of that.

Gilberto: It [inaudible 00:38:42] to hear the story.

Father Bob: It used to be so moving. The whole US society was shocked by this novel that came out. The movie was based on something that actually happened. But now it's [inaudible 00:38:57; and] we're the Nazis.

Gilberto: That's kind of my analysis right there.

Father Bob: Yeah.

Gilberto: Yeah.

Father Bob: Well, it's incredible in so many ways. I participated in the [inaudible 00:39:14]; it was one of the few things that we felt was effective in Chilean society, having these [inaudible 00:39:22] demonstrations that would only last five minutes, in front of the actual places of torture [inaudible 00:39:29] every single day during the seventeen years of the dictatorship, in every major city of the country. And we would invite the foreign press to come, and as many of the local press that were there to come and have these five-minute demonstrations in front of a torture center and then disperse, and then gather somewhere else to evaluate the action.

Gilberto: And the [inaudible 00:39:51] was to [inaudible 00:39:53]?

Father Bob: It was the key to not getting arrested.

Gilberto: Yeah.

Father Bob: Eventually, it took them several years to infiltrate us. We had a very good security system. You had to be invited by someone new in the [inaudible 00:40:08], and if someone turned up to these evaluation meetings that wasn't us and wanting to see what was going on, which actually happened, if they said something like "I came to this because I saw a notice on the parish bulletin board," [inaudible 00:40:26] and we would kick that person out because [inaudible 00:40:32].

Anyway, what's my point? Oh, so for years, from 1983 until about 1990 when the regime stopped, we would have this secret nonviolent movement against torture, and it was very demanding. Many of us were arrested several times. We tried to keep ourselves in the public eye as much as possible, and a safety measure. And, anyways, it took a lot out of us to even participate, and it's created a lot of fear. Sometimes we were beaten; some of us were sprayed with tear gas during the demonstrations or hosed with a water cannon, which is kind of funny; we discovered that if you're sitting on the ground, the water cannon couldn't really do any damage to you. There were certain chants where we would call for the water cannon 'cause it was so hot.

Anyway, so all this activity centered around torture; the one thing that people found themselves able to overcome their fear and mobilize against is now a problem here. I came back to the states in 2009 and found that the use of torture was debated in this country. It's something I never imagined. I remember the Chilean police, and they would repress us and see that there were foreigners in this movement. And they were saying, "Why don't you go back to your own country and protest torture?" and, of course, it would just roll off us because we're from the United States—we don't torture.

But now the shoe is on the other foot. I have to oppose torture because I protested in Chile, and how am I not going to protest it here?

Gilberto: This trajectory is making me think about the moment when the Bush administration brought it up.

Father Bob: Right. And I found myself living in a country where torture was practiced, which is huge.

Gilberto: Yeah.

Father Bob: But [inaudible 00:42:51] we used to be the country that would protest torture, but now we have no basis for that.

Gilberto: Right. You know, I didn't ask you this one thing, and it's very basic. Can I record this conversation?

Father Bob: You're doing it.

Gilberto: I know but [inaudible 00:43:11] can I have—

Father Bob: Yes, you may record this and use it as you like.

Gilberto: Okay, thank you. I have nothing else to ask you.

Father Bob: Okay.

Gilberto: I may follow up with an email here or there. You have a very affecting presence, Father. It's good, I needed that. I've been put down by what's going on in this country.

Father Bob: I'm really impr— [The recording ends abruptly here.]

■ Virginia Raymond Interview

Virginia: I am here with my good friend [crosstalk 00:00:08], tenured professor Gilberto Rosas, who I've known for many years and trust totally in my house. . . . I'm going to talk to him voluntarily. I have not been promised anything and will not receive anything except for the pleasure of Gilberto's company and that, perhaps, of his wife and two lovely children tonight for this. I'm just going to ask that if I get—just because I will get names of cases wrong and dates wrong, that if I make those kinds of booboos, that Gilberto will allow me to correct them before quoting me as a person who doesn't know what she's talking about.

Gilberto: And I'm here with a dear friend, colleague, activist, scholar, who I hold in the highest regard, Virginia Raymond, who has humbly agreed to share with me her experiences, her analysis of what is going on today in the United States, and the tension in courts along lines of asylum, withholding refugees, and similar reasons.

The book was going to be originally about asylum and the ethics testimony. It shifted two months ago to witnessing, given the broader dimension that witnessing implies. Now the field is so fraught, I just want to hear what you . . . what I just said, your thoughts, your deepest . . .

I'm sure it's very painful what you've experienced. Again, I really appreciate your willingness to share with me what you have seen and what you fought for and what you think is going on. I'm just going to say go at it. [inaudible 00:02:17] . . .

Back on. We're recording. I saw you in February and we . . .

Virginia: About a year ago.

Gilberto: Right. February 2018.

Virginia: 2018.

Gilberto: That was like the highlight of my career when we won that asylum case. Well, things have changed dramatically since then. Open there, on the issue of—

Virginia: Sure. Where to start? So you know that I came back to the practice of law very part-time in June 2018. I did so reluctantly. I think I was put on Earth to be a teacher, but I lost my job. I lost two jobs in 2011. So I taught for a year and a half at Austin Community College, but it wasn't. . . .

But in June 2012, when then president Obama signed the order that was going to allow for deferred action for childhood arrivals [DACA], I thought, That's wonderful, and a little scary, and it's going to take a lot of people processing a lot of applications, and we're going to need to be careful.

I had been involved in that kind of process before. For instance, after the American Baptist Church's settlement in 1990 and having to reopen—or being able to reopen many cases, working with TPS—temporary protected status—at different points during the first chapter of my law practice. So I called Barbara Hines, who was then still the director of the University of Texas Law School Immigration Law Clinic, and a mentor to many of us.

I said, "Barbara, what's the plan? This sounds like it's going to call for huge, mass processing on a lot of people." She said, "Well, good you ask. We're having a meeting next week" or whatever, soon, with a number of people, including the University Leadership Initiative, or ULI, a bunch of different people.

So from the summer of 2012 to December of 2012, I did a lot of work on DACA cases, DACA clinics, learning about DACA, helping to teach other people about DACA, what to watch out for, things like that. I spent a lot of time doing that. I was still teaching where I was in the fall semester, teaching at Austin Community College at the Eastview Campus here in Austin.

During that process of having all these clinics, I would see a lot of people, a lot of young people, a lot of lawyers that I had known from a long time ago who had been practicing immigration law in Texas when I started doing it, like Thomas Esparza, Paul Parsons, criminal defense lawyers. And other kinds of lawyers like Alberto Garcia, who has been a lawyer for a long time, but not strictly speaking an immigration lawyer, but very much aware of immigration lawyer[s] and the ways that it affects [their] clients on other kinds of cases. And numerous other people from American Gateways, which was a project that I'd helped start in 1987, '88. It was then called PAPA, the Political Asylum Project of Austin, or [Spanish language 00:06:13]. We chose that name because it was bilingual.

I heard earlier this year that American Gateways still has the legal orientation program. Some people in the detention centers, some people still refer to the American Gateways, people who go out and give those "Know your rights" kinds of talks, as [foreign language (Proyecto de Asilo Político de Austin); 00:06:38], because [crosstalk 00:06:38].

Gilberto: That's your imprint.

Virginia: Well, the name stuck. It's really—anyway, I don't want to get into that. I could tell lots of stories about PAPA.

But people kept saying, "You're back, you're back," and I was like, "No, I'm not," but two things. One is, Barbara Hines, at one of these clinics, said to me, "Hey, I want to talk to you. This young man I've just been speaking to qualifies for DACA, but I think that he also qualifies for VAWA, because he's gay and his father abused him and threw him out of the house when he came out, but he had been abused all his life for being, quote-unquote, 'feminine.'" I won't remember [crosstalk 00:07:21] . . .

Gilberto: So Violence Against Women—

Virginia: Yes, but the Violence Against Women Act [VAWA]—that's the name of the act, but it's always applied to people of any gender and not just to spouses but to children as well. Anyway, so she said, "He's also a VAWA case. He was abused. I think he could get VAWA, I think that would be better, because . . ." I'm tell[ing] you this now, I don't think she had to spell it out for me. With VAWA, if you get VAWA, you can adjust your status to become a legal permanent resident a year later if everything goes right. No arrests, no finding that you lied or something like that.

Gilberto: Change your status to what?

Virginia: To become a legal permanent resident. I was about to say, if all goes right, you can adjust your status within a year to become a legal permanent resident. That's also true of people who win asylum. That is not true of DACA. DACA was just like a hold-off. We're not going to—we could deport you now, but we're not going to unless we change our mind.

Barbara wanted me to represent this young man. I said, "Barbara, I've never done a VAWA case before." Also, I had stopped practicing law—well, a lot of changes had come to [inaudible 00:08:44]. As you know, I was in graduate school for a long time in there. There were many, many changes in graduate school to me, but there were many changes in immigration law during that period as well. But she said, "He's about to turn twenty-one." "Okay." Then he was going to, quote, "age out" of being able to apply.

Gilberto: For VAWA?

Virginia: For VAWA, or maybe he was about to turn eighteen. I can't even remember.

Gilberto: Why would the—I mean, does it not really [inaudible 00:09:14] . . . I'm curious. VAWA . . .

Virginia: He was a child, and so—

Gilberto: Okay, VAWA as a child.

Virginia: Yeah. Had he been abused by a spouse, he would have been experiencing the violence as an adult, and so that's a different kind of characterization, category. Anyway, so I agreed to do it. I'm still friends with that young man today. He's been a legal permanent resident for several years. He's charming. So it was an interesting case, but that's a different story.

I was teaching at the Austin Community College, Eastview Campus, in the fall of 2012. I had also taught for ACC in the fall of 2011 and the spring of 2012. At the end of 2012, they said, "Sorry, we don't have any courses for you in the spring," that is, 2013. They load up their beginning writing courses in the fall, because all students have to have it. It's how you treat it as a lecturer, or any kind of adjunct. You know that, unfortunately.

Gilberto: [crosstalk 00:10:38]

Virginia: Yeah. So here I had—I had been so depressed not being able to find a job. What kind of a loser has a PhD and a JD . . . and I'm not saying this to beat myself up, but this is how it felt. What kind of a loser must you be to have a JD and a PhD and a lot of experience in both fields and not be able to get a job? I was really down on myself, but I said, "There's a need for immigration lawyers, and I can learn." When I came back—so I started practicing immigration law full-time in January 2013, which was exactly eighteen years after the birth of [Luis 00:11:31], our youngest child. It was Luis's birth that told me, "I can't practice law anymore. I'm going to either malpractice my clients or my children." So we met during that period when I was doing other things, including going . . . [silence]
Was this the right kind of [inaudible 00:12:08]?

Gilberto: Yes. Is there one close by?

Virginia: Yes.

Gilberto: Oh, wonderful.

Virginia: I don't have a longer one.

Gilberto: I have one. I was about to . . .

Virginia: Well, whatever.

Gilberto: Yeah, thank you. Let me just tell them I'm—my father would talk to me all night if I [inaudible 00:12:32] . . .

Virginia: Oh, it was your dad.

Gilberto: Yeah, yeah, yeah. No, if it was a kid, I would definitely respond. There we go.

Virginia: So I'm back on. That's just backstory. I didn't plan on coming back to immigration law; I absolutely did not, but I have these skills, and I've got to do something.

Gilberto: You're very skilled.

Virginia: So, in January 2013, I went back to practicing law. One of the first cases I got was a friend-activist young person who I'd met during this DACA work who had a friend who [was] undocumented and who had [been] picked up and was in Pearsall, the South Texas detention center or facility in Pearsall, Texas, which is a horrible, horrible place. She asked me if I would try to bond him out and then work on something.

Long story short, it was an absolute disaster, absolute disaster. Not only did I not bond him out, but he had—ICE had set a really high bond for him, and we filed a motion to redetermine custody in the immigration court.

The ICE lawyer—people often call them trial attorneys. I try not to use that phrase, because those of us who go to trial are trial attorneys, and they're ICE attorneys. Call them what they are. They defend ICE, the decisions of ICE, and they're trying to deport people. So let's give them the name they deserve.

They argued that not only should they not lower the bond but, in fact, they should increase it, and, in fact, then the judge decided to deny bond altogether.

Gilberto: What year was this?

Virginia: It was 2013. It was my first detained case in 2013. It was a real shock; it was a real shock. I hadn't practiced this kind of law since—well, sort of since 1990, '91, because I still practiced law after [Becka 00:15:02] was born, our second child, but that was doing disability rights and other stuff. Anyway, it was a real shock. The law had changed so much and this was my first experience with it. That particular judge will not give, or would not give, bond to anybody who had a DWI. That was that. In 2013, I continued to learn doing different kinds of cases. In 2013, I saw on the National Immigration Project LISTSERV a call for somebody to represent and to try to at least bond out a young woman, a young Guatemalan woman, who was eighteen, but very young. Not a child, but very young, who was so called "detained." I now use the term "immcarcerated," I-M-M-carcerated.

Gilberto: Why do you use that term?

Virginia: I'm "detained" when I'm running out the door and my mom calls, and

I want to talk to my mother. So I am detained for the errand or the meeting that I was going to do. Or "detention" is appropriate—I don't know that it happens that often anymore, but [if] you act up in school, the consequence or punishment is that you're detained after school or you have to go to a detention center.

Gilberto: I remember those days.

Virginia: Right? "Detention" is a very mild term. It's way too mild, way too mild, for what is happening to immigrants and refugees. So I went to this so-called "detention center." It was run by LSC. It was called LSC, but I think it was originally Louisiana Corrections Corporation or something like that, and it was headquartered in Louisiana. The detention center–prison, it was an old jail, disgusting facility, was in Robstown, outside of [crosstalk 00:17:07]. . . .

Gilberto: Why was it disgusting? This is 20—?

Virginia: 2013.

Gilberto: This is well before the current moment?

Virginia: Mm-hmm [affirmative], but I mean, she was a young woman who had never . . . So at the current moment, the current moment keeps—as moments do, they keep moving forward. She was a young woman from Guatemala who had never come into the United States before, never come into the United States before. There was not any indication that she was trafficking, carrying weapons, carrying drugs, engaged in human trafficking or other forms of smuggling. She was a person who crossed the border and was looking for asylum. This was in 2013.

Gilberto: When she approached the border authorities to set up an—

Virginia: I do not remember whether she crossed . . . Well, no. She must have crossed. It must have been an EWI [entry without inspection] case, because as you know, people who approach the border and present themselves to a US official are called "arriving alien," and they are charged with being inadmissible. Not removable, but inadmissible. Because we did get around on bond, she must have crossed EWI. But she had asked for asylum—completely peaceable—young woman, barely not a child. She was locked up in this hellhole in Robstown.

When I say disgusting, I have never been able to see the places where people live. I'm not anybody special, I'm not a stakeholder, I don't direct a nonprofit, I'm not a senator or congress[person], so I don't get tours. I've only ever met people in the lobby, or in a so-called courtroom that's inside a prison, or in an attorney-client visiting area, or sometimes in a so-called regular, nonlegal visiting area. I've never been inside the places where people sleep or eat. I've never been inside the kitchens or the toilets. So everything I say about conditions—I don't have that firsthand. I don't have that firsthand. I can talk firsthand about access issues, access lawyers and legal assistants, and such—

Gilberto: I'm listening.

Virginia: Okay. Anyway, it was just repulsive. I'm not going to remember the details right now, but it was dark and dingy and it was an old jail. There was no client contact. It was like being in prison, where you're looking at somebody who's separated from you.

Gilberto: You're saying no client contact, you mean there was a—

Virginia: A wall.

Gilberto: A wall. A glass wall?

Virginia: No, I mean—

Gilberto: Plastic? [crosstalk 00:20:11] . . .

Virginia: There's a wall and then there's an opening in the wall. You're sitting on one side and the person is sitting on the other side. I cannot tell you right now whether it was—I don't remember. Well, it was never glass, because glass breaks.

Gilberto: [crosstalk 00:20:30] plexiglass, because that would [crosstalk 00:20:31] . . .

Virginia: Yeah. So, anyway, some kind of—

Gilberto: Transparent.

Virginia: Transparent, always very difficult to hear in those kinds of situations. There are some places where you can sit in a room with a client and you're sitting around a table. The place outside of—it's called Coastal Bend. Coastal Bend Detention Center, and it had been a jail in the past. It was run unusually, because the two big giants were CoreCivic and GEO.

But, anyway, long story short, we got her out. Although that was terrible, because it was one of my first understandings of how this privatized prison works, which is that I had a form of student, Manuel [inaudible 00:21:28], Manny [inaudible 00:21:29], who was living in Corpus. I had taught him when he took a [inaudible 00:21:33] class. I liked him a lot, and I knew he was really smart, and he lived in Corpus. I couldn't keep driving to Brownsville to visit with the [crosstalk 00:21:43], so I hired Manny as my paralegal, and he made some visits. They kept coming up with reasons why he couldn't visit her. Access is very, very difficult.

We finally got the hearing set. Corpus is in the Harlingen district. We right now are in the San Antonio immigration district. Harlingen-Brownsville district. The hearing was going to be at the Port Isabel Service Processing Center, which, back in the day, we used to call either [Spanish language 00:22:18] or Piss-Pee. It is one of the few nonprivate [centers]. It's run by the US government, not a private immigration prison. She was set for a bond hearing there. First, we went to Harlingen to deliver the paperwork. We didn't understand why that was, because I was new at this. Then we drove to Port Isabel for her bond hearing. When I went to the court, I found out that she wasn't there. ICE blamed the Coastal Bend private facility for not sending her. The private prison people blamed ICE for not putting her on some list. Meanwhile, we had spent all this time . . . We drove to Brownsville—we had spent the night; it was a long trip. Pick up Manny. It was just a big, big deal to drive to Brownsville.

Then I learned—because I didn't know this, because I was not working for anybody except for myself, so I was learning it all in a very difficult way—that the judge was actually in Harlingen. So we had been in Harlingen to drop off the papers at the court, to file the papers at the court, and we could have just stayed there and we would have seen the judge. I thought we were going to meet my client, but she wasn't there. Anyway, there was an agreed bond, and I just took it.

Gilberto: Agreed bond?

Virginia: "Agreed" meaning the ICE lawyer said, "What about X?" and I said, "Fine." Then the family came up with that amount of money, and she—Oh, it was disgusting. They dropped her off at a gas station which had a small convenience store attached to it on the highway. The bus wasn't going to come for hours, and she didn't have money for the bus ticket, and there had been no communication. Fortunately, the only saving grace in this story is that the young woman who was working in the convenience store allowed my client to use the phone to call her mother and to call me.

Gilberto: Are you suggesting this is a common practice?

Virginia: What I want to do, Gilberto, is just talk from my own personal experience. It's certainly not unheard of. But I feel like I'll be safer—you know, there's lots of articles written about this stuff, there's lots of testimony, there's lots of pleadings and lots of lawsuits. Let me just talk about my personal experience. We bought her ticket, and that's how we found out that you can buy tickets on Greyhound buses with a credit card. She came here first. Did she come here first? No, we just bought her a ticket for her to go all the way—and I won't say where she went, but a very, very, very, very distant part of the United States from here. Well, the person, she was indigenous. There are indigenous networks in the United States.

Gilberto: [inaudible 00:25:58]

Virginia: There are indigenous networks. So a shortish time later, I started getting calls from indigenous people. I should say Spanish-speaking indigenous people who had lived in the United States for some period of time, [long] enough to find a way to a lawyer who would then refer them to me. So my first complete merits case was somebody who was detained at Karnes. It was then the Karnes County Civil Detention Facility. Oh, no—Karnes County Civil Detention Center. So I represented this young man who was an indigenous young man who had come to the United States not knowing anything, was immediately removed in an expedited removal process, sent back to Guatemala, and within days, he was attacked again. He spent time hiding out in a confessional at a church until his brothers came, while people came and looked for him, members of the Guatemalan police force and gang members came and looked for him. He hid out in a confessional and survived until his brothers came and told him, "They're gone. You'd better go." He came back to the United States. Now he's in reinstatement of removal proceedings. Again, a very, very young man. I got to know him, because he was—this must have been November, maybe December. Let me pause and say there are two GEO facilities located right next to each other in Karnes.

Gilberto: G-E-O?

Virginia: GEO, G-E-O. Uh-huh. I don't remember—have you been to Karnes?

Gilberto: I have not.

Virginia: Okay. So one of them was the Karnes County Civil Detention Center and the other was . . . I don't remember what it was called; you can look it up, but it's on the map. It was very confusing, very, very confusing, because they are like—there's two streets that intersect, and one has an address on the larger street, and one has an address on the smaller street, and they back onto each other. The other one is much more—the US immigration people are there, some immigrants are there, but it's mostly run by the US marshals. Well, run by GEO for the US Marshals Service. So they're federal prisoners there. If there are immigrants there. . . .

I'll use the language that I've heard. I remember asking somebody who worked at GEO, "What's the difference?"—or, actually, this was an ICE officer I asked. "What's the difference between this facility and the one that's just right over there adjoining it?" He said, "Oh, that's for people where there's some kind of security issue. If they have anything, they're over there." If they have anything, meaning like any . . . He didn't spell it out, but I took it to mean like any indication. I said, "Oh, so my person I'm representing," I used his name, "is low security." He goes, "Oh, yeah, yeah. If he had anything, he'd be over there." So they've acknowledged it was very, very low-security place, the Karnes Civil Detention Center.

Very long story short, and I could tell you lots of details about this, he was detained for however long he had been there since before they called me—the indigenous community leader called me June of 2014.

Gilberto: Do you remember what people he—

Virginia: What people?

Gilberto: Yeah, I mean, indigenous [crosstalk 00:30:15] . . .

Virginia: [crosstalk 00:30:16] . . . I mean, he didn't speak K'ichee' as much as his uncle did and the community did. His merits hearing was in March of 2014. I'll never forget it, because it was right after [inaudible 00:30:46] funeral.

Gilberto: Do you want me to stop this?

Virginia: No, it's okay. If we stop every time I cry—we're now getting into the reality of detention. The judge had told me—so we're in Karnes, but we're within the San Antonio district. This was my first case in Karnes. Very young man, but an adult. Reinstatement of removal proceedings, so we have a higher burden: we have to show that it is more likely than not that he will be persecuted on one of the five factors, or we have to show that there's a probability, again more likely than not, that he will be tortured by the Guatemalan government or an entity the government cannot or will not control or protect him from.

Anyway, very interesting case on so many levels. So many stories I could tell you about this, but . . . Thank you. What I want to tell you is the hearing happened in March, I think, or I would have to look up and see when [inaudible 00:32:00] funeral was, because we pretty much were right there. We picked up his uncle, who ended up being an expert witness. This person is someone I would encourage you to talk to, because he had worked—

Gilberto: Would you like one?

Virginia: No. We paid for him to fly down from, well, north of here. That's all I want to say. Who told the history, which our client had never heard about what had happened to his family during the genocide. Then this person had also worked for the bishop's commission on human rights in Guatemala and had gone into the mountains, the communities, and encouraged people to tell their stories to the commission. But it was very difficult, because they had been told and they had seen people have their tongues cut out and they had seen people butchered and said, "This is going to happen to you if you tell anybody."

Anyway, we won that case, but we didn't know until June, because the hearing was held—everything was done on electronics. The tape recording is electronic. If you've been in immigration courts, you see the judge say, "Oh, excuse me. I've got to get this up and running," and blah blah blah blah blah. So there's no independent recording. The system had gone down for months, so there was no [EIR 00:33:35] hotline where you could call and find out what was going on with your case or when it was scheduled. Judges didn't have access to the record, because the whole system was down. So extra month. I mean, I don't know how long the judge would have taken to arraign his decision; I don't know how long it did take him, but our client was held unnecessarily for a month.

One of the first instances—I encountered them already in Robstown with Coastal Bend, sending Manny away saying he can't see her, with Coastal Bend not bringing the client to Port Isabel for her bond hearing. Now also, the system just going down so he's kept in there much longer than he should be. Everything's messed up in the spring of 2014 because the system is down. Now I wonder what's that about, just timing-wise, but of course at that time I had no idea of what was coming.

It was interesting. The judge—so I had gone to one of the hearings, the master calendar hearings in this case, to San Antonio where the judge, Bertha Zuniga, had said, "You have a right to be with your client in Karnes, or you can come to San Antonio and be here with me." She said, "It's up to you. I would prefer that you be here with me in this courtroom, but it's up to you." That's a terrible choice. It's a terrible choice, because normally of course you want to be with the client, the person who is having their big day in immigration court, such as it is. But there are times that you need to give the judge a piece of paper, a document. Just, things come up, and you don't know what's going to come up. So ever since then, I've tried, because we live in a beautiful community, and because we do this for each other, people will—I've tried to have somebody in the other court. But I always, if my client is testifying, if it's her or his or their hearing, I want to be with my client.

I made that decision, although this is the first time that this had ever come up for me, because I'd never been to a remote hearing before. I would have been for that client in Brownsville, because I didn't know that the judge was going to be in Harlingen, but that didn't happen. So, anyway, I just decided to go to Karnes to be with him, because it seemed like that was the most important thing, and because his uncle was coming in to testify, and I wanted them to be able to see each other in person.

Gilberto: The uncle was the expert?

Virginia: Uh-huh. Really a great uncle, but whatever. And we won. That was in June 2014. Meanwhile—so he got let out, then we saw that . . . The judge granted him CAT, Convention against Torture. When I met this young man, the only thing that he wanted to do, his goal in life, was to play music in a church. It's been several years since I've spoken to him, but I think he got his wish. Other things happened that year, other disasters, other heartbreaks, but I'm going to not go into all of that now. I'm just going to say that in about July of 2014, we went northeast to meet our kids at a vacation, since, as you know, two of them are no longer—well, none of them live here, but two of them are in the Northeast.

Gilberto: Before you proceed, you said that Karnes was "then called," past tense.

Virginia: Right.

Gilberto: "Civil Detention."

Virginia: Right.

Gilberto: And there's another Karnes facility. Can you talk about the—

Virginia: Transition?

Gilberto: Also the "civil," how immigration law is—can you speak to—

Virginia: Let me talk about the transition first. In June, meanwhile—

Gilberto: June?

Virginia: 2014. Reports started to trickle in, we started hearing about this place called Artesia. I had just won a case; other cases were on hold. I went away for two weeks to see my kids. Came back, so maybe that was July, whatever—come back in August.

Karnes had closed shortly after our client was released, having won CAT. It was closed, and then it reopened in late August of 2014 with a new name. It was no longer the Karnes County Civil Detention Center. It was now the Karnes Family Residential Center.

I will talk about the civil stuff later on, but I kind of wanted to talk about—because it's really important, with respect to something that happened this week during the Democratic debates. I'm actually very proud of Julián Castro for being the only one to bring this particular thing up.

So apparently [Karnes] had been empty for a certain amount of time. At a certain point, they painted over the sign, and for a while, all you could see was the paint over it. It might have said, "Karnes" and "Center." I have a photograph of the time that it was empty for a while, and I posted it on Facebook. A friend of mine filled it in with "Prison" or something. Anyway, that photo with the whited-out name during the transition time has made its way all over. I've seen it come up all over. I know that I'm the one who took it.

So in late August of 2014 is when a new chapter of family—I will now call it incarceration; we were then calling it family detentions—started in Texas. New—not the beginning of, because there had been an earlier period at Hutto, the former prison in Taylor during the more recent Bush administration when families had been detained there. Of course, if we're going to talk about families being separated and families being detained, there's a much longer history beginning with both the genocide of native peoples in what is now the United States and beginning with slavery. And believe me, the irony was not lost on me that this was happening in Karnes, because you know whose family was incarcerated in Karnes County.

Gilberto: I know, but I'll let you say it.

Virginia: The family of Gregorio Cortez. When Gregorio Cortez went on his ride on that little mare. Was it a mare? It was a mare that he was riding on while the Texas Rangers were looking at him. For a time, his family, including his wife and children and I don't know who else, was incarcerated in the Karnes County Jail, which is right across the main route through Karnes, or one of the [inaudible 00:42:03] from both the heavy-duty barbed-wire Karnes Detention Center, which has both people who are accused of federal crimes such as smuggling and bringing in drugs and whatever, and the security-light, low-security, minimum-security facility that was, up until the summer of 2014, the Karnes County Civil Detention Center. Then, magically after August, the Karnes Family Residential Center.

Gilberto: Karnes or Artesia?

Virginia: Residential, residential. It took them a while to paint that sign, but that's the sign they did. They put out some blue benches that they hadn't had before that were like right at the entrance to the lobby. They put up a covering that provided a minimal amount of shade and that's blue. So they made cosmetic changes. I have been told that they painted big vegetables on the cafeteria to make it more child friendly. I mean, I don't know.

Gilberto: You were told by people who are being held in there?

Virginia: Yes.

Gilberto: Or by—

Virginia: Both, and people who work there. I got to be friendly with some of the people who work there. I really did. Then there's different levels of friendship.

So that is when family detention restarted in Texas. It didn't begin, but it was a new chapter. From August of 2014 to February [2015], and I could look up the exact date, but it was the weekend my father died. You can see that this is a hard time. My dates are punctuated by things in my life.

ICE, DHS was refusing to set a bond for anybody. So let's talk about backlog for a second. ICE, the Department of Homeland Security, always has the discretion—despite the statutory language around, quote-unquote, mandatory detention—they always have the discretion to release somebody into the United States on parole. They can do that with such security measures as they deem necessary to get that person to show up for their hearings. So for a period between the closure of Family Detention in Hutto, which was shortly after Obama took office the first time, as a result of a huge amount of community pressure, and there was also a lawsuit pending, but it wasn't a court order, it was just [that] Obama ended family detention in Texas early in his first term.

June of 2014, when Artesia opened, there had been a policy, pretty much, if you came to the border, whether it was EWI, entry without inspection, or whether it was presenting yourself to an official and saying, "I'm here. I need to ask for asylum. I can't go home," there was a practice pretty much of if you were a woman with young children, they would take your photo, they would fingerprint you, they would assign you and your children A-numbers, you would say where you were going, they would hand you some paperwork, and [crosstalk 00:46:30] was to appear or what we now, per Justice Sotomayor—or at least I do think of as a putative notice to appear, because it didn't contain the time and date of the hearing. Then you were supposed to let DHS, Department of Homeland Security, know if you moved your address. Then you were supposed to show up for removal proceedings at some point in the future.

That was the practice. Some people were arrested and so-called detained. Some people ICE granted parole to on certain conditions to certain people, ICE DHS. You could ask for bond from immigration judges if you were in certain categories.

Judges do not have the authority by statue to grant bond to people who are presenting themselves at the border and asking for asylum. Those people are called arriving alien. They're in a different category than people who have crossed the border without inspection, etcetera. So that changed radically in June in New Mexico, but in August in Texas.

Gilberto: [crosstalk 00:48:01]?

Virginia: We're talking about 2014.

Gilberto: Sorry.

Virginia: Thank you. Still 2014. There was a radical change in August 2014 in Texas where they start arresting women with children who are presenting [crosstalk 00:48:16] . . .

Gilberto: Oh, sorry. Yeah, yeah, yeah. This is [inaudible 00:48:19] detention—

Virginia: 2014, who are presenting at the border. They are not setting bond for anybody, and they're not releasing people on parole, unless there are extraordinary circumstances.

What do I mean by extraordinary circumstances? Kate Lincoln-Goldfinch[, who] is a friend and a colleague and is in private practice here in Austin, found a woman whose daughter had brain cancer and after a lot of publicity and begging and shaming and bringing in lots of evidence about the child's condition, ICE let her go on parole. That's not out of the goodness of their hearts, that was because this child had very severe intense medical needs and there was a whole lot of publicity, very bad publicity. That's what I mean by extraordinary circumstances. There's some others, but I'll tell you about that later.

They were refusing—so ICE, as you know from my first experience in 2013, ICE can set bond, and then if the people are in certain categories and they think that the bond is too high or if ICE has refused to set bond, then people in certain categories can go to the immigration judge and ask for the judge to reconsider their custody status, i.e., set bond. Set a bond if no bond has been set or lower the bond if there has been a very high bond set. So ICE was refusing to set bond for any of these women and children starting in August 2014.

Then when we started saying that, they denied it, but I had talked to one of the ICE agents who was at Karnes, and I said, "So this is what I've done. I've put this together, this, this, this"—all the stuff that you would normally need for a bond packet: where the person is going to live, who they're going to live with, the immigration status of that person, whether they're a US citizen, have TPS, whatever, that that person has a stable place. That could be with a mortgage. In the best-case scenario, it could be a rent receipt that they live there that the person can support [themselves] and that person's family as well as their own family. So it could be a tax return, it could be a check, wages, etcetera, etcetera, etcetera. Also, they wanted to see that the person has a lawyer, more often than not, in the place that they were going, because people are more likely to show up for their hearings if they have a lawyer, etcetera.

I said to the ICE officer—I was talking about a particular client—"I've got this, I've got this, I've got this, this. What more do I need to do to get you to grant bond to this person?" That officer told me, "We are not setting bond for anybody." I said, "Is it true that you're not—" He said, "We're not setting bond for anybody unless a judge orders us to do so." I said, "What's your name?" I went to the car and I wrote it up in as much exact terms as I could, and that then later became an exhibit.

Speaker 3: [inaudible 00:51:56]

Virginia: Thank you so much.

Speaker 3: [inaudible 00:52:00]

Virginia: We'd better keep talking. We'd better keep talking. So between August 2014 and February of 2015, when a federal court in the District of Columbia said, "This is not due process," I said let's talk about backlog. So instead of ICE setting bond for people and people only needing to go to immigration courts, when ICE refused to set a bond or set a very high bond, for every single person who was arrested and placed in Karnes or Artesia, we had to go to immigration court. That's like—

Gilberto: Yeah, yeah, yeah. [inaudible 00:52:45]

Virginia: Well, no, I mean it just creates a huge, huge problem for the judges and for the courts and for everybody. It's a huge waste of time. When we go to court—I'll have to show you this. The ICE lawyer presents pages and pages and pages of—let's call it nonsense—arguing that all of these women and children, all of these Central American women and children, are a threat to the national security of the United States. The judges are like, "Why are they are a threat?" I remember very well Grace Garza saying, "They are drinking our water."

Gilberto: Grace Garza?

Virginia: A lawyer for ICE, so-called trial attorney. Their title is actually assistant chief counsel for [the] Department of Homeland Security.

Gilberto: She was saying that drinking our water is [crosstalk 00:53:54]?

Virginia: Yeah, I mean, what I'm saying is they had no answer. That's what she said in court one time. One of my earliest sets of clients, and I got these clients from—

So back up. So there had been a tour of the facility, and certain people were invited to go. I think Kate Lincoln-Goldfinch had some sort of position in ALA at that time. Anyway, she was one of the people allowed to go. I think Barbara Hines went, maybe Denise Gilman—people from the different immigration clinics, other people went.

So I called Kate and I said, "Bring me back something." She brought me back little pieces of papers with names. I think there were like six little pieces of paper. So four of those people became my clients. Then I got one from Jim Harrington at the Texas Civil Rights Project. One I would have to remember, from somebody else. The rest of my clients came from people telling each other. They'd come see me and say, "[foreign language 00:54:57]."

ICE was saying en masse that all of these people—. This is not due process. Due process means you look at each person individually. You look at the facts of each case individually. You do not say an entire group of people.

Gilberto: This is 2014.

Virginia: 2014.

Gilberto: This policy comes down and [inaudible 00:55:27] Obama era.

Virginia: No, Obama administration. The Obama administration. There were like . . . so crazy things . . .

Gilberto: This is for all immigrants?

Virginia: Central Americans.

Gilberto: Central Americans only?

Virginia: No, because there were a couple of Brazilians in Karnes, families.

Gilberto: How big is this order? All people who are trying to get—

Virginia: Let me explain two exceptions that I—so one of the first families I found out about, it was a family with five kids, mother and father and their five kids. When it comes time to cross, they are put in two separate floaty things, inner tubes, little boats, whatever.

Gilberto: Literally, okay, yeah, yeah.

Virginia: Little floaty things to cross the Rio Bravo, Rio Grande. The mother goes with the kids, who are what I call the age of reason, you know, like ten, eleven. They won't jump out. They're kids who can tie their own shoes, and, in our very privileged houses, can know how to make themselves toast. That kind of kid, bathe themselves, etcetera, etcetera. Then the dad went with the two oldest boys and the littlest kid, or maybe the littlest two kids, so that there was a big person, a dad, and teenage boys. I'm blanking on how many. But basically, the mother was with the kids who could sort of fend for themselves a little bit, but not totally, then the dad and teenage sons went with the littlest ones. They end up at different places on the river. The mother and the two sons are arrested and sent to Karnes. The dad, the littlest kid, and teenage boy or boys, I forget, are released. Why?

Gilberto: Yes, that's my next question to you.

Virginia: Because there's no family detention for dads yet. There's no family detention places at that point. Now, we're very sophisticated: we have family detention for dads and children, too. But in August 2014, we didn't.

Gilberto: What kind of—that's now law, that's policy.

Virginia: No, totally policy. Not even policy: practice.

Gilberto: Meaning . . . I mean . . .

Virginia: I don't think there was a policy "Release dads."

Gilberto: Okay, no. But who is saying—at what level are those kinds of—I have no idea, I'm asking [crosstalk 00:58:42] . . .

Virginia: Well, so there's a district director. There's Department of Homeland Security; there's Immigration Removal and Enforcement, ERO, and they make the decisions about—so, first, it's Customs and Border Protection. So I cannot tell you whether it was a Customs and Border Protection person, or it was somebody in Enforcement and Removal. I cannot tell you whether it was a field office director or an assistant field office director, AFOD. So the AFODs are in charge of—there's an AFOD . . . in charge of the Karnes Family, quote-unquote, Residential Center, and one in charge of the one in Hutto, and one in charge of Pearsall, and then I think there's on assistant field office director for all three of the Laredo immigration prisons.

Gilberto: Give me one minute. I'm going to pause.

Virginia: I'm going to make a note, I want to make sure I tell you everything. Where's the restroom? Oh, right here.

Gilberto: I'm going to put it back on, okay?

Virginia: Mm-hmm [affirmative].

Gilberto: Testing, one [inaudible 01:01:43]. . . . Okay.

Virginia: So that was a policy that I was aware of through beginning to represent families, that is women and children who were at Karnes in the low-security facility they were calling a residential facility. I could go on a lot about that. We're not going to even get close to finish.

Gilberto: We can always pick it up [crosstalk 01:02:28] . . .

Virginia: Yeah. But it wasn't everybody. The reason I know it's not everybody: I cannot tell you who made the decision not to lock up the dad and the oldest and youngest children, but I can imagine it was sort of a reversion to the policy of May 2014, which is, fingerprint them, give them an A-number, take a picture, give them a notice, tell them to show up. "Where are you going? Tell us the change of address when you get there if you move. You're going to have to show up at some point later for your removal proceeding."

Virginia: That's what they did with them—I imagine they did with them—because there was no place to send the dad and children. They weren't, contrary to what you will hear, they were not making a policy of taking the dad and sending him off to an adult immigration facility and the teenage boys and sending them to a different facility and the little girl. That was not happening on any kind of large scale, to my knowledge or that I've ever heard of, during the Obama administration.

Gilberto: There's a lot of debate about this very question.

Virginia: What I will tell you is I do know that there were cases. I represented a client who I came to realize had been abusing her daughter and abused a child in Karnes. That woman was separated from her teenage daughter. That was right. That was the appropriate thing to do. I couldn't keep representing her until I lost touch with the whole story, because at that point, I was representing both that mother and daughter and the mother and daughter of the child who was abused in the shower by this woman. So I had a conflict of interest and I couldn't represent either family anymore, so I don't know what the end of that story is.

You did hear stories like that, but when I heard about it or when I saw it happening, there was a reason. It wasn't widespread. Now, I will give you another example of separation that was stupid, but it's not the same thing as what started happening last year en masse.

I represented—let's see what it was. They leave their country in Central America. It's a young woman in her earlier twenties and her little daughter, her toddler daughter, and her younger sister who's fourteen or fifteen. The three of them arrive at the border. They ask who they are. They say, "This is me, this is my daughter, and this is my sister." They bond out the young woman and her toddler daughter. They take the younger teenager, the minor teenager, and they send her on a tour of ORR facilities because that wasn't her mom.

Gilberto: How do they know?

Virginia: Well, I think they were honest. This is [inaudible 01:06:02].

Gilberto: They declared [inaudible 01:06:04]. . . .

Virginia: I mean, I don't think anybody was—I mean, despite what you hear from the right, and I'm not saying you believe this, but there's this assumption that people lie. It's like, "We had to get out of Honduras." "Where are you going to live?" "With our mom."

Gilberto: They declared, it sounds like, that they're related.

Virginia: It wasn't an issue at that point. It was not an issue at that point that they thought or that—. Then I'm thinking, "Oh, that's what happened." Then they finally release the younger sister and she moves into the house where her mom, her dad—who've come to Honduras earlier, a decade or so ago—and her sister, and her sister's toddler are all living. So it was a waste, it was stupid, but if you're saying, "We are going to send children who are not accompanied by their mom, dad, or legal guardian," it makes sense. So that was taking place, but it's very different.

Gilberto: Yeah, yeah, yeah. On the scale or the maliciousness of the—

Virginia: Yes, yeah. I mean, really different. And there were sometimes judges—so, in fact, the immigration judges at that point—. So I had the set of clients—actually, let me get to that point later. I want to say—.

So this one family of seven: the man and the kids get released; the mother and two kids are held in Karnes. We go to the immigration court and say, "We need to release these people on bond." I make an equal protection argument. The judge says, "What does the government have to say about this?" I'm like, "Well, that's just the decision they made." "But what was the reason?" "That's just what they felt was in the best interest" or whatever. I mean, just complete drivel nonsense.

I mean, it's clear that the reason why they didn't lock up the dad and the kids is they didn't have such a facility. They had, at that point, one family so-called residential facility in Texas, and it was at Karnes, and it was women and children. They weren't prepared to accept a grown man and teenage boys with the little—so they let them go, and they went off to their extended family in another state, and they won asylum later. But the judge—

Gilberto: [crosstalk 01:08:54] . . . They let them go with the stipulation that they go back for a hearing later.

Virginia: Yeah, hold on. So the judge, in that case, I had asked—the judge let them, the part of the family that I was representing, he let them go without [inaudible 01:09:09], no bond, because it was so egregious and because the government attorney could not articulate a reason for this.

Gilberto: Okay, I hear you.

Virginia: So that's one example. This other thing I didn't find out until much later. I'm representing a family. Dad came first to the United States, comes to the US, is arrested, bonds out, pays the bond, goes to live with people in Houston, never goes back to court. A year passes without him filing asylum. Never goes back to court. He's never asked to come to court, but he also doesn't know. This was the subject of a lawsuit, because nobody ever tells him that if he wants asylum, he has to apply within one year. So this has happened to lots and lots and lots of people. Then the people who were threatening him start threatening his wife, so she and the kids come. Then he had a friend in Houston, so he was staying in Houston. She has family in Austin, so she comes to Austin—mom, two children.

They tell him, "Come to Austin." They meet up and they all come to Austin, then they find me. I represent them. I have the wife be the primary person—they're Salvadorian—because she's the one who's going to file the asylum. She's just got here and somebody tells her, "You've got to get a lawyer; you've got to file asylum." [I] file asylum for her within the one year with the husband and the two minor children as derivatives. The judge, who everybody says is a horrible, horrible, horrible judge, he really had to work to give me this decision, but he granted them all asylum. He granted the woman asylum, and he granted the husband and children asylum as derivatives of her. Their legal permanent applications are pending.

But when I asked the dad, the husband, to bring in his papers, it was really interesting to me, because he came in in the fall of frickin' 2014, and they let him bond out. It wasn't an exceptionally high bond. At the same moment when they're refusing to set bond for any women and children—single man, adult, and he's a big guy. I think that at some level, this was about maximizing pain.

Gilberto: In 2014?

Virginia: I mean, I don't have an explanation for it. I only found this out several years after. I would have to look up, and I will look up, and if I can find his bond paperwork, I will redact it and send it to you, because I think this is really interesting.

Gilberto: I appreciate that if you find it.

Virginia: I should have it. And I'm still friends with him, so if I don't have it, I can ask him to find it for me. In February, a district court in—. Oh.

Gilberto: If you're getting . . . Do you want to take a break or—

Virginia: So in February of 2015—. So meanwhile, you know about credible and reasonable fear interviews?

Gilberto: Tell me about it. I'm a fly on the wall right now.

Virginia: So credible and reasonable fear interviews are kind of the compromise creation between the 1996 so-called immigration reform—anyway, IIRIRA, IIRIRA, Immigration Reform and Responsibility Act of 1996, which provides, for the first time, for expedited removal and reinstatement of removal. That wasn't a thing before 1996. Thank you very much, US Congress. Thank you very much, Bill Clinton. It was, as you know, one of the three most horrible omnibus bills that Congress passed on Clinton's watch. That one, the welfare one, and Antiterrorism and Effective Death Penalty Act, which kind of cuts off civil liberties for most prisoners most of the time. So we have a responsibility under our international treaties and under the

1980 Refugee Act to provide asylum for people, and yet we have IIRIRA that provides for expedited removal. How do we resolve that?

So the compromise is credible fear interviews and reasonable fear interviews. So, if you're arrested by immigration officials within a certain number of miles from the border—and there's been creep, right? IIRIRA gave them a lot of discretion, a lot of room for how many miles and how many days and how much time, which they didn't use all of it at the beginning. At the beginning, they only used it in like ports. Water, boats, ports, as I understand it. But there was creep, and they started to expand, because they had the authority under IIRIRA. There was a good article that talked about the expansion of that. I don't know if I can find it.

But anyway, so under the terms of expedited removal, if you have just come in, they can remove, aka deport, you immediately, without you ever seeing a judge unless you say to an official, "I'm afraid to go back; I want asylum" or something clearly along those lines. Then what is supposed to happen is that you are supposed to get an interview with an asylum officer. If the asylum officer believes that you have a fear of persecution based on one of these five factors or fear of torture by the government or by [inaudible 01:16:15] government is unwilling or unable to control that, you will then be re-placed in removal proceedings.

You will have the right to have, such as it is, more due process. You have the right to a lawyer at your own expense. The government will not provide you one, because this is a civil proceeding. You will have a right to examine witnesses against you, to inspect the evidence against you, and to respond to it. There will be a so-called neutral fact finder, who is the immigration judge. You will have the right to present evidence on your own behalf to testify, etcetera, etcetera, etcetera, to bring in witnesses, and so forth.

The credible fear interview is really going to determine—largely, not completely—whether or not you get to move to step two or whether you will be sent back immediately: reinstatement-of-removal proceedings if you have already been removed or deported previously from the United States, like that young Guatemalan man that I told you about, then you are placed in reinstatement proceedings. Same kind of process except for a higher burden of proof.

I will just send you some information about that because the words don't make any sense. I can never remember what they mean, because they don't have any inherent sense to them.

So what was happening was, is usually we'd hurry up and—we had the best-case scenario when people had passed their credible fear interviews, which meant an asylum officer agreed with them. "Yes, it looks like you have an asylum case that you should at least be able to take to court." So then we would say, "Okay, she passed her credible fear interview. She got a place to go, a firm place to go, and lined up a lawyer in Boston, Colorado," wherever, wherever, "so please set a bond. No criminal history, no danger. Please set a bond."

The judges would do that. Some judges really took what I would say, would take the job very seriously, and would sort of look at all the factors. If it looked like your case was a strong case and the person you were going to stay with was a US citizen—mom or child or a legal permanent resident brother—then that would be—you know, who has a job and who owns his house—you might get a lower bond, because the security of that situation would be more than if you had a cousin with DACA who was renting an apartment and living hand to mouth.

There were other judges who would [say], "$8,000" for everybody. You'd be sitting there listening to all the stories and all the facts and be like "$8,000," "$8,000," "$8,000."

Gilberto: [crosstalk 01:19:37] . . .

Virginia: It didn't matter, it didn't matter. Sometimes it was like an $8,000 day and sometimes it would be an $8,500 day. So some judges—. I forgot my train of thought now.

Gilberto: I'm good, just—.

Virginia: Let's pause. Let's pause for a second. I have to go back to where I was.

Gilberto: I'm going to check on the fam. Okay.

Virginia: This is what's going on between August—and here I'm speaking of Texas—between August and February. August 2014, February 2015.

Not everybody's getting a credible fear interview, though. Who do you suppose that might be? Indigenous peoples, because they don't have enough asylum officers to conduct the interviews. It seemed to me—although I never had the bird's-eye view and I kept trying to get reporters interested and no reporter was interested. We tried to do a Freedom of Information Act request. It seemed to me that they were getting higher bonds.

The reason makes sense, even though it's discriminatory, because if you just get passed onto the removal proceeding without going through the credible fear interview process with an asylum officer, the asylum officer is not going to say, "Blah blah blah blah blah, this is what happened," and the judge is not going to be able to read it and say, "Oh, this sounds like a good case." It's just like a bond package. It's just a bond package. The judge signs off on it, but can't say, "Oh, wow. This is really a winner. You're definitely coming back to court for this."

There's debate about how much of a factor should the validity or strength of the claim be, because, for instance, the strength of the claim depends in part on where you are in the country. Like, the claim might look pretty lousy here in San Antonio in the Fifth Circuit, but it might be a pretty good claim somewhere else in the country. So that's an issue. But I think that judges were looking sort of at the claims. When they didn't believe the claims were very strong, that that was sort of like having a DACA relative rather than a legal permanent resident or US citizen. That was kind of a factor that tended to say, "Okay, there's not as much chance that you're going to come back. Therefore, we're going to set the bond higher to make the incentive—whoever is paying that bond for you is going to really put the pressure on you to go back and show up for court."

Now what I have to say—. So I think that it seemed to me that indigenous people were getting set higher bonds because they weren't going through the CFI [credible fear interview] process, because there weren't people. The other thing that was happening was that I think that if you look at who's deported, I would bet you almost anything that it's been indigenous people whose first language is an indigenous Mayan language [more] than other people, because there were no legal orientation program materials available in K'ichee' or any of [crosstalk 01:23:22]. . . .

Or any of the languages. It was all European languages, colonial languages. And because there was nobody there who could talk to them, and because there were so few lawyers, and because—. Most of the indigenous communities that I knew of were concentrated in places where, like, somebody knew one lawyer. So they went to that one lawyer they knew in Chicago or New York or Los Angeles.

That lawyer is used to calling in to ICE and negotiating the bond, not aware of the fact—because ICE has never made this policy public, and in fact it has been denying it, that ICE is not setting any bond. So the family pays $5,000 to Dewey, Screwum, & Howe law firm in Los Angeles [which is] saying, "Yeah, I'll take care of it. $5,000, I'll do the bond hearing." They do the bond hearing by telephone, having talked to the family but unlikely to the client, or if they do, it's on a telephone at Karnes, and then calling into the immigration court. The judge may or may not accept a telephonic hearing. They're not able to do anything with ICE, because ICE just says, "No," and there's no negotiating.

Gilberto: So, just to be clear about this: judges are not required to accept telephonic hearings?

Virginia: Mm-mm [negative].

Gilberto: How about interpretation?

Virginia: No, I mean—

Gilberto: Telephonic.

Virginia: No, they do it. The interpretation is always done by the court. The court has the responsibility for the hearing.

Gilberto: It's often through [inaudible 01:25:06].

Virginia: Well, it depends on where you are and what the language is. So, in San Antonio, normally—although there was a slowdown because the court was screwing with the interpreters. The interpreters' union got mad. It was a slowdown, so there were actual days that we didn't have Spanish interpreters in San Antonio, Texas.

One time, I had a judge bring in—. The judges have a lot of discretion. Normally, they use this language line, but they can say, "No, I want . . ."

Gilberto: [crosstalk 01:25:47] . . . I'm sorry, this is important to me. Normally, they use a language line. Is that a national hotline?

Virginia: I think so. Hotline—

Gilberto: Well, I mean, it's like a [crosstalk 01:25:58] . . .

Virginia: It's a national service. You usually have to make a reservation. So, on January 19, I have a K'ichee' client who's going to appear on my master calendar. So the judges will take them first or take them last, try to bunch up the same language speakers so that people are not—. Anyway. So you're not calling an interpreter back and people waiting and stuff like that. Anyway, the judges can also insist on—. But there were simply not enough language speakers to accommodate—I think this is still true—the asylum office interviews, so they were just dispensing with them, dispensing with the CFI process. There were no materials whatsoever, legal orientation program materials, for the people inside the detention centers. who are like, "What's going on? What do I need to do?"

Gilberto: What year is this again?

Virginia: That was 2014, but I would venture to say it's still true. Not every place even has a legal orientation program. So, anyway, the court says in February of 2015 that ICE has to start—DHS has to start setting bond for people who are otherwise qualified for bond, which would leave out three categories of people. [1] People who have not passed a CFI, which theoretically would exclude indigenous people, but it in practice didn't. They just let them go, which is—well, I'll tell you more about that. [2] Which would exclude arriving aliens, because they're not eligible for bond, and [3] it would exclude withholding people and withholding only proceeding—

Gilberto: Wait, back up on that last twenty, about arriving aliens.

Virginia: Those are the people who arrive at a bridge or another port of entry and say, "Hi, my name is Virginia." [inaudible 01:28:18]. . .

"I'm applying for asylum." Okay, they're arriving aliens. They are charged with being inadmissible rather than being removable. By statute, judges have no ability to change their custody status—let me say immigration judges. And the third category was people who are with only proceedings, which is people who were previously deported.

As a practical matter from what I observed, they did, in fact, release some of my clients who were arriving aliens. They did set bond for them, and the family scrambled and came up with it. They did, starting in February 2015, because I was talking to some of these people on the frickin' phone from the hospital when my father had just died, or while he was dying. They were having bonds hearings the next day, and we were trying to somehow—. Anyway, there was that going on. Or merits hearings the next day, and we were trying to get them out beforehand.

As a practical matter, they did release indigenous people who spoke no Spanish who had not had CFIs. Why is that? Why was that? What are the unintended consequences of that? Unfortunately, I think a lot of those people had no idea what was going on and thought that when their families paid the money for bond, they had now paid to be in the United States.

Gilberto: Then they would not go back to court.

Virginia: And they *would* not. They had no material that was in their languages. I know that it happened to at least one family who I was representing. The reason I found out that they thought they had purchased a right to stay in the United States is because of—I should remember his name, Sergio, professor at UT, who teaches K'ichee' and who's in the Spanish—. Anyway, nice guy. I got so little help from [inaudible 01:30:34]. I was appalled. I was appalled. I mean, here we are at the University of Texas, supposed flagship, with all these people studying Latin American studies. I could hardly get anybody to go to a detention center. It was too far for them. Basically, two professors who are no longer at UT would agree to be experts.

Gilberto: [inaudible 01:31:03]

Virginia: Mm-hmm (affirmative). I mean, Charlie told me it was not worth his time, and Juliet Hooker just said, "No." I wrote her a "I know you're busy, blah blah blah." "No," like not—she doesn't owe me any explanation in one sense. It's not like I'm—. Anyway, just, "No."

When I tell you, Gilbert, that you're special, I'm not making shit up. I would probably love you even if you weren't doing this. I would love you even if you weren't doing this work, but I also—. Academics have not shown up for this work in general at all. You are the exception; Ellen is an exception; Lisa is an exception; Alfonso is an exception; Jen is an exception.

So let me tell you the other thing that's really changing the whole scenario before I get back to what happened to the withholding people, because that's a big deal. Withholding only people. In August, it was like the same frickin' week that Karnes opened, we opened, ARCG [*Matter of A-R-C-G- et al., Respondents*] came down. ARCG came down for the BIA that said married women in Guatemala who cannot get out of their relationship may constitute a particular social group. This felt like the saying, "The Lord giveth and the Lord taketh away." It was like, "Oh my God," because all of these people who were escaping from violent-household spousal sort of relationships were now going to have a chance, a prayer. It just turned over right away, and then that ended just as quickly. Only not by a board of immigration appeals, but by Dicta-Head Sessions.

I want a footnote that that's my term, "Dicta-Head." I'll tell you why I call him Dicta-Head, because he purported to say that there was no more domestic violence or gang asylum cases, but what he said was in general, domestic violence and gang violence will not be grounds for asylum. Immigration judges do not decide cases in general, they decide cases one at a time. So what he says is dicta. Dicta, d-i-c-t-a, is like superfluous language that is not central to your decision. So he's not just a dickhead, but a dicta-head.

Gilberto: Gratuitous.

Virginia: Superfluous. Anyway, so I spent time in Philly, and I find that—. So I just want to say these are my words: InKarcerated, with a capital K. Immcarcerated. Dicta-Head. ICE-holds.

Gilberto: One word, the term?

Virginia: Yeah, like that person is a fracking ice-hold.

Gilberto: Okay, okay.

Virginia: I've met so many of them. Fracking, particularly because South Texas—

Gilberto: I remember that. First DHS attorney, who did the first case—he was a caricature on [inaudible 01:35:15], cowboy boots, tall, [inaudible 01:35:18].

Virginia: He's now an immigration judge.

Gilberto: Everybody knows, he was . . . Anyway.

Virginia: I said one nice thing to him about a month ago or two months ago. Stuart Alcorn.

Gilberto: Yeah, it was him.

Virginia: He's now an immigration judge at Pearsall. I saw him leaving the building. I was still in the waiting lobby area, because I'd been there for hours and I was going to be there for hours. I said, "Judge Alcorn," and he looked at me like, "What?" I said, "My name is Virginia Raymond. I just want to tell you how sorry I am. I heard that your wife has passed." He said, "Thank you very much. I really appreciate that." I think he was sincere. He said she was sick for a long time. It was not a surprise, but thank you. I had a human being moment with Stuart Alcorn, which I never thought I would have, but the death of a spouse warrants a human bring moment. [inaudible 01:36:30], but we're not even going to talk about that.

So ARCG comes down in August of 2014, and it felt like, "Okay, at least we have this." So the February decision could have left indigenous women screwed, because they weren't getting CFIs, and it could have left arriving alien women and children screwed, because they were not statutorily—I mean, they were eligible for bonds, but judges did not have the power to give it to them. But as a practical matter, those people were released from Karnes on bonds that ICE set. So we stopped having to go to immigration court for every single family to ask for bond, but now we still have these women who—. This gets back to the point about family separation. This is why I have to tell you this, because it's really important to understand what Obama was doing wrong and what he wasn't doing wrong, okay.

There were three families that I represented all the way to the bitter end where the moms had come to the United States and been deported previously, but their children were in the United States for the first time. It was a really high burden for the moms to meet to the—they had a higher burden than their kids in terms of the reasonable fear process. There was this one family who were on the brink of deportation. I swear to God they were on the removal—. Let's turn off the phone for a second.

■ Declaration of Luis H. Zayas, PhD

I, Luis H. Zayas, declare as follows:

I make this declaration based on my own personal knowledge and if called to testify I could and would do so competently as follows:

I. Qualifications

1. I am a licensed psychologist and licensed clinical social worker in the State of Texas. Previously, I held psychology licenses in New York and Missouri and a clinical social work license in New York. I hold a master of science degree in social work (1975), and a master of arts (1984), master of philosophy (1985), and PhD (1986) in developmental psychology, all from Columbia University in the City of New York. I have been a practicing clinician since 1975 in child and adolescent psychiatry and primary care medicine.

2. I am presently the Dean of the School of Social Work at the University of Texas at Austin. I also occupy the Robert Lee Sutherland Chair in Mental Health and Social Policy. A copy of my curriculum vitae is attached hereto as Exhibit A.

3. Previously, I was the Shanti K. Khinduka Distinguished Professor of Social Work and Professor of Psychiatry, School of Medicine, at Washington University in St. Louis. I was also founding director of the Center for Latino Family Research. Prior to my ten years at Washington University, I was professor of social work at Fordham University, where I also directed the Center for Hispanic Men-

tal Health Research; visiting associate professor of family medicine and visiting associate professor of psychiatry at Albert Einstein College of Medicine; and assistant professor of social work at Columbia University in the City of New York.

4. My background encompasses clinical practice, teaching, and research in child and adolescent mental health, child development, child-rearing, and family functioning. I have been a clinician in general acute care hospitals and in outpatient mental health clinics in inner city settings. My specialty has been on minority and immigrant families and their children. I have conducted research in prenatal and postpartum depression, child-rearing values, alcohol use among Hispanic men, the influence of ethnicity on psychiatric diagnosis, and the suicide attempts of young Hispanic females. My research has been funded by the National Science Foundation and the National Institutes of Health (National Institute of Mental Health and National Institute of Child Health and Human Development). Since 2006, I have focused my clinical and research attention on the U.S.-born and foreign-born children [and] undocumented children of undocumented immigrants, mostly from Mexico and Central America.

5. I have published over 100 papers in scientific and professional journals and two books, *Latinas Attempting Suicide: When Cultures, Families, and Daughters Collide* (Oxford University Press, 2011) and *Forgotten Citizens: Deportation, Children, and the Making of American Exiles and Orphans* (Oxford University Press, 2015). A complete list of my publications issued in the last ten years is included in my CV.

6. I have previously testified as an expert witness in the following cancellation of removal cases in immigration court:

In the Matter of Jose Alejo (Kansas City, 2012)
Cristina Carlos (Kansas City, 2011)
Reyna Canseco-Ibaficz (Kansas City, 2011)
Fernando Garcia Cruz (Kansas City, 2011)
German Garcia (Kansas City, 2011)
Delio Lemuz-Hernandez (Kansas City, 2012)
Salvador Licea (San Antonio, 2014)
Ismael Limon (Kansas City, 2011)
Jose Rosario Lira-Correa (Orlando, 2013)
Ricardo Lopez (San Antonio, 2014)
Arturo Lopez Arrellano (Kansas City, 2006)

I also provided an affidavit as expert witness but did not testify *In the Matter of Fuentes* (San Antonio, 2014) on children's psychological functioning, Attention-Deficit/Hyperactivity Disorder, and childhood trauma.

7. I am making this declaration to provide my considered opinions concerning the psychological and developmental impact of detention on the immigrant families that I observed at the Karnes Detention Facility. My opinions derive from my interviews on August 19 and 20, 2014, with immigrant families detained at the Karnes County Residential Center.

8. My opinions are also based on 39 years of experience as a licensed social worker and psychologist conducting evaluation and treatment of children, adolescents, and families. This includes experience conducting evaluations for immigration courts since 2006 and conducting federally funded research on the mental health effects of the deportation of undocumented Mexican immigrants on their U.S.-born children since 2011. This research is currently being published in scientific journals and the aforementioned book.

9. I also reviewed relevant scientific literature in forming my conclusions, including the following publications:

Abram, K. M., Zwecker, N. A., Welty, L. I., Hershfeld, M. A., Dulcan, M. K., & Teplin, L. A. (2014). Comorbidity and continuity of psychiatric disorders in youth after detention: A prospective longitudinal study. *Journal of the American Medical Association.*

American Psychiatric Association (2013). *Diagnostic and statistical manual of mental disorders.* Fifth edition. Washington, DC: American Psychiatric Press.

Byrne, M. W., Goshin, L., & Blanchard-Lewis, B. (2012). Maternal separation during the reentry years for 100 infants raised in a prison nursery. *Family Court Review.*

Dallaire, D. H., Zeman, J. L., & Thrash, T. M. (2014). Children's experiences of maternal incarceration–specific risks: Predictions of psychological maladaptation. *Journal of Clinical Child and Adolescent Psychology.*

Evans, G. W., & Kim, P. (2013). Childhood poverty, chronic stress, self-regulation, and coping. *Child Development Perspectives, 7,* 43–48.

Foster, H., & Hagan, J. (2013). Maternal and paternal imprisonment in the stress process. *Social Science Research, 42,* 650–669.

McLaughlin, K. A., Sheridan, M. A., & Lambert, H. K. (2014). Childhood adversity and neural development: Deprivation and threat as distinct dimensions of early experience. *Neuroscience and Biobehavioral Reviews, 47*, 578–591.

Murray, J., & Farrington, D. P. (2005). Parental imprisonment: Effects on boys' antisocial behaviour and delinquency through the life-course. *Child Psychology and Psychiatry, 46*, 1269–1278.

Nesmith, A., & Ruhland, E. (2008). Children of incarcerated parents: Challenges and resiliency, in their own words. *Children and Youth Services Review, 30*, 1119–1130.

II. Summary of Findings and Opinions

10. Detention has had serious and long-lasting impacts on the psychological health and wellbeing of the families I interviewed at Karnes. This was evident even though the families I interviewed had been detained at Karnes for a relatively limited period of time—i.e., two to three weeks. In general, mothers and children showed high levels of anxiety—especially separation anxiety for the children—symptoms of depression, and feelings of despair. Children showed signs that detention had caused developmental regression, such as reversion to breastfeeding, and major psychiatric disorders, including suicidal ideation. Teenagers showed signs of depression and anxiety and, in some cases, major depressive disorders. The impacts of detention are exacerbated by the fact that families have already experienced serious trauma in their home countries and in the course of their journey to the United States.

11. The psychological traumas experienced by these mothers and children—in their home countries, during their travel to the United States, and upon their detention in the United States—will require years of mental health services to alleviate. Moreover, the ongoing stress, despair, and uncertainty of detention—for even a relatively brief period of time—specifically compromises the children's intellectual and cognitive development and contributes to the development of chronic illness in ways that may be irreversible. Detention at Karnes puts children at risk of recurrent and distressing memories, nightmares, dissociative reactions, prolonged psychological distress, and negative alterations in cognition.

III. Background of Evaluation

12. On August 19 and 20 of 2014, I met with ten families (mothers with children) detained at the Karnes County Residential Center in Karnes City, Texas, in order to assess their mental health status and evaluate the impact that their detention was having upon their psychological, educational, and emotional development. Without divulging confidential or client-specific data, I am able to share the following information.

13. Typically, my assessments began with a family meeting to get an overall picture of the family's pre-migration conditions and experiences; the conditions they experienced in traveling to the United States; and their post-migration encounters and experiences with U.S. Customs and Border Protection (CBP) and Immigration and Customs Enforcement (ICE) officials and employees of GEO Group, Inc., the private company that operates the Karnes County Residential Center.

14. In all, I evaluated ten mothers, ranging in age from 24 years to 47 years, and their children, who ranged in age from 2 years to 17 years. Eight of the families were from El Salvador. One was from Guatemala and one was from Honduras.

15. There were 23 children in these families; I interviewed or spoke with and asked some questions to 21 of the children, which includes all of the children who were able to speak. There were 13 males, ranging in age from 2 years to 17 years. The two 2-year-old children were breastfeeding, although one had apparently been weaned but reverted to breastfeeding after being placed in detention, according to his mother. There were 10 female children, ages 9 to 17 years.

16. In most instances, the families were first detained by U.S. officials near the border and subsequently transferred to the Karnes detention center. Those families with older children—adolescent boys and girls—were separated at Karnes such that the older children slept in other rooms with young people their age rather than sleeping near their parents.

17. At the time of my interviews, most families had been in the Karnes detention center for two to three weeks but had entered the United States some time earlier. All families identified at least one family member who resided in the United States, in such places as Texas, Ohio, Maryland, Virginia, Colorado, and other locations, with whom they could stay if released from detention.

IV. Findings

18. Without divulging confidential or client-specific information, I am able to describe the families' post-migration experiences that they encountered upon reaching the United States and, in most instances, their detention by U.S. border patrol agents and other law enforcement at the border and their processing by U.S. officials to their arrival and detention in Karnes.

19. In all cases, the families I interviewed fled severe violence in their home countries in order to seek refuge in the United States. The pre-migration histories of most [of] the families included domestic violence and sexual abuse of the mothers by their partners. Several of the mothers also reported being raped, robbed, and/or threatened by gang members. The teenage children appeared to suffer the greatest difficulties because of the gangs. Adolescent girls reported being accosted by gang members who insisted on forcibly taking them as their "girlfriends." While adolescent boys reported being told that they must become members of the gangs. In both cases, the teenagers reported that the consequence or refusal would be their own death or the death of a parent or sibling. (Teenage females were naturally more reluctant to discuss the situations of their sexual assaults with a male interviewer.) As for younger children, mothers I spoke to reported that their younger children were exposed to gang and street violence, or the aftermath, such as cadavers on the street.

20. At the time that I interviewed them, all of the families had been held at the Karnes detention facility for between two and three weeks. Their fears were not allayed by CBP or ICE: on the contrary, the families I interviewed all exhibited signs of elevated levels of anxiety, depression, and despair. Most mothers described elation when they were apprehended by U.S. officials because they initially felt safe in their hands. However, thereafter, the mothers and adolescents told of verbally rough treatment by U.S. border officials, such as being spoken sternly to and told to move faster, and admonished when they did not. Families stated that they did not always understand the orders given as they were told in English or in limited Spanish by some U.S. officials. All mothers and older children provided relatively uniform descriptions of the conditions in the *hieleras* (roughly translated as ice boxes) in which they were placed early in detention. The *hielera* is a large, very cold cell housing large groups of immigrants (women,

girls, and younger children) that provides no privacy, including a toilet used by everyone that was exposed to the view of everyone in the cell. The *hielera* was also intensely cold. Most told of being held in this setting for 48 hours or so. After that stop, the immigrants told of going to another location in which they were given aluminum-foil-like blankets that did warm them.

21. From there, they were moved to Karnes detention facility. While some families reported initially receiving friendly and caring treatment by U.S. officials, they also described punitive and verbally abusive treatment. They described the employees of the detention facility as "mean," "rude," "bullies," along with other negative terms. Staff at Karnes called for census counts three times a day and if a child, typically an adolescent, was found in her or his mother's cell and not in the one assigned to the teenager, they were given some sort of demerit. This was the case with one teenage female who was separated from her mother and two younger female siblings and was often weepy and fearful of being separated from her family. When I met her, the girl had received two warnings and was told that a third time would bring upon her a serious penalty (one that neither her mother nor she could describe).

22. In each conversation I held with mothers and older children, the feelings of despair and uncertainty were quite evident and voiced by them. Among the younger children I detected high levels of anxiety, especially separation anxiety (fear of being away from their mother; fearful that they would be moved and children not told; fear of losing their mother). The mothers showed mostly signs of depression with such vegetative signs as lack of sleep, loss of appetite and weight loss, and hopelessness. Some of the same symptoms were evident in the adolescents, especially girls.

23. Mothers and older children expressed varying levels of despair about their futures: how long they would be detained; what would be the conditions of their release; and whether they would ever see their families in the U.S. or back home again. Mothers exhibited anxiety about the health of their children, who they reported had lost weight, [had] become listless, and in some cases had reverted to infantile behaviors. At least three mothers with young children were distraught in thinking that they brought their children from one nightmarish situation to another.

24. Among the children, I witnessed signs that detention had caused regression or arrests in their development and major psychiatric disorders, including suicidal ideation. One of the two infants I observed had regressed developmentally: although he had previously been weaned, he had reverted back to breastfeeding and needed to be held by his mother constantly. Older children showed separation anxiety and regressions in their behaviors (e.g., staying attached to their mothers, worrying if their mother did not return from an errand). Several children reported nightmares.

25. Teenagers who were detained showed, primarily, signs of depression and anxiety. At least three of the teenagers with whom I spoke showed signs of major depressive disorders. At least one teenage male I interviewed expressed suicidal ideation, telling me that he would rather take his life than to return to his hometown and face the gangs that had tried to recruit him. In my clinical experience, and supported by scientific literature, suicidal ideation is not uncommon among detained or incarcerated persons. Research shows that suicidal ideation and attempts most commonly emerge during even brief periods of incarceration, in the early days and weeks of the person's imprisonment. This young man at Karnes showed classic symptoms of major depression: anhedonia (i.e., marked loss of interest or pleasure); psychomotor retardation (i.e., slow cognitive, verbal, and physical responses and movements); fatigue; feelings of worthlessness; and diminished ability to concentrate. His depressed mood was evident to me through these signs as well as his flat affect and "lifelessness" in his eyes.

26. In addition, both mothers and children expressed concern about the impact of detention on their educational development. One mother related that she had asked to organize a school for the children with other mothers but was rebuffed. Inasmuch as they did not know how long they would be in detention, several older children who had educational aspirations to go to college expressed concern about their future education.

V. Opinions

27. Based on my professional experience and background, and on the interviews and evaluations I conducted while at Karnes Family Detention Center, I conclude that the psychological traumas experienced by these mothers and chil-

dren—in their home countries, during their travel to the United States, and after their arrival in the United States when they found themselves locked up in immigration detention facilities—will require years of mental health services to alleviate. The ongoing stress, despair, and uncertainty of detention compromises children's intellectual and cognitive development and contributes to the development of chronic illnesses. Institutionalized children and the threats they face are similar to those of trauma, and result in recurrent, distressing memories, nightmares, dissociative reactions, prolonged psychological distress, and negative alterations in cognition. My conclusions arc well supported by medical and psychiatric research.

28. The scientific literature is very uniform in its findings about the impact of maternal incarceration or detention on children. Research (Byme et al., 2012) shows that infants and children who live in detention with their mothers often have more maladaptive social and emotional development, academic failure, and later criminal involvement compared to other children. With infants, the disruption of their emotional attachment to their mothers can lead to insecure bonding of the infant with the mother. Since attachment also predicts future behavior, insecure levels of attachment will result in suboptimal development. Indeed, disruptions in attachment affect general growth and development of the brain as well as social functioning, aggression, and reactions to stress. Children of incarcerated parents face many adverse outcomes and show difficulties in social interactions, such as making friends and navigating social situations, and research shows that maternal incarceration predicts the children's future antisocial and delinquent outcomes (Murray & Farrington, 2005; Nesmith & Ruhland, 2008).

29. Detention or institutionalized living, and child-rearing in prisons is a major childhood traumatic stressor, even under conditions of short or brief detentions (Foster & Hagan, 2013). Findings show that the childhood trauma from maternal incarceration increases depressive symptoms among children. Specifically, children 5 to 10 years and 11 to 14 years show increased risk for dropping out of high school, while the risks for children birth to 5 years and 11 to 16 years show high levels of depression and other internalizing behaviors (i.e., withdrawal, rumination) as well as externalizing behaviors (i.e., aggression, defiance and oppositionalism, fighting, vandalism, cruelty). Such externalizing behaviors in children

often mask clinical depressive symptoms and suicidality (often seen in aggressive, provocative behavior toward persons in authority, often police and law enforcement, that can lead to fatal encounters, commonly known as "suicide by cop").

30. Likewise, the scientific literature shows the negative effects of children's detention or incarceration on their future psychological health. Of 1,829 youth who were in juvenile detention during their teen years, 27% of males and 14% of females had what are known as "comorbid" psychiatric disorders, that is, co-occurring problems (Abram et al., 2014). Most commonly, the comorbidity involved major depression and anti-social behavior (oppositional defiant disorders) with alcohol abuse among males. The comorbidities for females were post-traumatic stress, anxiety, and anti-social personality disorder and substance abuse. Note that in this comorbidity, depression occurs with an externalizing disorder (oppositionalism). We see therefore that both internalizing and externalizing disorders are likely to be the outcomes of maternal and/or child detention. This has led researchers to conclude that incarceration-specific experiences place children at higher risk for maladjustment than exposure to general environmental risk in community settings (Dallaire et al., 2014).

31. However, there are more than the external indicators of the effects of detention—even [for] short periods—on children that should give us great reason for concern and worry. Rather, adverse childhood experiences, such as trauma and detention, have detrimental effects on children's brain growth and neural development. Research in the neurobiology of trauma and brain development shows that as childhood adversity increases, the likelihood of psychopathology also increases (McLaughlin, Sheridan, & Lambert, 2014).

32. Institutional rearing, that is, growing up in detention even for short periods of time—and particularly following the traumatic circumstances of migration—is one of the most adverse environments that scientists have studied, commonly called in the literature "complex adverse experiences." The two distinct but powerfully determinant elements of the trauma of these adverse experiences are *deprivation* (i.e., absence of expected developmentally appropriate environmental inputs and complexity) and *threat* (i.e., the presence of experiences that represent an immediate or ongoing threat to the child's physical integrity and psychological security).

Under the conditions of prolonged and intense stress, the body's natural stress responses (and release of specific hormones that aid in the flight-fight response and coping) arc over-used. The condition of chronic deprivation and threat stresses affect neural or brain development which in turn determines cognitive and behavioral functioning in children. Stress under prolonged and intense conditions activates the release of hormones that lead to structural and functional changes of some brain regions that are essential for self-regulation and other behaviors. As a result of the ongoing stress, despair, and uncertainty of detention, children's brain development is compromised, impairing not just their intellectual and cognitive development but also contributing to the development of chronic illnesses which can last into adulthood (Evans & Kim, 2013). The deprivation common in institutionalized children and the threats they face are similar to those of trauma as defined in the *Diagnostic and Statistical Manual of Mental Disorders* (2013) that include recurrent and distressing memories, nightmares, dissociative reactions, prolonged psychological distress, avoidance of people or other reminders of the trauma, and negative alterations in cognition such as not being able to remember important events or aspects of the traumatic events.

33. For adolescent development, when the sense of autonomy is emerging in preparation for adult roles, the loss of any autonomy—not just from the parents which all adolescents complain about but by being detained and lacking basic freedom—will have devastating effects on the adolescents once they enter the world outside the detention center. Unlike other adolescents in the communities they will be released to or returned to, they will have lost a part of their key developmental time in confinement with younger children and adult women.

34. Although I was not privy to any allegations of sexual abuse at the hands of the detention guards and employees by any of the mothers or children at the time of my interviews, I understand that such allegations have been made and that formal complaint or complaints were lodged. Should an investigation confirm the allegations of sexual abuse, that abuse will likely cause more maternal depression, signs of which will he evident to the children. Should a mother have experienced a sexual groping, rape, or coerced sexual favor near her children or within minutes of seeing their children, it is likely that the mothers will "reveal" their distress visibly which will be detected by their children. This can be very confusing to children and leave them feeling more vulnerable as well.

35. Taking this scientific background into consideration and combining it with the impressions I gathered in my interviews with mothers and children in the Karnes facility, I can unequivocally state that the children in the Karnes facility are facing some of the most adverse childhood conditions of any children I have ever interviewed or evaluated. Untold harm is being inflicted on these children by the trauma of detention. What is more is that the children at Karnes are experiencing *trauma upon trauma upon trauma*. That is, they not only suffered the trauma of having their lives threatened and disrupted by fleeing their native countries but they also experienced, witnessed, and heard of violent, traumatic events in their crossing through Mexico. On top of these serial and often long-term traumatic experiences, the children are exposed to the deprivation and constant threat of living in a facility in which they have no sense of their future. Complicating the children's development are the disrupted family roles and dynamics in which children see their mothers treated very poorly by staff and witnessing their mothers' vulnerability and helplessness. Children need the security and protection of their parents, and the conditions of detention militate against mothers' capacity to provide that kind of comfort for their children.

36. Based on my professional background and expertise, my knowledge of the scientific literature on child development and psychopathology and parenting and family functioning, and based on my conversations, with mothers and children detained at Karnes, I can say with certainty that detention is inflicting emotional and other harms on these families, particularly the children, and that some of these effects will be long lasting, and very likely permanent as adduced by the scientific literature.

37. The healing process, in my view, cannot begin while mothers and young children are detained. Indeed, my interviews led me to conclude that even a few weeks of detention has exacerbated the trauma experienced by these families and added a new layer of hardship that, with respect to the children in particular, may be irreversible.

VI. Compensation

38. I have received no compensation for my participation in this case.

39. I reserve the right to amend or supplement this report as appropriate upon receipt of additional information or documents.

I declare under penalty of perjury under the laws of the United States and the District of Columbia that the foregoing is true and correct.

Executed this 10th day of December, 2014, at Austin, Texas.

Signed Luis H. Zayas, Ph.D.

ACKNOWLEDGMENTS

To write about what happened in my hometown on August 3, 2019, means to struggle with monsters. I write in a moment of legal and political in-betweenness. I write amid multiple, intersecting crises, be they our public health, a looming large-scale war, ecological deterioration, policing, patriarch, or white supremacy. These crises tell of crimes licensed by cascading concentrations of power and wealth, crimes that too often befall marginalized populations.

To write about what happened in my hometown also means that I must honor the dead and those who have experienced the afflictions of US-Mexico border policy. This book and the analysis it puts forth are an effort to do that.

The book emerged from a series of conversations and travels between my old home and my new one. I grew up in El Paso, Texas. I now live in Champaign, Illinois. The book could not have happened without the luminous support of my family in both places. My mother and father, Gilbert Arthur Rosas and Cecilia Mora Rosas, put up with my fitful research trips to El Paso for a project that began with questions about refuge back in the mid-2010s and transformed into one on political violence. Gilberto and Angelina, Ignacia, Estela and Raul, Hector, Marie, Monica, Tommie, Pat, Stella, Anthony, and others supported me throughout the research and writing of this book. The patience and support of my co-conspirator and partner in crime, Korinta Maldonado, nourished my project and my soul, as did her acute insights, through dizzying twists and turns. Her influence resounds through the book. Our children, Teo and Maya, put up with my bouts of writerly angst, as did our multiple nonhuman companions, particularly Pulga, our Labrador mix.

The book would not have been possible without the support of community workers in El Paso. Diana Martinez was instrumental in helping me think through what happened in August 2019 and the context surrounding it. Her point of view is informed by her work as a community activist, particularly for the Coalition to End Childhood Detention, and her keen understanding of and long-standing ties to the area. She also authored this book's interlude. Ashley Heidebrecht, whom I first reached out to online through the Witness for Peace group on Facebook, also provided invaluable support. Crystal Massey, a human rights worker with training in anthropology, went out of her way to share her firsthand accounts of the immediate context around the events of August 3, 2019, as did Guillermo Glen, another community activist. Padre Robert Mosher of the Detained Migrant Solidarity Committee provided a gripping analysis of migrant detention and shared his experiences in confronting political violence in the Americas. This book would not be the same without profesora Yolanda Leyva, who organized the wonderful exhibit *Uncaged Art* on child detention, or without her expertise and commitments to the El Paso community.

I must acknowledge the contributions of several attorneys in the Office of the Federal Public Defender, Western District of Texas, El Paso. Federal public defender Maureen Scott Franco and assistant public defenders Alejandro Almanzan and Sergio Garcia shared their experiences with me to the betterment of this book.

Scholars, colleagues, and friends, near and far, including Ana Aparicio, Lisa Cacho, Howard Campbell, Ben Chappell, Alex Chavez, Marisol de la Cadena, Miguel Diaz-Barriga, Margaret Dorsey, Julie Dowling, Adriana Garriga López, Alma Gottlieb, Joe Heyman, Jonathan Inda, Sergio Lemus, Mireya Loza, Alejandro Lugo, Ania Muller, Neni Panougia, Gina Perez, Marc Perry, Dave Roediger, Jonathan Rosa, Audra Simpson, Aimee Villareal, Paige West, Pat Zavella, and many others, influenced this project with their scholarship, their collegiality, their conversations, and other forms of support. Virginia Raymond has been a wonderful friend and fellow traveler ever since one of my first courses in graduate school at the University of Texas in Austin. It is fantastic to have drawn on her astute expertise and experiences for this book.

At the University of Illinois at Urbana-Champaign, colleagues in the Department of Anthropology helped me think through some of the book's complexities. They include Jenny Davis, Jane Desmond, Virginia Dominguez, Brenda Farnell, Jessica Greenberg, Faye Harrison, Ripan Malhi, Jeff Martin, Ellen Moodie, Andy Orta, and Krystal Smalls. In Latina/o Studies, my other appointment at the university, colleagues Elizabeth Velasquez and Isabel Molina made important contributions, as did wonderful staff members Alicia Rodriguez and Laura Castañeda and my "accomplices" elsewhere at the University of Illinois, including Antoinette Burton, Cynthia Oliver, and Charles Roseman. Naomi Paik, who left the institution recently, and Erik McDuffie also helped me keep it real.

In addition, I had the benefit of working with wonderful, committed graduate students. Alana Ackerman and Brenda Garcia aided me as research assistants during the book's development. My spring seminar in 2020, Critical Border Studies, taught virtually at the height of lockdown, provided me with an opportunity to work through some complex questions that surfaced in the course of writing.

At Johns Hopkins University Press, acquiring editor Laura Davulis was quick to respond to my queries and regularly offered great writerly advice.

I would be remiss if I didn't acknowledge land claims without which this book would have been impossible to produce. The first is from the Borderland Rainbow Center, an LGBTQ community center that serves queer people in El Paso. The center's land acknowledgment reminds us how borders are superimposed on stolen land:

> We would like to recognize and pay our respects to the Indigenous people of what is now known as the State of Texas upon whose land we are living and working. We honor the Lipan Apache, Mescalero Apache, Piro, Manso, Suma, Jumano, Ysleta del Sur Pueblo, Piro/Manso/Tiwa Indian Tribe of the Pueblo of San Juan de Guadalupe, Tortugas Pueblo, the Carrizo & Comecrudo, Coahuiltecan, Caddo, Tonkawa, Comanche, Alabama-Coushatta, Kickapoo, and the peoples of Chihuahua and northern Mexico from whom many of our El Paso area colleagues and friends descend, such as the Rarámuri, Tepehuan, Wixarrika and Nahuatlaca peoples.
>
> We recognize and honor all Indigenous people of Turtle Island and acknowledge their right to this land.[1]

The second comes from the university where I work:

> As a land-grant institution, the University of Illinois Urbana-Champaign has a responsibility to acknowledge the historical context in which it exists. In order to remind ourselves and our community, we will begin this event with the following statement. We are currently on the lands of the Peoria, Kaskaskia, Piankashaw, Wea, Miami, Mascoutin, Odawa, Sauk, Mesquaki, Kickapoo, Potawatomi, Ojibwe, and Chickasaw Nations. It is necessary for us to acknowledge these Native Nations and for us to work with them as we move forward as an institution. Over the next 150 years, we will be a vibrant community inclusive of all our differences, with Native peoples at the core of our efforts.[2]

■ I am indebted to these communities; to my family, friends, and colleagues; and to many others I haven't named here. All errors or omissions in the book are my own.

NOTES

INTRODUCTION

1. Stephens, "El Paso Shooter."
2. Aguilar, "El Paso Again Tops List."
3. I am indebted here to Aisha M. Beliso–De Jesús and Jemima Pierre's introduction to the 2019 *American Anthropologist* special section "Anthropology of White Supremacy." "White nationalism" speaks to a particular iteration of white supremacy informing the killer and related purveyors of white supremacy in our present time. See Beliso–De Jesús and Pierre, "Special Section: Anthropology of White Supremacy."
4. Eligon, "El Paso Screed."
5. Eligon, "El Paso Screed."
6. Hartman, "'Passing of the Great Race.'"
7. Cacho, *Social Death*, 17.
8. Paik, *Bans, Walls, Raids, Sanctuary*, 26–27.
9. Paik, 28.
10. *Time* Staff, "Here's Donald Trump's Presidential Announcement Speech."
11. Trouillot writes of the "savage slot" as a foundational category for modern anthropology. See Trouillot, "Anthropology and the Savage Slot." The article advances the complex argument that within the Western and North Atlantic global imaginary, this slot was to be viewed as part of a triad of savageness, utopia, and dis-

order. This position echoes the ways certain sites and populations are similarly slotted in daily life.

12. I am not taking race as a biological fact. Rather, it is fundamentally a social relation. It constitutes the "embodiment of social inequality," embedded in relations of power that too often become misrecognized as biological, genetic, or some other innate difference. See Gravlee, "How Race Becomes Biology." I am particularly persuaded by the position that racism constitutes "the state-sanctioned or extralegal production and exploitation of group-differentiated vulnerability to premature death," as advanced by Ruth Wilson Gilmore, in *Golden Gulag*, 28. The articulation of these positions goes far beyond flip discussions of "race as a social construct" that strangle critical thought in the contemporary academy. For other productive studies on race and racism and how they inform the unsettling present, see, for example, Robinson, *Black Marxism*; and Lowe, *The Intimacies of Four Continents*.

13. See, for example, Speed, *Incarcerated Stories*; Morgensen, "Biopolitics of Settler Colonialism"; Wolfe, "Settler Colonialism and the Elimination of the Native"; Wolfe, "On Being Woken up"; Wolfe, *Traces of History*; Mamdani, "Good Muslim, Bad Muslim"; Hernández, *City of Inmates*; and Simpson, *Mohawk Interruptus*. The innovations in this body of scholarship often come from Native and Indigenous scholars.

14. See, for example, Luibhéid, *Entry Denied*; and Manalansan, *Global Divas*.

15. Here I am in conversation with recent scholarship on "ethnonationalism," "national populism," and related terms, much of which is underpinned by the seminal work of Stuart Hall in 1980 on what he termed "authoritarian populism." Ethnonationalism invites contemplation of how certain elements in the Latinx communities see themselves as natives and thus may support white nationalist movements and border-policing campaigns. Even so, deep consideration must be given to how the US Border Patrol offers political and economic opportunities to long-impoverished members of largely "Hispanic" border communities. See Chávez, "Gender, Ethnonationalism, and the Anti-Mexicanist Trope"; Gusterson, "From Brexit to Trump"; and Hall, "Popular Democratic versus Authoritarian Popularism."

16. Settler colonialism marks an apocalypse in the Americas, as argued by Horne, in *Apocalypse of Settler Colonialism*.

17. The scholarship on dispossession is multifaceted and rich. It includes Chakravartty and Da Silva, "Accumulation, Dispossession, and Debt"; Dayan, "Legal Terrors"; West, *Dispossession and the Environment*; and Loperena, "Settler Violence?"

18. Otero, "Neoliberal Reform and Politics in Mexico," 22–23.

19. Rosas, *Barrio Libre*, 50–51.

20. Rosas, 51.

21. Inspiration here comes in part from Césaire, *Discourse on Colonialism*.

22. US Border Patrol, "Border Patrol Strategic Plan," 7 See also Rosas, *Barrio Libre*, 103–5.

23. See "Fatal Encounters with CBP."

24. See Budd, "How Border Control Agents Get Away with Murder—Part 1."

25. Greg Grandin and Elizabeth Oglesby, "Washington Trained Guatemala's Killers for Decades," *The Nation*, January 25, 2019, https://www.thenation.com/article/archive/border-patrol-guatemala-dictatorship/.

26. Heyman, "President and Immigration Law Series."

27. For significant analyses on the politics of movement, see Mbembe, "Idea of a Borderless World"; Kotef, *Movement and the Ordering of Freedom*.

28. The multifaceted scholarship on borders and frontiers is complex. It includes Abrego, *Sacrificing Families*; Bebout, *Whiteness on the Border*; Campbell, *Drug War Zone*; Grandin, *The End of the Myth*; Lugo, *Fragmented Lives, Assembled Parts*; Hernández, *Coloniality of the US/Mexico Border*; Heyman, *Life and Labor on the Border*; Aretxaga, "What the Border Hides"; Simpson, *Mohawk Interruptus*; Stephen, *Transborder Lives*; Nicholas De Genova, "Migrant 'Illegality' and the Metaphysics of Antiterrorism: 'Immigrants' Rights' in the Aftermath of the Homeland Security State," *Items* (blog), July 28, 2006, https://items.ssrc.org/border-battles/migrant-illegality-and-the-metaphysics-of-antiterrorism-immigrants-rights-in-the-aftermath-of-the-homeland-security-state/; Mezzadra and Neilson, *Border as Method*; Walia, *Border and Rule*; Besteman, "Militarized Global Apartheid."

29. See Stevenson, "Looking Away."

30. See Behar, *The Vulnerable Observer*; Scheper-Hughes, *Death without Weeping*.

31. See Beverly, *Testimonio*; Menchu, *I, Rigoberta Menchu*; and Luiselli, *Tell Me How It Ends*.

32. This book thus engages anthropology's regular crises of legitimacy. Indeed, some have called for "letting it burn." Expressions that "gay couples can kiss in public now" and "racism is stupid" play into the liberal myth of progress and inclusion that diminishes anti-Blackness and white supremacy as an everyday violence for too many people and negate colonial histories of violence. For a discussion, see Jobson, "The Case for Letting Anthropology Burn," 261. Such liberal presuppositions account for the "shock" that gripped the United States over Trump's election, and for related accounts that consider violence as unjust events rather than the consequences of racial democracy and racial capitalism that fuel US empire. See Rosa and Bonilla, "Deprovincializing Trump," 202.

33. For a deeper look history of border enforcement and its defiance, see Levario, *Militarizing the Border*; and Loza, *Defiant Braceros*. For related long-standing questions, as well as contemporary ones, involving migration, see Ngai, *Impossible Sub-*

jects; Stuesse, *Scratching Out a Living*; Roediger, *Working toward Whiteness*; and Jones, *White Borders*.

34. See Malkki, "National Geographic."

35. See Anderson, *Imagined Communities*.

KINDLING

1. These crimes are tied the Chinese Exclusion Acts. Historian Erika Lee has shown how racist cartoons and newspaper reports of Chinese migrants merged "the illegal aspect of their migration with coexisting charges that Chinese were either cunning criminals or 'coolies,' casting Chinese immigration as a harmful invasion of inferior and unassimilable aliens," while ignoring "the role of U.S. immigration laws" in forcing their illegal immigration. Lee, "Enforcing the Borders," 68. Characters like John Chinaman "reinforced the popular representation of Chinese immigrants as . . . 'pollutants' who endangered American society with their alien presence and . . . threatened the white working class." The US government and "common knowledge" as illuminated by the media dehumanized Chinese migrants as "aliens," an "invasion" and "threatening." See Lee, "Enforcing the Borders," 69–70.

2. Khosravi, "Stolen Time."

3. See Benjamin, "Critique."

4. Contemporary practices of detention can in part be traced to the Immigration Reform and Control Act (IRCA). Passed in November 1986, after some fourteen years of acrimonious debate, the IRCA, as scholars and policy makers typically remember it, coupled the legalization of several million undocumented persons with a largely ineffective regime of employer regulation. White nationalist or Great Replacement–like fears of the wrong bodies seeping through the "backdoor" of the border, bearing their medical risks, their "contagion possibilities," their so-called "cultural enclavism," and their fiscal burdens, smolder in the congressional record of the debates on the IRCA. The act increased monies for ground and aerial surveillance hardware, fencing, roads, and border-policing practices under the joint control of the Departments of Justice, the Treasury, and Defense and melded with expanding practices of detention. The measure augmented the deployment of military troops and the National Guard in the border region. These developments are captured in the important work Dunn, *Militarization of the U.S.-Mexico Border*, 19, among many others.

5. Asylum seekers and other orders of border crossers who flee persecution and related conditions in their own countries too often confront confinement. The freedom and security of refugees are sacrificed in the name of the freedom and security

of "proper" citizens. Even in countries proud of their democratic values, the value of an open society quickly closes itself off. Oliver, *Carceral Humanitarianism*, 44.

6. Pitzer, *One Long Night*, 5–6. See also Müller, *If the Walls.*

7. For a discussion of deportation, "removal," and political imprisonment, see Davis, *Freedom Is a Constant Struggle*, 32.

8. See appendix Statement of Barbara Hines.

9. See appendix Statement of Virginia Raymond.

10. See appendix Declaration of Luis H. Zayas.

11. See appendix Statement of Virginia Raymond.

12. See Paredes, *"With His Pistol in His Hand"*; and Limón, *Dancing with the Devil.*

13. See appendix Statement of Barbara Hines.

14. See appendix Declaration of Luis H. Zayas.

15. See appendix Declaration of Luis H. Zayas.

16. See appendix Declaration of Luis H. Zayas.

17. Immigrant rights activist Crystal Massey, interviewed by Gilberto Rosas, July 26, 2019.

18. Rosas and Raymond, "Migrant Detention Turns Deadlier."

19. Rosas and Raymond.

20. Rosas and Raymond.

INTERLUDE. White Supremacy in El Paso before August 3, 2019

1. BCFS Health and Human Services operated the Tornillo immigrant detention facility on behalf of the Department of Health and Human Services' Office of Refugee Resettlement (ORR). The facility opened in June 2018, with a capacity for 400 minors. At its highpoint, the facility held some 2,800 teenagers, making it one of the ORR's largest of such facilities. See Graham Kates, "'Tent City' for Unaccompanied Migrant Children to Remain Open Longer than Planned;" *CBS News*, July 9, 2018, https://www.cbsnews.com/news/tornillo-texas-tent-city-for-unaccompanied-migrant-children-to-remain-open-longer-than-planned/; Daniel Levinson, Inspector General, to Lynn Johnson, Assistant Secretary, Administration for Children and Families, Department of Health and Human Services, Office of Inspector General, November 27, 2018, https://oig.hhs.gov/oas/reports/region12/121920000.pdf; Madlin Mekelburg, "Official: No Migrant Children Remain at Tornillo Tent Shelter as It Heads toward Closure," *El Paso Times*, January 11, 2019, https://www.elpasotimes.com/story/news/politics/2019/01/11/tornillo-shelter-no-migrant-children-closed-january/2547461002/.

THE LLORONX

1. Some interpretations of La Llorona and related figures suggest they transgress strict gender norms that permit and sometimes encourage the objectification, displacement, and disposability of women and their bodies. See, among many others, Paz, *The Labyrinth of Solitude*; Anzaldúa, *Borderlands*; Renee Perez, "The Politics of Taking."

2. Sergio Garcia, interview by the author, July 19, 2019, El Paso County Public Defender Office.

3. Maureen Scott Franco, interview by the author, July 17, 2019, El Paso County Public Defender Office.

4. Crystal Massey, interview by the author, July 17, 2019, Las Cruces, New Mexico.

5. See Milian, *LatinX*.

6. Department of Justice, "Review of the DOJ's Planning and Implementation of Its Zero Tolerance Policy," 39.

7. Miroff, "Honduran Father Who Died in Texas Jail Was Fleeing Violence."

8. Scott Franco, author interview.

9. Golash-Boza, *Immigration Nation*, 54–55.

10. Golash-Boza, 54–55.

11. See James, *Black Jacobins*. For related exemplary work on the African diaspora, see, among many others, Perry, *Negro Soy Yo*; McDuffie, *Sojourning for Freedom*; and Pierre, *The Predicament of Blackness*.

12. Loyd and Mounts, *Boats, Borders, and Bases*, 169–72.

13. *A Culture of Cruelty*, 5.

14. Wessler, *Shattered Families*, 6.

15. See Iturralde, "Neoliberalism and Its Impact on Latin American Crime Control Fields."

16. Emphasis added. Indeed, per the Department of Justice report, the Office of the Attorney General under Sessions's direction initiated discussions with the Department of Justice and the Department of Homeland Security about changing policy to address the number of apprehensions on the Southwest border. These included explicitly considering the prosecution of adults apprehended at the border in family units, as well as the separation of the children from adults in those units, and noting that by "placing the adults in detention . . . minors under the age of 18 . . . will see the definition of 'unaccompanied alien child,' i.e., (1) has no lawful immigration status in the U.S.; (2) has not attained the age of 18; and (3) has no parent or legal guardian in the U.S., or no parent or legal guardian in the U.S. is available to provide care and physical custody." Department of Justice, "Review of the DOJ's Planning and Implementation of Its Zero Tolerance Policy," 11–12.

17. There are echoes here of the emergent work of Sophia Balakian. See her "Of Aunts and Mothers."

18. Many of these accounts are corroborated in the Department of Justice's review of the Trump administration's practices of family separation, "Review of the DOJ's Planning and Implementation of Its Zero Tolerance Policy." For example:

> On Friday, May 11, the five Southwest border U.S. Attorneys, the EOUSA [Executive Office United States Attorney] Liaison, and two ODAG officials [Office of the Deputy Attorney General] were scheduled to speak with Hamilton to discuss the zero-tolerance policy and the DHS referrals of family unit adults. However, shortly before the call was to begin, the EOUSA Liaison sent an email to the U.S. Attorneys stating that Hamilton would not be able to join the call. The five U.S. Attorneys, who had already dialed into the conference line, decided to stay on the line to discuss their concerns about family unit prosecutions and the separation of children from the parents. The EOUSA Liaison and one of the ODAG officials were also on the conference call.
>
> Following the U.S. Attorneys' discussion, the EOUSA Liaison sent an email to Hamilton, two ODAG officials, and an EOUSA Assistant Director and EOUSA Deputy Director, describing the U.S. Attorneys' concerns about the policy change. The EOUSA Liaison wrote that Bash [recently confirmed as US attorney for the Western District of Texas] recommended that the Department develop and coordinate talking points regarding the prosecution of family units and the separation of children. The liaison also stated that all of the U.S. Attorneys agreed that the Department should have a consistent message and strategy on these issues. The liaison wrote that all of the districts had received media inquiries about family separations and were requesting guidance and assistance in responding to the inquiries. The liaison noted that the WDTX [Western District of Texas] Federal Public Defender was not waiving preliminary and detention hearings on family unit cases, that this would "clog up the system," and that the SDCA [Southern District of California] was also facing legal challenges to the new policy. Finally, the EOUSA Liaison highlighted the U.S. Attorneys' primary concern:
>
> BIG CONCERN: What is happening with these children when they are being separated from the parent? It appears that once DHS turns the child over to HHS [Department of Health and Human Services], DHS is out of the picture and cannot give information. What are the safeguards to

the children. . . . Also, what is the age cut-off for children and parents to be separated? So far, there are representations that if the child/children are 5 years and older that the parents/child will be separated.

How is DHS arranging for Central and South American family units to be deported after the misdemeanor prosecution of the parent? How are they getting the child back to the parent? Mexico will not allow them to be turned over to Mexico. Will these individuals all be released into the US pending removal? Where are the kids during that time?

The EOUSA Liaison concluded, "US Attorneys are deeply concerned about this issue and will make themselves available for a call later tonight . . . or this weekend. I can arrange."

After receiving the email from the EOUSA Liaison, one of the ODAG officials forwarded it to Bash, asking, "Is there anything key missing from your perspective?" Bash responded, "No. We need a complete understanding of what happens to children when the parents are prosecuted and then craft that into talking points for the press and potentially filings for courts." The ODAG official forwarded Bash's response to Hamilton, stating, "I double checked with USA Bash to get his take on the call. Please see below for his take on the bottom line, in case helpful for you too."

Later that afternoon, then acting U.S. Attorney for the DAZ [District of Arizona] Strange wrote an email to a USAO official in her office, stating that it was her understanding that family members prosecuted in her district were not being reunited with their children immediately after the defendants received time-served sentences. She added that this was contrary to what Sessions had communicated, noting, "My understanding is that even though the parents will be sentenced to 'time served' for the misdemeanor, they will not be immediately reunited with their children (which USA John Bash and I recalled was not the AG's understanding in the call with the [Southwest border] Districts last week)."

After Hamilton received the email on May 11 from the EOUSA Liaison expressing the concerns of the five Southwest border U.S. Attorneys, Sessions scheduled a conference call with them for later that same day, May 11. Based on notes from the call taken by multiple U.S. Attorneys, Sessions thanked the U.S. Attorneys for "stepping up" and said that there had been "lots of progress" made on immigration. Sessions offered to get the Southwest border USAOs additional personnel and urged them to "move rapidly" on hiring. According to the notes, Sessions also told the U.S. Attorneys that the Department was committed to prosecuting individuals who enter the country illegally to ensure a conviction was on their record. The notes further recorded Sessions telling the U.S. Attorneys, "we need to take away children; if care about kids, don't bring them in; won't give amnesty ~~to kids~~; to people with kids" (strikethrough in original).

SDTX U.S. Attorney Patrick sent an email to his staff soon after the call with Sessions. In his email, he stated: "I just got off the phone with the Attorney General. He praised our office on ramping up so quickly on the new zero tolerance stance. . . . He wants an honest assessment of conditions, but he doesn't want excuses, and he isn't hearing them from us."

That evening, Hamilton emailed the Chief of Staff and Acting Deputy Chief of Staff of ICE, the CBP Chief of Staff, and the Director of ORR asking for a telephone call in the next few days "to confirm some logistical matters for our U.S. Attorneys on the Southwest border about the handling of minors whose parents are criminally prosecuted for illegal entry—and issues related to their reunification after they serve time for any criminal offense." After reviewing a draft of this report, Hamilton told us that, although he did not recall the specifics of those conversations with the four officials, he asked generally about reunification practices and had received assurances, as he said he had received in prior months, that DHS and HHS were working together to address such matters.

WITNESSING TORTURE

1. See Levin et al., "Trump Policy of Detaining Children 'May Amount to Torture' "; Oberg et al., "Treatment of Migrant Children on the US Southern Border Is Consistent with Torture."

2. Caitlin Dickerson, " 'There Is a Stench': Soiled Clothes and No Baths for Migrant Children at a Texas Center," *New York Times*, June 21, 2019, https://www.nytimes.com/2019/06/21/us/migrant-children-border-soap.html.

3. Recent scholarship analyzes the centrality of pain and suffering in racial and other kinds of socially and politically produced difference in public life. See Beltrán, *Cruelty as Citizenship*; Ralph, *The Torture Letters*; Puar, *Terrorist Assemblages*; Taussig, *Shamanism*; Scarry, *The Body in Pain*; James, *Resisting State Violence.*

4. Dickerson, " 'There Is a Stench.' "

5. Hooks, "The Cruelty at the Border Is Increasingly Pointless."

6. Department of Homeland Security, "Concerns about ICE Detainee Treatment and Care," 3–4.

7. Such practices have disturbing echoes. In Abu Ghraib, Iraq, during the early stages of the Iraq War, for example, members of the US Army and the Central Intelligence Agency committed a series of human rights violations and war crimes against detainees. See Puar, "On Torture."

8. See, for example, "Sexual Abuse in Immigration Detention."

9. When I first began researching this book, people from Latin America constituted some 90 percent of those being incarcerated in such sites. Gradually, however, the demographics changed. Migrants from Latin America were sent into the Migrant Protection Protocols, where they were put into encampments, often in Mexico. A second development is more recent. For the most part, DHS has not been placing African asylum seekers in the Migrant Protection Protocols program, also known as "Remain in Mexico," and it has not been using Asylum Cooperative Agreements, or so-called safe third-country deals, to force them to wait for hearings in El Salvador, Guatemala, or Honduras. Instead, DHS seems to be reserving these programs for presumed Spanish-speakers—Cubans, Guatemalans, Hondurans, Salvadorans, Nicaraguans, Venezuelans, and Ecuadorians, some of whom speak Indigenous languages primarily or exclusively—and caging them in third countries. MPP has not, however, emptied out immigration detention. The intent behind MPP may not have been to separate asylum seekers by "race," but such separation is one of its effects. The length and nature of these asylum seekers' journey also results in the disproportionate incarceration of Black Africans. For example, many migrants arrive without any identity documents, such as passports, which frequently have been stolen, as I note in chapter 1. Without such documents, DHS often denies parole. See Rosas and Raymond, "Migrant Detention Turns Deadlier."

10. I am situated in what some such as Poblete have termed "critical Latin American and Latino studies," and thus follow the Latinx-influenced work of scholars who study Latin America, such as Saldaña-Portillo, *Revolutionary Imagination in the Americas*; and Gómez *Revolutionary Imagination of Greater Mexico*.

11. Grandin, *Empire's Workshop*, 79.

12. Spira, "Neoliberal Captivities," 131–32.

13. Grandin, *Empire's Workshop*, 79–80.

14. Spira, "Neoliberal Captivities," 133.

15. In terms of tactics used in Chile, Mosher explains, "One of the few things that we felt was effective in Chilean society was having these demonstrations that would only last five minutes, in front of the actual places of torture every single day during

the 17 years of the dictatorship, in every major city of the country. And we would invite the foreign press to come, and as many of the local press that were there to come and have these five-minute demonstrations in front of a torture center and then disperse, and then gather somewhere else to evaluate the action. Oh, so for years, from 1983 until about 1990 when the regime stopped, we would have this secret nonviolent movement against torture, and it was very demanding. They arrested many of us several times. We tried to keep ourselves in the public eye as much as possible, and a safety measure. And anyway, it took a lot out of us to even participate, and it created a lot of fear. Sometimes we were beaten, some of us were sprayed with tear gas during the demonstrations or hosed with a water cannon, which is kind of funny—we discovered that if you're sitting on the ground, the water cannon couldn't really do any damage to you. There were certain chants where would we call for the water cannon 'cause it was so hot."

16. Such practices have become a normal part of the US border and immigration, as seen in Jason De León's analysis in *The Land of Open Graves*.

17. See US Border Patrol, "Border Patrol Strategic Plan."

18. See Cavallaro and Collins, "Frontier Injustice." Immigrant rights activist and community historian Lupita Castillo, a member of a Tucson based immigrant's rights group, Derechos Humanos / Arizona Border Rights Project, sought to bring national attention to the Elmer case. The organization sought to draw an analogy between the Rodney King incident in California, the murder of Miranda Valenzuela, and other human rights violations at the hands of immigration authorities. Castillo recalls that when she approached a *New York Times* correspondent to complain about the newspaper's lack of interest in the story, she was told that the American people do not care about the border: "It's a Third World country."

19. The INS, before it became ICE, estimated that 7 million unauthorized immigrants were living in the United States in January 2000 and that on average this population grew by about 350,000 per year from 1990 through 1999. Indeed, this population is twice as large as it was in the early 1990s. See Inda, *Targeting Immigrants*, 113.

20. The dramatic demographic transformation occurring in the United States analyzed in the scholarship of illegality and Indigenous transnationality suggests that many of the immigrants who attempt to circumvent militarized border enforcement succeed. Nicholas De Genova argues that the US-Mexico border provides a spectacular example. See De Genova, "Migrant 'Illegality' and Deportability in Everyday Life." See also, among this voluminous literature, Kearney, "The Local and the Global"; Mountz and Wright, "Daily Life in the Transnational Migrant Community of San Agustín."

21. Eschbach et al., "Death at the Border."

22. There is much compelling and critical work on Central America and Central Americans. See, for example, Heidbrink, *Migranthood*; Goett, *Black Autonomy*; Moodie, *El Salvador in the Aftermath of Peace*; Estrada, "Grassroots Peacemaking"; Zilberg, *Space of Detention*; Copeland, *The Democracy Development Machine*.

23. This episode is taken from Rosas, *Barrio Libre*.

24. *Culture of Cruelty*, 4.

25. *Culture of Cruelty*, 6.

26. *Culture of Cruelty*, 22.

27. *Culture of Cruelty*, 24

28. *Culture of Cruelty*, 25–27.

29. Wessler, *Shattered Families*, 5.

30. For this section of the chapter, I draw extensively on the complaint. See Family Members of Anastasio Hernández-Rojas, Petitioners. Page references appear in parentheses in the text.

31. Cheryl W. Thompson and Mark Berman, "Improper Technique, Increased Risks," *Washington Post*, November 26, 2015.

32. See Muñiz de la Peña, "Statement."

33. Muñiz de la Peña, 5–6.

34. Hitler, as many have noted, took inspiration from the anti-Blackness foundational to the United States. See, for example, Whitman, *Hitler's American Model*.

WITNESSING THE JOAQUIN DEAD

Much of this chapter is adapted from Rosas, "Necro-subjection."

1. See Rosas, *Barrio Libre*.

2. See Rosas, "Cholos, Chúntaros, and the 'Criminal' Abandonments of the New Frontier."

3. See Paredes, *With a Pistol in His Hand*.

4. See Rosas, *Barrio Libre*.

5. See De León, *The Land of Open Graves*.

6. See Berlant, "Cruel Optimism"; Viego, *Dead Subjects*; Muñoz, "Feeling Brown, Feeling Down."

7. See Rosas, "The Thickening Borderlands"; Rosas, "Managed Violences of the Borderlands"; Inda, "Borderzones of Enforcement."

8. See De Genova, "Legal Production of Mexican/Migrant 'Illegality' "; Buff, *Against the Deportation Terror*.

9. See Hale, "What Is Activist Research."

10. See Visweswaran, *Fictions of Feminist Ethnography*; and Zavella, "Feminist Insider Dilemmas."

11. See Murakawa, *First Civil Right.*

12. See Mills, "Racial Liberalism."

13. For a genealogy of abolitionist anthropology, see Shange, *Progressive Dystopia.*

14. I am invoking Ruth Wilson Gilmore's prescient and abolitionist-inspired definition of racism. Gilmore, *Golden Gulag*, 28.

15. I echo other anthropologists who follow legal proceedings, including Lynn Stephen, who has developed the concept of "gendered embodied structures of violence" to document the complex, multiple, legal, and extralegal realms of violence that Mam women from Guatemala experience. See Stephen, "Fleeing Rural Violence."

16. See Gonzalez and Fernandez, *Century of Chicano History.*

17. Brute force and the social facts of violence no longer constitute an anomaly of racial liberal rule, if they ever did, for those forming or inhabiting its colonial "dark" side. They include, for Sylvia Wynter, "a category defined at the global level by refugee/economic migrants stranded outside the gates of the rich countries." Wynter, "Unsettling the Coloniality of Being/Power/Truth/Freedom," 261.

The wretched at the borders reaffirm that, as Aníbal Quijano notes, the idea of race has become the "most efficient instrument of social domination in the last 500 years." Quijano, "¡Que tal raza!" 141. No longer content to stay cordoned off in the hinterlands, the new refugees encounter global structures of white supremacy. They move despite an increasingly globalized nativism that demands the contortions of death and life.

18. I discuss the practices of testimony in immigration proceedings as one example of "fugitive work." See Rosas, "Fugitive Work." Maya Berry, Claudia Chavez Argüelles, Shanya Cordis, Sarah Ihmoud, and Elizabeth Velásquez Estrada, in their unsettling account of sexual violence in the field, hold that a decolonizing and "fugitive" anthropology likely demands breaking with one's "intellectual home." See Berry et al., "Toward a Fugitive Anthropology."

19. See Mbembe, "The Idea of a Borderless World."

20. See Paik, *Rightlessness.*

21. Paik.

22. The echoes of the carnivalesque, or the way power relations may be temporarily inverted in festivities, between Limón, *Dancing with the Devil*, and Mbembe, "The Banality of Power and the Aesthetics of Vulgarity in the Postcolony," are noteworthy.

23. See Stephen, "Fleeing Rural Violence."

24. See Loyd and Mountz, *Boats, Borders, and Bases.*

25. See Zavala, *Los cárteles no existen*; and Wright, "Epistemological Ignorances and Fighting for the Disappeared."

26. See Farmer, "Anthropology of Structural Violence."
27. See Simon, "Michel Foucault on Attica."
28. See West, *Dispossession and the Environment.*
29. See Marx, *Capital*; and Fazio, *Estado de Emergencia.*
30. See Foucault, *Society Must Be Defended.*
31. See Gilmore, "Fatal Couplings of Power and Difference."
32. Mbembe, "Necropolitics," 13 (emphasis in original).
33. Mbembe, "Necropolitics," 40.
34. Mbembe, "Necropolitics," 39.
35. See Foucault, *Discipline and Punish*, 90.
36. See Robinson, *Black Marxism.*
37. Mbembe, "Necropolitics," 38.
38. See Newton, *Genius of Huey P. Newton*; and Heiner, "Foucault and the Black Panthers."
39. See Michel Foucault, "The Subject and Power."
40. See Visweswaran, *Un/common Cultures*; Federici, *Caliban and the Witch.*
41. For literature on refusal and related concepts, see Simpson, *Mohawk Interruptus*; Ortner, "Resistance and the Problem of Ethnographic Refusal"; and Cohen, "Deviance as Resistance."
42. See Vega, *Latino Heartland.*
43. Chavez, *Covering Immigration.*
44. See Balaguera, "Trans-migrations."
45. See Ortner, "Dark Anthropology and Its Others."

GRIEF AND BORDER CROSSING RAGE

This chapter is adapted from Rosas, "Grief and Border-Crossing Rage."

1. Aisha M. Beliso–De Jesús and Jemima Pierre urge anthropologists to speak to a global system of white supremacy, how it structures global capitalism, neocolonial relations, and a host of other factors. See Beliso–De Jesús and Pierre, "Anthropology of White Supremacy."
2. Mica Rosenberg and Julian Cardona, "Ten Thousand Dead and Counting: Ciudad Juarez, the Mexican City That's Deadlier than Afghanistan," *National Post*, December 27, 2011, https://nationalpost.com/news/ciudad-juarez-10000-killed-in-four-years-as-mexicos-toothless-war-on-drugs-goes-on.
3. This is anthropology that breaks the heart, as discussed in Behar, *Vulnerable Observer.*
4. See Briggs, *Taking Children.*

5. Megan Sheets, "El Paso Walmart Employee and Customer Who Helped 140 Panicked People Escape the Store When Gunman Patrick Crusius Opened Fire," *Daily Mail*, updated August 6, 2019, https://www.dailymail.co.uk/news/article-7329001/El-Paso-Walmart-employee-customer-helped-140-escape-gunman-Patrick-Crusius-opened-fire.html.

6. David Gilbert, "'No One Really Knew Him': Everything We Know about the El Paso Mass Shooting Suspect," *Vice*, August 4, 2019, https://www.vice.com/en/article/7x5z4a/el-paso-shooting-suspect-patrick-crusius.

7. See Beliso–De Jesús and Pierre, "Anthropology of White Supremacy."

8. See Rosaldo, "Grief and a Headhunter's Rage."

9. Alejandro Lugo recognized *Culture and Truth* as "the culmination of [Rosaldo's] analytical and theoretical arguments . . . [about] human social life." See Lugo, "Dossier." For more recent work in anthropology on the affective, see Ramos-Zayas, *Street Therapists*.

10. See Brodkin, Morgen, and Hutchinson, "Anthropology as White Public Space."

11. See Cisneros, *The House on Mango Street*.

12. See Harrison, *Decolonizing Anthropology*.

13. See McGranahan, Roland, and Williams, "Decolonizing Anthropology."

14. See Gutmann, *Meanings of Macho*.

15. Rosas, *Barrio Libre*, 135.

16. See Lorde, "Uses of the Erotic"; Moraga and Anzaldúa, *This Bridge Called My Back*.

17. See "The Anthropoliteia #BlackLivesMatterSyllabus Project, Week 8."

18. Callahan, "Zapatismo beyond Chiapas"; Saramago, "Chiapas, Land of Hope and Sorrow."

19. See Mora, *Kuxlejal Politics*.

20. Rosaldo, *Culture and Truth*, 208.

21. See Galemba, *Contraband Corridor*; and Jusionyte, *Savage Frontier*.

22. Related works—such as those that interrogate the practices of racial segregation in the border region of Texas or California, or that document the poetics of transborder music making, or that recognize the complex relations between addiction and coloniality in Puerto Rico, the cultivation of militarized Latino youth—perhaps lead to the recognition that what "brings flesh to theory," to follow Moraga, and what brings theory to flesh may be the emotional force of materialist histories of colonialism, caste relations, and related histories of dispossession. See, among many others, Nájera, *Borderlands of Race*; Menchaca, *Mexican Outsiders*; Chávez, *Sounds of Cross-*

ing; Garriga-López, "The Coloniality of Addiction in Puerto Rico"; Perez, *Citizen, Student, Soldier*; Ambikaipaker, *Political Blackness in Multiracial Britain*; Lemus, "Performing Power *en las Yardas*"; and Chappell, *Lowrider Space*.

23. See, among other works, Shange, *Progressive Dystopia*; and Mbembe, "Idea of a Borderless World."

24. See Rosas, "Las fronteras que se engrosan."

25. See Rosas, "Necro-subjection."

26. See De Genova, "Migrant 'Illegality' and Deportability in Everyday Life"; *and* Rios Contreras, "The Role of Drug-Related Violence and Extortion in Promoting Mexican Migration."

27. See Nevins, "Border Death-Trap—Time to Tear Down America's Berlin Wall," *La Prensa San Diego*, August 2, 2002, https://www.laprensa-sandiego.org/archieve/augusto2-02/border.htm; Dunn, *Militarization of the U.S.-Mexico Border*.

28. See Rosas, *Barrio Libre*.

29. See, among the many powerful works in this vein, Muehlmann, *When I Wear My Alligator Boots*; Estévez, *Guerras necropolíticas y biopolítica de asilo en América del Norte*; and Vogt, "Crossing Mexico."

30. See Rosas, "Necro-subjection"; and Speed, *Incarcerated Stories*.

31. See Chavez, *Latino Threat*.

32. See Varela Huerta et al., "Notes for an Anti-racist Feminism in the Wake of the Migrant Caravans."

33. See Besteman, "Militarized Global Apartheid."

34. See Díaz-Barriga and Dorsey, *Fencing in Democracy*.

35. See Paredes, *With His Pistol in His Hand*; Khosravi, *"Illegal" Traveller*.

36. De León, *The Land of Open Graves*; Jusionyte, "Called to 'Ankle Alley.'"

37. Rosas, "The Managed Violences of the Borderlands."

38. In these scenarios, those who surreptitiously enter the United States engender analytical interventions, raising the question of the parallels of settler and migration formations. See Nájera and Maldonado, "Transnational Settler Colonial Formations and Global Capital."

39. As Rosa contends, a racio-linguistic perspective conceptualizes the conaturalization of linguistic and racial borders. It analyzes the current rearticulation of colonial distinctions between populations and modes of communication that come to be positioned as more or less normatively European. These semiotic distinctions organize "the joint governance of markets and difference within modernist projects of racial capitalism and liberal democracy." Rosa, *Looking like a Language, Sounding like a Race*, 5.

40. "Ana," interviewed by the author, July 25, 2014, at her place of business.

41. Ghassan Hage has noted that Foucauldian theorists of governmentality presume that the governmental apparatus works directly on the governed population. Settler-colonial government, however, works through the mediation of the extremist mob, highlighting an often-neglected dimension of governmental technology. The philosopher Giorgio Agamben is thus correct in asserting that for neoliberal governmentality, "we are all virtually homines sacer but there remains a difference in this virtuality... necropolitical collaborators become the 'sacrificers' in the face of those to be 'sacrificed,'" and I would argue this is inextricably tied to racism and related settler logics. See Hage, "État de Siège," 42.

42. See, among other works, Zavella, *I'm Neither Here nor There*; and Du Bois, *The Souls of Black Folk.*

43. See Lugo, *Fragmented Lives, Assembled Parts.*

44. This analysis emerges from one of the numerous conversations I had with Diane Martinez. Among other reportage about the raids, see Rogelio V. Solis and Jeff Amy, "Largest US Immigration Raids in a Decade Net 680 Arrests," Associated Press, April 20, 2021, https://apnews.com/article/donald-trump-us-news-ap-top-news-arrests-immigration-bbcef8ddae4e4303983c91880559cf23.

ON THE BANALITY OF CROSSING

1. Compelling visions of abolitionist possibilities and radical sanctuary are integral to my looking to everyday practices for a reimagining of borders and what they could be. See Shange, *Progressive Dystopia*; Paik, *Bans, Walls, Raids, Sanctuary*; Villarreal, "Sanctuaryscapes in the North American Southwest"; Vitale, *End of Policing*; Gilmore and Gilmore, "Beyond Bratton"; and LeBrón, *Policing Life and Death.*

2. See Rosas, "Thickening Borderlands"; Varela Huerta et al., "Notes for an Antiracist Feminism."

3. See Lugo, "Theorizing Border Inspections."

4. See Rosas, *Barrio Libre*; Rubio-Goldsmith et al., "The 'Funnel Effect' and Recovered Bodies of Unauthorized Migrants"; De León, *Land of Open Graves.*

5. A significant nexus between sovereignty and the biopolitical body in modern liberal democracies reveals how what was originally excluded from politics as the outstanding exception that nevertheless founds the law has now become the norm: what jostles contemporary states may not be rooted in obscure historical figures found in Western law but in mobile lives whose excessive movement provokes deep unease, disruption, and invites contemplation of a coming political community. See Agamben, *Homo Sacer.*

6. See Rosas, "Refusing Refuge at the United States–Mexico Border."

7. I draw from the work of Savannah Shange, particularly this scholar's insistence that Black children at a progressive school in San Francisco refuse "burdened individuality." They live amid the ongoing pressures and normative notions of the "Black girl ordinary" but do not accept them. See Shange, "Black Girl Ordinary." Indeed, refusal rejects the easy answers, the pat outcomes taken as the political, particularly for mobile populations that in themselves do not want, that refuse, or that have been overstudied. See Simpson, "Consent's Revenge." Indeed, to analyze refusal demands an analytical push away from normative analysis of what counts as research in anthropology, allied disciplines, and other dominated knowledge formations toward post- or anti-disciplinary formations such as queer, ethnic, or Latinx studies. To analyze refusal demands a deep accounting of the demands of research to the communities of the overstudied, a reckoning with their concerns, their agendas, a coming to grips with the colonial underpinnings of anthropology and other disciplines and postdisciplines, a recognition that too much of academic research on marginal communities has become ventriloquism: the subaltern, the Latinx, and other communities know prisons, borders, factories better than the traditional intellectual. Ethnography then confirms this with the rejoinder that they know how to struggle.

AFTERWORD. Rifling in the Unsettling Present

1. Chege Karomo, "What Is Salvador Ramos' Ethnicity? His Upbringing and Parents Explored," TheNetline, May 26, 2022, https://thenetline.com/salvador-ramos-ethnicity/.

ACKNOWLEDGMENTS

1. "Land Acknowledgement," Borderland Rainbow Center, https://www.borderlandrainbow.org/about-us.

2. "Land Acknowledgement Statement," Office of the Chancellor, July 26, 2018, https://chancellor.illinois.edu/land_acknowledgement.html.

■ BIBLIOGRAPHY

Abrego, Leisy J. *Sacrificing Families: Navigating Laws, Labor, and Love across Borders*. Stanford, CA: Stanford University Press, 2014.

Agamben, Giorgio, and Daniel Heller-Roazen. *Homo Sacer: Sovereign Power and Bare Life*. Stanford, CA: Stanford University Press, 1998.

Aguilar, Julián. "El Paso Again Tops List of Safest U.S. Cities." *Texas Tribune*, February 5, 2013. https://www.texastribune.org/2013/02/05/el-paso-again-ranked-countrys-safest-city/.

Ambikaipaker, Mohan. *Political Blackness in Multiracial Britain*. Philadelphia: University of Pennsylvania Press, 2018.

"The Anastasio Hernández Rojas Case Timeline." Alliance San Diego. Accessed June 4, 2022, https://www.alliancesd.org/the_anastasio_hernandez_rojas_case_timeline.

Anderson, Benedict R. *Imagined Communities: Reflections on the Origin and Spread of Nationalism*. Revised ed. London: Verso Books, 1991.

"The Anthropoliteia #BlackLivesMatterSyllabus Project, Week 8: Bianca C. Williams on 'The Uses of Anger' by Audre Lorde," Anthropoliteia, November 3, 2016. https://anthropoliteia.net/2016/11/03/the-anthropoliteia-blacklivesmatter syllabus-project-week-8-bianca-c-williams-on-the-uses-of-anger-by-audre-lorde/.

Anzaldúa, Gloria. *Borderlands: La Frontera*. San Francisco: Aunt Lute Books, 1999.

Aretxaga, Begoña. "What the Border Hides: Partition and the Gender Politics of Irish Nationalism." *Social Analysis: The International Journal of Social and Cultural Practice* 42, no. 1 (1998): 16–32.

"Asylum in the United States." American Immigration Council. August 27, 2014. https://www.americanimmigrationcouncil.org/research/asylum-united-states.

Balaguera, Martha. "Trans-migrations: Agency and Confinement at the Limits of Sovereignty." *Signs: Journal of Women in Culture and Society* 43, no. 3 (2018): 641–64.

Balakian, Sophia. "Of Aunts and Mothers: Refugee Resettlement, the Nuclear Family, and Caring for 'Other' Children in Kenya." *Ethnic and Racial Studies*, forthcoming.

Bebout, Lee. *Whiteness on the Border: Mapping the US Racial Imagination in Brown and White.* New York: New York University Press, 2016.

Beltrán, Cristina. *Cruelty as Citizenship: How Migrant Suffering Sustains White Democracy.* Minneapolis: University of Minnesota Press, 2020.

Behar, Ruth. *The Vulnerable Observer: Anthropology That Breaks Your Heart.* Boston: Beacon Press, 1996.

Beliso–De Jesús, Aisha M., and Jemima Pierre. "Anthropology of White Supremacy." *American Anthropologist* 122, no. 1 (2020): 65–75.

Benjamin, Walter. "Critique of Violence." In *Reflections: Essays, Aphorisms, Autobiographical Writings*, edited by P. Demetz, 268–85. New York: Harcourt, Brace, Jovanovich, 1978.

Berlant, Lauren. "Cruel Optimism." *Differences* 17, no. 3 (January 1, 2006): 20–36.

———. "Slow Death (Sovereignty, Obesity, Lateral Agency)." *Critical Inquiry* 33, no. 4 (2007): 754.

Berry, Maya J., Claudia Chávez Argüelles, Shanya Cordis, Sarah Ihmoud, and Elizabeth Velásquez Estrada. "Toward a Fugitive Anthropology: Gender, Race, and Violence in the Field." *Cultural Anthropology* 32, no. 4 (2017): 537–65.

Besteman, Catherine. "Militarized Global Apartheid." *Current Anthropology* 60, no. S19 (February 1, 2019): S26–S38.

Beverly, John. *Testimonio: On the Politics of Truth.* Minneapolis: University of Minnesota Press, 2004.

Briggs, Laura. *Taking Children: A History of American Terror.* Oakland: University of California Press, 2020.

Brodkin, Karen, Sandra Morgen, and Janis Hutchinson. "Anthropology as White Public Space?" *American Anthropologist* 113, no. 4 (December 25, 2011): 545–56.

Bruner, Edward M., ed. *Text, Play, and Story: The Construction and Reconstruction of Self and Society*. Washington, DC: American Ethnological Society, 1984.

Budd, Jenn. "How Border Control Agents Get Away with Murder—Part 1," *DemCast*, July 29, 2021. https://demcastusa.com/2021/07/28/border-patrol-part-1/.

Buff, Rachel Ida. *Against the Deportation Terror: Organizing for Immigrant Rights in the Twentieth Century*. Philadelphia: Temple University Press, 2017.

Byrd, Jodi A. *The Transit of Empire: Indigenous Critiques of Colonialism*. Minneapolis: University of Minnesota Press, 2011.

Cacho, Lisa M. *Social Death: Racialized Rightlessness and the Criminalization of the Unprotected*. New York: New York University Press, 2012.

Callahan, Manuel. "Zapatismo beyond Chiapas." Catalyst Project: Antiracism for Collective Liberation. Accessed March 11, 2021. https://collectiveliberation.org/wp-content/uploads/2013/01/Callahan_Zapatismo_Beyond_Chiapas.pdf.

Campbell, Howard. *Drug War Zone: Frontline Dispatches from the Streets of El Paso and Juárez*. Austin: University of Texas Press, 2009.

Capps, Randy, Rosa Maria Castañeda, Ajay Chaudry, and Robert Santos. "Paying the Price: The Impact of Immigration Raids on America's Children." Urban Institute. 2007. https://www.urban.org/sites/default/files/publication/46811/411566-Paying-the-Price-The-Impact-of-Immigration-Raids-on-America-s-Children.PDF.

Cavallaro, James L., Jr., and Allyson Collins, "Frontier Injustice: Human Rights Abuses along the US Border with Mexico Persist amid Climate of Impunity." *News from Americas Watch* 5, no. 4 (May 5, 1993). https://www.hrw.org/sites/default/files/reports/US935.PDF.

Césaire, Aimé. *Discourse on Colonialism*. New York: Monthly Review Press, 1972.

Chakravartty, Paula, and Denise Ferreira Da Silva. "Accumulation, Dispossession, and Debt: The Racial Logic of Global Capitalism—an Introduction." *American Quarterly* 64, no. 3 (2012): 361–85.

Chappell, Ben. *Lowrider Space: Aesthetics and Politics of Mexican American Custom Cars*. Austin: University of Texas Press, 2012.

Chávez, Alex E. "Gender, Ethno-Nationalism, and the Anti-Mexicanist Trope." *Journal of American Folklore* 134, no. 531 (2021): 3–24.

———. *Sounds of Crossing: Music, Migration, and the Aural Poetics of Huapango Arribeño*. Durham, NC: Duke University Press, 2017.

Chavez, Leo R. *Covering Immigration*. Oakland: University of California Press, 2020.

———. *The Latino Threat: Constructing Immigrants, Citizens, and the Nation*. Stanford, CA: Stanford University Press. 2008.

Cisneros, Sandra. *The House on Mango Street*. Houston: Arte Publico Press, 1989.

Cohen, Cathy. "Deviance as Resistance: A New Research Agenda for the Study of Black Politics." *Du Bois Review: Social Science Research on Race* 1, no. 1 (January 1, 2004): 27–45.

Copeland, Nicholas. *The Democracy Development Machine*. Ithaca, NY: Cornell University Press, 2019.

A Culture of Cruelty: Abuse and Impunity in Short-Term US Border Patrol Custody. No More Deaths/No Más Muertos (Tucson, AZ). 2011. https://nomoredeaths.org/wp-content/uploads/2014/10/CultureOfCruelty-full.compressed.pdf.

Davis, Angela Y. *Freedom Is a Constant Struggle: Ferguson, Palestine, and the Foundations of a Movement*. Chicago: Haymarket Books, 2016.

Dayan, Colin. "Legal Terrors." *Representations* 92, no. 1 (2005): 42–80.

De Genova, Nicholas. "The Legal Production of Mexican/Migrant 'Illegality.'" *Latino Studies* 2, no. 2 (January 1, 2004): 160–85.

———. "Migrant 'Illegality' and Deportability in Everyday Life." *Annual Review of Anthropology* 31, no. 1 (October 1, 2002): 419–47.

De Genova, Nicholas, and Ana Yolanda Ramos-Zayas. *Latino Crossings: Mexicans, Puerto Ricans, and the Politics of Race and Citizenship*. New York: Routledge, 2003.

De León, Jason. *The Land of Open Graves: Living and Dying on the Migrant Trail*. Berkeley: University of California Press, 2015.

Debrix, François. *Global Powers of Horror: Security, Politics, and the Body in Pieces*. New York: Routledge, 2016.

Department of Homeland Security, Office of Inspector General. "Concerns about ICE Detainee Treatment and Care at Four Detention Facilities." June 3, 2019. https://www.oig.dhs.gov/sites/default/files/assets/2019-06/OIG-19-47-Jun19.pdf.

Department of Justice, Office of the Inspector General. "Review of the DOJ's Planning and Implementation of Its Zero Tolerance Policy and Its Coordination with the DHS and DHHS." Evaluation and Inspections Division, January 2021.

Díaz-Barriga, Miguel, and Margaret E. Dorsey. *Fencing in Democracy: Border Walls, Necrocitizenship, and the Security State*. Durham, NC: Duke University Press, 2020.

Du Bois, W. E. B. *The Souls of Black Folk: Essays and Sketches*. Great Illustrated Classics. New York: Dodd, Mead, 1979.

Dunn, Timothy J. *The Militarization of the U.S.-Mexico Border, 1978–1992: Low-Intensity Conflict Doctrine Comes Home*. Austin: Center for Mexican American Studies, 1996.

Eligon, John. "The El Paso Screed and the Racist Doctrine Behind It." *New York Times*, August 7, 2019. https://www.nytimes.com/2019/08/07/us/el-paso-shooting-racism.html.

Eschbach, Karl, Jacqueline Hagan, Nestor Rodriguez, Ruben Hernandez-Leon, and Stanley Bailey. "Death at the Border." *International Migration Review* 33, no. 2 (1999): 430–54.

Estévez, Ariadna. *Guerras necropolíticas y biopolítica de asilo en América del Norte*.

Mexico City: Universidad Nacional Autónoma de México, Centro de Investigaciones sobre América del Norte, 2018.
Estrada, Ruth Elizabeth Velásquez. "Grassroots Peacemaking: The Paradox of Reconciliation in El Salvador." *Social Justice* 41, no. 3 (2015): 69–86.
Family Members of Anastasio Hernández-Rojas, Petitioners v. United States, Respondent. Complaint filed with the Inter-American Commission on Human Rights. March 2016. https://d3n8a8pro7vhmx.cloudfront.net/alliancesandiego/legacy_url/1324/Anastasio-Complaint-FINAL-160329.pdf?1490744367.
Farmer, Paul. "An Anthropology of Structural Violence." *Current Anthropology* 45, no. 3 (January 1, 2004): 305–25.
"Fatal Encounters with CBP." Southern Border Communities Coalition. Updated June 21, 2022. https://www.southernborder.org/deaths_by_border_patrol.
Fazio, Carlos. *Estado de emergéncia: De la guerra de Calderón a la guerra de Peña Nieto*. Mexico City: Grijalbo, 2016.
Federici, Sylvia. *Caliban and the Witch: Women, the Body, and Primitive Accumulation*. London: Pluto Press, 2003.
Foucault, Michel. *Discipline and Punish: The Birth of the Prison*. Translated by Alan Sheridan. Vintage Books, 1995.
———. *Society Must Be Defended: Lectures at the Collège de France, 1975–76*. Edited by M. Bertani, A. Fontana, F. Ewald, and D. Macey. Vol. 1. New York: Picador USA, 2003.
———. "The Subject and Power." *Critical Inquiry* 8, no. 4 (1982): 777–95.
Galemba, Rebecca B. *Contraband Corridor: Making a Living at the Mexico-Guatemala Border*. Stanford, CA: Stanford University Press, 2018.
Garriga-López, Adriana. "The Coloniality of Addiction in Puerto Rico." In *Ethnographies of U.S. Empire*, edited by Carole McGranahan and John F. Collins, 126–59. Durham, NC: Duke University Press, 2018.
Gilmore, Ruth Wilson. "Fatal Couplings of Power and Difference: Notes on Racism and Geography." *Professional Geographer: Journal of the Association of American Geographers* 54, no. 1 (February 1, 2002): 15–24.
———. *Golden Gulag: Prisons, Surplus, Crisis, and Opposition in Globalizing California*. Berkeley: University of California Press, 2007.
Gilmore, Ruth Wilson, and Craig Gilmore. "Beyond Bratton." In *Policing the Planet: Why the Policing Crisis Led to Black Lives Matter*, edited by Jordan T. Camp and Christina Heatherton, 173–99. London: Verso, 2016.
Goett, Jennifer. *Black Autonomy*. Stanford, CA: Stanford University Press, 2020.
Golash-Boza, Tanya Maria. *Immigration Nation: Raids, Detentions, and Deportations in Post-9/11 America*. Boulder, CO: Paradigm, 2011.

Gómez, Alan Eladio. *The Revolutionary Imaginations of Greater Mexico: Chicana/o Radicalism, Solidarity Politics, and Latin American Social Movements*. Austin: University of Texas Press, 2016.

Gonzalez, Gilbert G., and Raul A. Fernandez. *A Century of Chicano History: Empire, Nations, and Migration.* New York: Routledge, 2003.

Grandin, Greg. *Empire's Workshop: Latin America, the United States, and the Rise of the New Imperialism*. The American Empire Project. New York: Metropolitan Books, 2006.

———. *The End of the Myth: From the Frontier to the Border Wall in the Mind of America.* New York: Metropolitan Books, 2019.

Gravlee, Clarence C. "How Race Becomes Biology: Embodiment of Social Inequality." *American Journal of Physical Anthropology* 139, no. 1 (May 2009): 47–57.

Gusterson, Hugh. "From Brexit to Trump: Anthropology and the Rise of Nationalist Populism." *American Ethnologist* 44, no. 2 (May 2017): 209–14.

Gutmann, Matthew C. *The Meanings of Macho: Being a Man in Mexico City*. Berkeley: University of California Press, 1996.

Hage, Ghassan. "État de Siège: A Dying Domesticating Colonialism?" *American Ethnologist* 43, no. 1 (February 2016): 38–49.

Hale, C. R. "What Is Activist Research?" *Items and Issues: Social Science Research Council* 2, nos. 1–2 (January 1, 2001): 13–15.

Hall, Stuart. "Popular Democratic versus Authoritarian Popularism." In *Marxism and Democracy*, edited by Alan Hunt, 157–87. London: Lawrence & Wishart, 1980.

Harrison, Faye Venetia, ed. *Decolonizing Anthropology: Moving Further toward an Anthropology for Liberation*. Arlington, TX: American Anthropological Association, 1998.

Hartman, Noel. "'The Passing of the Great Race' @ 100." *Public Books*, July 1, 2016. https://www.publicbooks.org/the-passing-of-the-great-race-at-100/.

Heidbrink, Lauren. *Migranthood.* Stanford, CA: Stanford University Press, 2020.

Heiner, Brady Thomas. "Foucault and the Black Panthers." *Cityscape* 11, no. 3 (December 1, 2007): 313–56.

Hernández, Kelly Lytle. *City of Inmates: Conquest, Rebellion, and the Rise of Human Caging in Los Angeles, 1771–1965*. Chapel Hill: University of North Carolina Press, 2017.

Hernández, Roberto D. *Coloniality of the US/Mexico Border: Power, Violence, and the Decolonial Imperative.* Tucson: University of Arizona Press, 2018.

Heyman, Josiah. *Life and Labor on the Border: Working People of Northeastern Sonora, Mexico, 1886–1986.* Tucson: University of Arizona Press, 1991.

———. "The President and Immigration Law Series: The Consequences of the Free Rein of Enforcement on Borderlands Society." Just Security, October 13, 2020. https://www.justsecurity.org/72742/the-president-and-immigration-law-series-the-consequences-of-the-free-rein-of-enforcement-on-borderlands-society/.

Hooks, Christopher. "The Cruelty at the Border Is Increasingly Pointless." *Texas Monthly*, July 5, 2019. https://www.texasmonthly.com/news-politics/the-cruelty-at-the-border-is-increasingly-pointless/.

Horne, Gerald. *The Apocalypse of Settler Colonialism: The Roots of Slavery, White Supremacy, and Capitalism in 17th Century North America and the Caribbean.* New York: New York University Press, 2018.

Inda, Jonathan Xavier. "Borderzones of Enforcement: Criminalization, Workplace Raids, and Migrant Counterconducts." In *The Contested Politics of Mobility: Borderzones and Irregularity*, edited by Vicki Squire, 74–91. London: Routledge, 2011.

———. *Targeting Immigrants: Government, Technology, Ethics.* Malden, UK: Blackwell, 2006.

Iturralde, Manuel. "Neoliberalism and Its Impact on Latin American Crime Control Fields." *Theoretical Criminology* 23, no. 4 (2019): 471–90.

James, C. L. R. *The Black Jacobins*. New York: Random House, 1963.

James, Joy. *Resisting State Violence: Radicalism, Gender, and Race in U.S. Culture.* Minneapolis: University of Minnesota Press, 1996.

Jobson, Ryan Cecil. "The Case for Letting Anthropology Burn: Sociocultural Anthropology in 2019." *American Anthropologist* 122, no. 2 (June 2020): 259–71.

Jones, Reece. *White Borders: The History of Race and Immigration in the United States from Chinese Exclusion to the Border Wall.* Boston: Beacon Press, 2021.

Jusionyte, Ieva. "Called to 'Ankle Alley': Tactical Infrastructure, Migrant Injuries, and Emergency Medical Services on the US-Mexico Border." *American Anthropologist* 120, no. 1 (March 1, 2018): 89–101.

———. *Savage Frontier: Making News and Security on the Argentine Border.* Oakland: University of California Press, 2015.

Kearney, Michael. "The Local and the Global: The Anthropology of Globalization and Transnationalism." *Annual Review of Anthropology* 24, no. 1995 (January 1, 1995): 547–65.

Khosravi, Sharam. *"Illegal" Traveller: An Auto-ethnography of Borders.* Basingstoke, UK: Palgrave Macmillan, 2010.

———. "Stolen Time." *Radical Philosophy* 2, no. 3 (December 2018): 38–41.

Kotef, Hagar. *Movement and the Ordering of Freedom: On Liberal Governances of Mobility.* Durham, NC: Duke University Press, 2015.

LeBrón, Marisol. *Policing Life and Death: Race, Violence, and Resistance in Puerto Rico*. Oakland: University of California Press, 2019.

Lee, Erika. "Enforcing the Borders: Chinese Exclusion along the US Borders with Canada and Mexico, 1882–1924." *Journal of American History* 89, no. 1 (2002): 54–86.

Lemus, Sergio. "Performing Power *en Las Yardas* (at the Yards): The Body, Capitalist Discipline, and the Making of Mexican Yardero Lives in South Chicago." *Anthropology of Work Review* 38, no. 2 (2017): 104–12.

Levario, M. A. *Militarizing the Border: When Mexicans Became the Enemy*. College Station: Texas A&M University Press, 2012.

Levin, Sam, Amanda Holpuch, Nina Lakhani, Rory Carroll, Oliver Laughland, Lauren Gambino, Simon Tisdall, and Tom Phillips. "Trump Policy of Detaining Children 'May Amount to Torture,' UN Says—as It Happened." *The Guardian*, June 22, 2018. http://www.theguardian.com/us-news/live/2018/jun/22/trump-family-separation-crisis-immigration-border.

Limón, José E. *Dancing with the Devil: Society and Cultural Poetics in Mexican-American South Texas*. Madison: University of Wisconsin Press, 1994.

Lira, Natalie. *Laboratory of Deficiency: Sterilization and Confinement in California, 1900–1950s*. Oakland: University of California Press, 2022.

Loperena, Christopher A. "Settler Violence? Race and Emergent Frontiers of Progress in Honduras." *American Quarterly* 69, no. 4 (2017): 801–7.

Lorde, Audre. "Uses of the Erotic." In *Sister Outsider: Essays and Speeches*, 53–59. Trumansburg, NY: Crossing Press, 1984.

———. "The Uses of Anger." *Women's Studies Quarterly* 25, nos. 1–2 (1997): 278–85.

Lowe, Lisa. *The Intimacies of Four Continents*. Durham, NC: Duke University Press, 2015.

Loyd, Jenna M., and Alison Mountz. *Boats, Borders, and Bases: Race, the Cold War, and the Rise of Migration Detention in the United States*. Berkeley: University of California Press, 2018.

Loza, Mireya. *Defiant Braceros: How Migrant Workers Fought for Racial, Sexual, and Political Freedom*. Chapel Hill: University of North Carolina Press, 2016.

Lugo, Alejandro. "Dossier: Celebrating and Engaging Renato Rosaldo's *Culture and Truth*." *Aztlan* 37, no. 1 (January 1, 2012): 119–43.

———. *Fragmented Lives, Assembled Parts: Culture, Capitalism, and Conquest at the US-Mexico Border*. Austin: University of Texas Press, 2008.

———. "Theorizing Border Inspections." *Cultural Dynamics* 12, no. 3 (January 1, 2000): 353–73.

Luibhéid, Eithne. *Entry Denied: Controlling Sexuality at the Border.* Minneapolis: University of Minnesota Press, 2002.

Luiselli, Valeria. *Tell Me How It Ends: An Essay in Forty Questions*. Minneapolis: Coffee House Press, 2017.

Malkki, Lisa. "National Geographic: The Rooting of People and the Territorialization of National Identity among Scholars and Refugees." *Cultural Anthropology: Journal of the Society for Cultural Anthropology* 7, no. 1 (January 1, 1992): 24–44.

Mamdani, Mahmood. "Good Muslim, Bad Muslim: Post-apartheid Perspectives on America and Israel." *POLAR: Political and Legal Anthropology Review* 27, no. 1 (January 1, 2004): 1–15.

Manalansan, Martin F. *Global Divas: Filipino Gay Men in the Diaspora*. Durham, NC: Duke Univ Press, 2003.

Marx, Karl. *Capital: A Critique of Political Economy*, 3 vols. New York: Penguin Classics, 1976.

Mbembe, Achille "The Banality of Power and the Aesthetics of Vulgarity in the Postcolony." *Public Culture* 4, no. 2 (January 1, 1992): 1–30.

———. "The Idea of a Borderless World." Africa Is a Country, November 11, 2018. https://africasacountry.com/2018/11/the-idea-of-a-borderless-world?fbclid=IwARocyScyyMMPqSMSSqMLdoyaVJmV17UiBhTQUPMGdoBGYt9X-ocmFKNMLGQ.

———. "Necropolitics." *Public Culture* 15, no. 1 (January 1, 2003): 11–40.

McDuffie, Erik S. *Sojourning for Freedom: Black Women, American Communism, and the Making of Black Left Feminism*. Durham, NC: Duke University Press, 2013.

McGranahan, Carole, Kaifa Roland, and Bianca C. Williams. "Decolonizing Anthropology: A Conversation with Faye V. Harrison, Part I." Savage Minds, May 2, 2016. https://savageminds.org/2016/05/02/decolonizing-anthropology-a-conversation-with-faye-v-harrison-part-i/.

Mckiernan-Gonzalez, John Raymond. *Fevered Measures: Public Health and Race at the Texas-Mexico Border, 1848–1942*. Durham, NC: Duke University Press, 2012.

Menchaca, Martha. *The Mexican Outsiders: A Community History of Marginalization and Discrimination in California*. Austin: University of Texas Press, 1995.

———. *Recovering History, Constructing Race: The Indian, Black, and White Roots of Mexican Americans*. Austin: University of Texas Press, 2001.

Menchu, Rigoberta. *I, Rigoberta Menchu: An Indian Woman in Guatemala*. London: Verso Books, 2010.

Mezzadra, Sandro, and Brett Neilson. *Border as Method; or, The Multiplication of Labor*. Durham, NC: Duke University Press, 2013.
Milian, Claudia. *LatinX*. Minneapolis: University of Minnesota Press, 2019.
Mills, Charles W. "Racial Liberalism." *PMLA* 123, no. 5 (2008): 1380–97.
Miroff, Nick. "Honduran Father Who Died in Texas Jail Was Fleeing Violence, Consul Says." *Washington Post*, June 11, 2018. https://www.washingtonpost.com/world/national-security/honduran-father-who-died-in-texas-jail-was-fleeing-violence-consul-says/2018/06/11/89c3c2ac-6daa-11e8-bd50-b80389a4e569_story.html.
Mora, Mariana. *Kuxlejal Politics: Indigenous Autonomy, Race, and Decolonizing Research in Zapatista Communities*. Austin: University of Texas Press, 2017.
Moraga, Cherríe. *Loving in the War Years: Lo que nunca pasó por sus labios*. Cambridge, MA: South End Press, 2000.
Moraga, Cherríe, and Gloria Anzaldúa. *This Bridge Called My Back: Writings by Radical Women of Color*. Watertown, MA: Persephone Press, 1981.
Moodie, Ellen. *El Salvador in the Aftermath of Peace: Crime, Uncertainty, and the Transition to Democracy*. The Ethnography of Political Violence. Philadelphia: University of Pennsylvania Press, 2010.
Morgensen, Scott Lauria. "The Biopolitics of Settler Colonialism: Right Here, Right Now." *Settler Colonial Studies* 1 (2011): 52–76.
Mountz, Allison, and Richard A. Wright. "Daily Life in the Transnational Migrant Community of San Agustín, Oaxaca, and Poughkeepsie, New York." *Diaspora* 5, no. 3 (January 1, 1996): 403–28.
Muehlmann, Shaylih. *When I Wear My Alligator Boots: Narco-trafficking in the US-Mexico Borderlands*. Berkeley: University of California Press, 2013.
Müller, Anna. *If the Walls Could Speak: Inside a Women's Prison in Communist Poland*. Oxford: Oxford University Press, 2017.
Muñiz de la Peña, Cristina, on behalf of American Psychological Association. Statement of Cristina Muñiz de La Peña, Ph.D. Hearing on Examining the Failures of the Trump Administration's Inhumane Family Separation Policy, February 7, 2019. American Psychological Association. https://www.apa.org/news/press/releases/2019/02/muniz-testimony.pdf.
Muñoz, José Esteban. "Feeling Brown, Feeling Down: Latina Affect, the Performativity of Race, and the Depressive Position." *Signs* 40, no. 1 (January 1, 2014).
Murakawa, Naomi. *The First Civil Right: How Liberals Built Prison America*. Oxford: Oxford University Press, 2014.
Nájera, Jennifer R. *The Borderlands of Race: Mexican Segregation in a South Texas Town*. Austin: University of Texas Press, 2015.

Nájera, Lourdes Gutiérrez, and Korinta Maldonado. "Transnational Settler Colonial Formations and Global Capital: A Consideration of Indigenous Mexican Migrants." *American Quarterly* 69, no. 4 (2017): 809–21.

Nevins, Joseph. *Operation Gatekeeper: The Rise of the "Illegal Alien" and the Making of the U.S.-Mexico Boundary*. New York, London: Routledge, 2002.

Newton, Huey P. *The Genius of Huey P. Newton, Minister of Defense*. San Francisco: Black Panther Party, 1970.

Ngai, Mae M. *Impossible Subjects: Illegal Aliens and the Making of Modern America*. Princeton, NJ: Princeton University Press, 2004.

Oberg, Charles, Coleen Kivlahan, Ranit Mishori, William Martinez, Juan Raul Gutierrez, Zarin Noor, and Jeffrey Goldhagen. "Treatment of Migrant Children on the US Southern Border Is Consistent with Torture." *Pediatrics* 147, no. 1 (January 2021). https://doi.org/10.1542/peds.2020-012930.

Oliver, Kelly. *Carceral Humanitarianism: Logics of Refugee Detention*. Minneapolis: University of Minnesota Press, 2017.

Ortner, Sherry B. "Dark Anthropology and Its Others: Theory since the Eighties." *HAU: Journal of Ethnographic Theory* 6, no. 1 (July 16, 2016): 47–73.

———. "Resistance and the Problem of Ethnographic Refusal." *Comparative Studies in Society and History* 37, no. 1 (January 1, 1995): 173–93.

Otero, Gerardo. "Neoliberal Reform and Politics in Mexico: An Overview." In *Neoliberalism Revisited: Economic Restructuring and Mexico's Political Future*, edited by Gerardo Otero, 1–26. Boulder, CO: Westview Press, 1996.

Paik, A. Naomi. *Bans, Walls, Raids, Sanctuary: Understanding U.S. Immigration for the Twenty-First Century*. Oakland: University of California Press, 2020.

———. *Rightlessness: Testimony and Redress in U.S. Prison Camps since World War II*. Chapel Hill: University of North Carolina Press, 2016.

Paredes, Américo. *"With His Pistol in His Hand": A Border Ballad and Its Hero*. Austin: University of Texas Press, 1958.

Paz, Octavio. *The Labyrinth of Solitude: The Other Mexico, Return to the Labyrinth of Solitude, Mexico and the USA, the Philanthropic Ogre*. Vol. 13. New York: Grove Press, 1994.

Perez, Gina. *Citizen, Student, Soldier: Latina/o Youth, JROTC, and the American Dream*. New York: New York University Press, 2015.

Perry, Marc D. *Negro Soy Yo: Hip Hop and Raced Citizenship in Neoliberal Cuba*. Durham: Duke University Press, 2015.

Phillips, Amber. "'They're Rapists': President Trump's Campaign Launch Speech Two Years Later, Annotated." *Washington Post*, June 16, 2017. https://www.washingtonpost.com/news/the-fix/wp/2017/06/16/theyre-rapists-presidents-trump-campaign-launch-speech-two-years-later-annotated/.

Pierre, Jemima. *The Predicament of Blackness: Postcolonial Ghana and the Politics of Race*. Chicago: University of Chicago Press, 2013.

Pitzer, Andrea. *One Long Night: A Global History of Concentration Camps*. Boston: Little Brown, 2017.

Poblete, Juan, ed. *Critical Latin American and Latino Studies*. Cultural Studies of the Americas 12. Minneapolis: University of Minnesota Press, 2003.

Puar, Jasbir K. "On Torture: Abu Ghraib." *Radical History Review*, no. 93 (January 1, 2005): 13–38.

———. *Terrorist Assemblages: Homonationalism in Queer Times*. Durham, NC: Duke University Press, 2007.

Quijano, Aníbal. "¡Que tal raza!" *Ecuador Debate* 141 (February 5, 2014): 152.

Ralph, Laurence. *The Torture Letters: Reckoning with Police Violence*. Chicago: University of Chicago Press, 2020.

Renee Perez, Domino. "The Politics of Taking: La Llorona in the Cultural Mainstream." *Journal of Popular Culture* 45, no. 1 (February 22, 2012): 153–72.

Rios Contreras, Viridiana. "The Role of Drug-Related Violence and Extortion in Promoting Mexican Migration: Unexpected Consequences of a Drug War." *Latin American Research Review* 49, no. 3 (January 1, 2014): 199–217.

Robinson, Cedric J. *Black Marxism: The Making of the Black Radical Tradition*. Chapel Hill: University of New Carolina Press, 2020.

Roediger, David R. *Working toward Whiteness: How America's Immigrants Became White—The Strange Journey from Ellis Island to the Suburbs*. New York: Basic Books, 2018.

Romo, David Dorado. *Ringside Seat to a Revolution: An Underground Cultural History of El Paso and Juárez, 1893–1923*. El Paso: Cinco Puntos Press, 2014.

Rosa, Jonathan. *Looking like a Language, Sounding like a Race: Raciolinguistic Ideologies and the Learning of Latinidad*. Oxford: Oxford University Press, 2019.

Rosa, Jonathan, and Yarimar Bonilla. "Deprovincializing Trump, Decolonizing Diversity, and Unsettling Anthropology." *American Ethnologist* 44, no. 2 (2017): 201–8.

Rosaldo, Renato. *Culture and Truth: The Remaking of Social Analysis*. Boston: Beacon Press, 1993.

———. "Grief and a Headhunter's Rage: On the Cultural Force of Emotions." In *Text, Play, and Story: The Construction and Reconstruction of Self and Society*, edited by Edward M. Bruner, 178–95. Washington, DC: American Ethnological Society, 1984.

Rosas, Gilberto. *Barrio Libre: Criminalizing States and Delinquent Refusals of the New Frontier*. Durham, NC: Duke University Press, 2012.

———. “Cholos, Chúntaros, and the ‘Criminal’ Abandonments of the New Frontier.” *Identities* 17, no. 6 (December 15, 2010): 695–713.

———. “Fugitive Work: On the Criminal Possibilities of Anthropology.” Society for Cultural Anthropology, September 26, 2018. https://culanth.org/fieldsights/fugitive-work-on-the-criminal-possibilities-of-anthropology.

———. “Grief and Border-Crossing Rage.” *Anthropology and Humanism* 46, no. 1 (June 2021): 114–28.

———. “Las fronteras que se engrosan y las nuevas pesadillas del neoliberalismo moribundo.” In *Desafiando fronteras: Control de la movilidad y experiencias migratorias en el contexto capitalista*, edited by Alejandra Aquino, Amarela Varela, and Frédéric Décosse, 55–64. Oaxaca, Mexico: Frontera Press, 2013.

———. “The Managed Violences of the Borderlands: Treacherous Geographies, Policeability, and the Politics of Race,” *Latino Studies* 4, no. 4 (December 1, 2006): 401–18.

———. “Necro-subjection: On Borders, Asylum, and Making Dead to Let Live.” *Theory and Event* 22, no. 2 (2019): 303–24.

———. “Refusing Refuge at the United States–Mexico Border.” *Humanity: An International Journal of Human Rights, Humanitarianism, and Development* 8, no. 3 (2017): 535–37.

———. “The Thickening Borderlands: Bastard Mestiz@s, ‘Illegal’ Possibilities, and Globalizing Migrant Life.” In *Critical Ethnic Studies: A Reader*, edited by Nada Elia, David M. Hernández, Jodi Kim, Shana L. Redmond, Dylan Rodríguez, and Sarita Echavez See, 344–59. Durham, NC: Duke University Press, 2016.

Rosas, Gilberto, and Virginia Raymond. “Migrant Detention Turns Deadlier.” *NACLA Report on the Americas* 52, no. 3 (July 2, 2020): 289–95.

Rubio-Goldsmith, Raquel, M. Melissa McCormick, Daniel Martinez, and Indez Magdalena Duarte. “The ‘Funnel Effect’ and Recovered Bodies of Unauthorized Migrants Processed by the Pima County Office of the Medical Examiner, 1990–2005.” Tucson: Binational Migration Institute, Mexican American Studies and Research Center at the University of Arizona, October 1, 2006.

Saldaña-Portillo, María Josefina. *The Revolutionary Imagination in the Americas and the Age of Development*. Latin American Otherwise: Languages, Empires, Nations. Durham, NC: Duke University Press, 2003.

Saramago, José. “Chiapas, Land of Hope and Sorrow,” *Le Monde diplomatique*, March 1, 1999. https://mondediplo.com/1999/03/08sarama.

Scarry, Elaine. *The Body in Pain: The Making and Unmaking of the World*. New York: Oxford University Press, 1985.

Scheper-Hughes, Nancy. *Death without Weeping: The Violence of Everyday Life in Brazil*. Berkeley: University of California Press, 1992.

"Sexual Abuse in Immigration Detention." American Civil Liberties Union. Accessed February 25, 2022. https://www.aclu.org/issues/immigrants-rights/immigrants-rights-and-detention/sexual-abuse-immigration-detention-0.
Shange, Savannah. "Black Girl Ordinary: Flesh, Carcerality, and the Refusal of Ethnography." *Transforming Anthropology* 27, no. 1 (2019): 3–21.
———. *Progressive Dystopia: Abolition, Antiblackness, and Schooling in San Francisco*. Durham, NC: Duke University Press, 2019.
Simon, John K. "Michel Foucault on Attica: An Interview." *Telos* 19, nos. 154–61 (January 1, 1974).
Simpson, Audra. "Consent's Revenge." *Cultural Anthropology* 31, no. 3 (2016): 326–33.
———. *Mohawk Interruptus: Political Life across the Borders of Settler States*. Durham, NC: Duke University Press, 2014.
Speed, Shannon. *Incarcerated Stories: Indigenous Women Migrants and Violence in the Settler-Capitalist State*. Chapel Hill: University of North Carolina Press, 2019.
Spira, T. L. "Neoliberal Captivities: Pisagua Prison and the Low-Intensity Form." *Radical History Review* 2012, no. 112 (January 1, 2012): 127–46.
Stephen, Lynn. "Fleeing Rural Violence: Mam Women Seeking Gendered Justice in Guatemala and the U.S." *Journal of Peasant Studies* 46, no. 2 (February 23, 2019): 229–57.
———. *Transborder Lives: Indigenous Oaxacans in Mexico, California, and Oregon*. Durham, NC: Duke University Press, 2007.
Stephens, Alain. "El Paso Shooter Coveted 'Most Lethal' Rifle Ammunition on the Market." *The Trace*, August 4, 2019. https://www.thetrace.org/2019/08/el-paso-mass-shooting-8m3-ammunition/.
Stern, Alexandra Minna. *Proud Boys and the White Ethnostate: How the Alt-Right Is Warping the American Imagination*. Boston: Beacon Press, 2019.
Stevenson, Lisa. "Looking Away." *Cultural Anthropology: Journal of the Society for Cultural Anthropology* 35, no. 1 (February 14, 2020): 6–13.
Stoll, David. *Rigoberta Menchú and the Story of All Poor Guatemalans*. Boulder: Westview Press, 1999.
Stuesse, Angela. *Scratching Out a Living: Latinos, Race, and Work in the Deep South*. California Series in Public Anthropology 38. Oakland: University of California Press, 2016.
Taussig, Michael T. *Shamanism, Colonialism, and the Wild Man: A Study in Terror and Healing*. Chicago: University of Chicago Press, 1986.
Trouillot, Michel-Rolph. "Anthropology and the Savage Slot: The Poetics and Poli-

tics of Otherness." In *Recapturing Anthropology: Working in the Present*, edited by Richard Fox, 7–28. Santa Fe, NM: School of American Research Press, 1991.

US Border Patrol. "Border Patrol Strategic Plan: 1994 and Beyond." Homeland Security Digital Library. Accessed September 12, 2020. https://www.hsdl.org/?view&did=721845.

Valencia Triana, Sayak. "Tijuana Cuir." *Queer Geographies. Beirut, Tijuana, Copenhagen, Dinamarca, Museet for Samtidskunst* (2014): 90–95.

Varela Huerta, Amarela, Verónica Gago, Marta Malo, and Liz Mason-Deese. "Notes for an Anti-racist Feminism in the Wake of the Migrant Caravans." *South Atlantic Quarterly* 119, no. 3 (2020): 655–63.

Vega, Sujey. *Latino Heartland: Of Borders and Belonging in the Midwest.* New York: New York University Press, 2015.

Viego, Antonio. *Dead Subjects: Towards a Politics of Loss in Latino Studies.* Durham, NC: Duke University Press, 2007.

Villarreal, Aimee. "Sanctuaryscapes in the North American Southwest." *Radical History Review* 2019, no. 135 (October 1, 2019): 43–70.

Visweswaran, Kamala. *Fictions of Feminist Ethnography.* Minneapolis: University of Minnesota Press, 1994.

———. *Un/common Cultures: Racism and the Rearticulation of Cultural Difference.* Durham, NC: Duke University Press, 2010.

Vitale, Alex. *The End of Policing.* London: Verso Books, 2021.

Vogt, Wendy A. "Crossing Mexico: Structural Violence and the Commodification of Undocumented Central American Migrants." *American Ethnologist* 40, no. 4 (2013): 764–80.

Walia, Harsha. *Border and Rule: Global Migration, Capitalism, and the Rise of Racist Nationalism*, Chicago: Haymarket Books, 2021.

———. *Undoing Border Imperialism.* Anarchist Interventions. Washington, DC: AK Press, 2013.

Wessler, Seth Freed. *Shattered Families: The Perilous Intersection of Immigration Enforcement and the Child Welfare System."* New York: Applied Research Center, 2011.

West, Paige. *Dispossession and the Environment: Rhetoric and Inequality in Papua New Guinea.* New York: Columbia University Press, 2016.

Whitman, James Q. *Hitler's American Model: The United States and the Making of Nazi Race Law.* Princeton, NJ: Princeton University Press, 2017.

Wolfe, Patrick. "On Being Woken Up: The Dreamtime in Anthropology and in Australian Settler Culture." *Comparative Studies in Society and History* 33, no. 2 (April 1991): 197–224.

———. "Settler Colonialism and the Elimination of the Native." *Journal of Genocide Research* 8, no. 4 (January 1, 2006): 387–409.

———. *Traces of History: Elementary Structures of Race*. London: Verso Books, 2016.

Wright, Melissa W. "Epistemological Ignorances and Fighting for the Disappeared: Lessons from Mexico." *Antipode* 49, no. 1 (January 2017): 249–69.

Wynter, Sylvia. "Unsettling the Coloniality of Being/Power/Truth/Freedom: Towards Human, After Man, Its Overrepresentation—an Argument." *New Centennial Review* 3, no. 3 (January 1, 2003).

Zavala, Oswaldo. *Los cárteles no existen: Narcotráfico y cultura en México*. Barcelona: Malpaso Ediciones SL, 2018.

Zavella, Patricia. "Feminist Insider Dilemmas: Constructing Ethnic Identity with Chicana Informants." In *Feminist Dilemmas in Fieldwork*, edited by Diane L. Wolf, 138–59. London: Taylor and Francis, 2018.

———. *I'm Neither Here nor There*. Durham, NC: Duke University Press, 2011.

Zilberg, Elana. *Space of Detention: The Making of a Transnational Gang Crisis between Los Angeles and San Salvador*. Durham, NC: Duke University Press, 2011.

■ INDEX